Inconsistency and Indecision in the United States Supreme Court

The United States Supreme Court exists to resolve constitutional disputes among lower courts and the other branches of government, allowing elected officials, citizens, and businesses to act without legal uncertainty. American law and society function more effectively when the Court resolves these ambiguous questions of constitutional law. Since lower courts must defer to its reasoning, the Court should also promulgate clear and consistent legal doctrine, giving a reason for its judgment that a majority of justices support.

Yet a Court that prioritizes resolving many disputes will at times produce contradictory sets of opinions or fail to provide a rationale and legal precedent for its decision at all. In either case, it produces an unreasoned judgment. Conversely, a Court that prioritizes logically consistent doctrine will fail to resolve many underlying disputes in law and society. *Inconsistency and Indecision in the United States Supreme Court* demonstrates that over time, institutional changes, lobbied for by the justices, substantially reduced unreasoned judgments in the Court's output, coinciding with a reduction in the Court's caseload. Hence, the Supreme Court historically emphasized the first goal of dispute resolution but evolved into a Court that prioritizes the second goal of logically consistent doctrine. As a result, the Court today fails to resolve more underlying questions in law and society in order to minimize criticism of its output from other elites. In so doing, the modern Court often fails to live up to its constitutional obligation.

Matthew P. Hitt is Assistant Professor of Political Science at Colorado State University.

Inconsistency and Indecision in the United States Supreme Court

Matthew P. Hitt

University of Michigan Press
Ann Arbor

Published in the United States of America by the
University of Michigan Press
Printed and bound by CPI Group (UK) Ltd, Croydon, CR0 4YY

First published May 2019

A CIP catalog record for this book is available from the British Library.

ISBN 978-0-472-13136-5 (hardcover : alk. paper)
ISBN 978-0-472-12522-7 (ebook)

To Jen, with love and thanks.

Contents

Digital materials related to this title can be found on the Fulcrum platform via the following citable URL: https://doi.org/10.3998/mpub.10087106

List of Figures

List of Tables

Acknowledgements

This project began in early 2011 while I was a third-year PhD student at Ohio State when William Minozzi asked me if I'd ever heard about the discursive dilemma. I hadn't. Professor Minozzi, a wonderful mentor, suggested that I might do some reading and thinking about the idea. I devoured the works of Philip Pettit and Christian List, among many others, and quickly became fascinated by the impossibility of guaranteeing group-level consistency between reasons and judgment. Professor List, though he had never met this green graduate student from Ohio, generously shared a copy of his doctoral dissertation on the topic with me during this time, which proved enormously helpful to me.

I obsessed over the idea that the U.S. Supreme Court was producing discursive dilemmas/doctrinal paradoxes, and I wanted to know whether these phenomena were common and what consequences these sorts of decisions had for American law and society. As time went by, and encouraged by my mentors at Ohio State, I began to conceptualize the notion of judgments without reasons more broadly, ending with the definition of unreasoned judgment presented here. I undertook this project as a doctoral dissertation. Looking back now, more than half a decade later, I am amazed by two things. First, I am humbled by the intellect and generosity of my mentors, colleagues, and friends in the discipline of political science. This little project may not have deserved so much of their time, thought, care, and assistance, but it is so much the better for it. Second, I am amazed that after all this time, I remain as fascinated by the phenomenon of collective judgments without reasons as I was in 2011. My students in undergraduate judicial politics courses at Louisiana State University and Colorado State University would attest to that, I think. I thank all of my former students for humoring their professor's intellectual obsessions and horrifically bad white board artwork.

I now wish to publicly thank, in particular, a number of individuals who supported this project intellectually, financially, and personally. This book is immeasurably better for their assistance and guidance.

First, I thank my graduate advisor, Gregory Caldeira, for his feedback, advice, and for frequent and invaluable conversations regarding this project and many other topics. I also thank my other graduate school mentors: Lawrence Baum, Janet Box-Steffensmeier, William Minozzi, and Michael Neblo. Their guidance shaped this project in its earlier days as a doctoral dissertation, and their mentorship helped me become the academic I am today.

Critical financial support for this research came from the National Science Foundation's Decision, Risk, and Management Sciences Program, grant #1259252, The Ohio State University, Louisiana State University, the State of Louisiana Board of Regents, and Colorado State University. I offer my sincerest thanks to these funders for their generosity. I could never have spent luxurious weeks at the Library of Congress, nose deep in Harry Blackmun's cursive, without this assistance.

Through the years, a number of outstanding research assistants aided me substantially. I thank Alexis Elio, Cassie Knott, Aubrey Patterson, Mary Lou Ranney, and Thomas Varacalli for terrific work on this project. Alexis in particular deserves special mention: an undergraduate student at CSU, she volunteered as an unpaid research assistant on this project in the summer of 2017. The vignettes that begin each chapter are undergirded by her excellent research on the historical background of the cases of Willie Francis, Sandra Lockett, Robert Watts, and others.

In April 2016, supported by Louisiana State University and the ATLAS program of the State of Louisiana Board of Regents, a book conference for this project occurred at The Ohio State University. I thank Lawrence Baum, Ryan Black, Gregory Caldeira, William Massengill, Vittorio Mérola, William Minozzi, Michael Neblo, and Michael Zilis for their incredibly helpful engagement and feedback. The book improved tremendously as a direct result of this conference.

Additionally, a number of terrific scholars generously offered comments and conversation on portions of this project over the years. Given that this effort began in early 2011, and I've added two kids, a spouse, a PhD, a minivan, three home purchases (with two home sales), and two interstate moves in the intervening years, I am certain this list is underinclusive. Nevertheless, I thank Brandon Bartels, Bethany Blackstone, Jeff Budziak, Pam Corley, Courtenay Daum, Nick Davis, Paul Debell, Jessy Defenderfer, Johanna Dunaway, Nick Felts, Jim Garand, Shane Gleason, Jess Goode, Vlad

Kogan, Daniel Lempert, Yonatan Lupu, Lauren Mattioli, Irfan Nooruddin, Katy Powers, Chinnu Parinandi, Kyle Saunders, Kathleen Searles, Anand Sohkey, Kathleen Winters, and Jack Wright for their thoughts, suggestions, and questions over the years.

Thank you to Elizabeth Demers, Meredith Norwich, Danielle Coty, and the entire staff at the University of Michigan Press for their support of this book. I also thank the three anonymous referees for their thoughtful and helpful feedback.

I thank the Panera Bread Company, in particular their stores in Dublin, Ohio, and Fort Collins, Colorado, for their generous policies of free wifi and refills on coffee, which I shamelessly abused and exploited for years on end while writing this book. I'm not sorry.

I wish to thank my entire family for their patience in hearing out my research ideas and for keeping me grounded and connected through the solitary and monastic periods of academic life. Thanks to my parents for their love and support and for instilling in me the value of a great education from the very start. Thank you to my brothers Luke and Travis for their encouragement and support as I prove, consistently, to be by far the nerdiest of the three of us. Thank you to my precious young children Theodore and Caroline, without whom this book would have been completed several years earlier. Thanks to Teddy for introducing me to Disney's "The Lion Guard," and to Caroline for reintroducing me to 5:20 a.m.

Finally, thank you to my wife Jen, whose love and companionship make the highs of life feel so much higher. Strictly speaking, this book project is older than our marriage; we tied the knot back home in Colorado in August 2012. In that time, Jen witnessed firsthand the stress and struggles of graduate school, the academic job market, and the tenure track. She also endured the weather that accompanies a tailgate party on a late November morning outside Ohio Stadium. She always centered me after long, exhausting days that sometimes felt like I had very little to show for it. Whether it was a game of tennis, conversation over Chipotle burritos, or a glass of red wine on a patio, Jen's presence in my life always reminded me that I have a best friend and partner, no matter how the academic rat race turned out. Without Jen's patience, help, and positivity, I never would have been able to get this thing finished. I dedicate this book to her, with love and thanks.

Preface

While campaigning for the office of president of the United States, Donald J. Trump called publicly for a "total and complete shutdown" of the entry of Muslims to the United States. Upon gaining the office, his first executive order banned travel into the United States from several majority-Muslim countries. This order blocked citizens of Iran, Iraq, Syria, Libya, Somalia, Sudan, and Yemen from entering the country for ninety days and permanently blocked the entry of Syrian refugees. Protests exploded across the country, with marchers chanting their opposition to, in their words, President Trump's "Muslim Ban".

Several lower federal courts ruled that this first executive order was motivated by religious animus, likely rendering it unconstitutional on the merits. These courts granted injunctions blocking the ban from being enforced while these issues were litigated. Rather than continue defending the original order, the administration issued a revision. On March 6, 2017, the president announced a new travel ban, aimed at defeating the legal difficulties of the original. Iraq was dropped from the list of banned countries, and Syrian refugees were now blocked for 120 days instead of permanently. This order contained language stressing national security concerns as a primary motivator for the bill (Order No. 13780, 82 Fed. Reg. 13209), arguing that "nationals [of these countries] continue to present heightened risks to the security of the United States (§1(e))."

However, lower federal courts continued to rule against the constitutionality of this revised executive order, and injunctions against its enforcement remained in place. Unusually, these opinions cited the president's own Twitter account (@realDonaldTrump) as evidence of religious animus, due to his statements made during the presidential campaign (*Hawaii v. Trump*, _____

F.Supp. 3d_____, 2017 WL 1167383). The administration filed a petition for a writ of certiorari to the Supreme Court, asking the Court to take the case. Of course, the goal of this action was the reinstatement of the ban and a declaration of its constitutionality via a favorable judgment of the Supreme Court.

On June 26, 2017, the Court allowed elements of this second ban on travel from six majority-Muslim countries to go into immediate effect (582 U.S. _____ (Slip Op.), *Trump v. International Refugee Assistance Project*). The Court granted cert on the question of whether this second ban was constitutional. The justices issued special instructions stipulating that arguments ought to be held in October 2017 (i.e., as soon as ordinarily possible). Crucially, the justices had to decide whether to keep the injunctions in place or to allow the ban to go into effect in the interim period between the granting of certiorari and the issuance of a final judgment on the merits.

The justices issued their judgment on this issue per curiam. In a brief, unsigned opinion, the justices resolved this question by focusing only on what a reasonable outcome in the instant case would be, avoiding a broader doctrinal analysis altogether. In a mixed judgment, the Court allowed the ban to go into effect during the intervening period, but only for individuals lacking a "bona fide" connection to the United States—that is, an immediate familial, educational, or occupational connection (Slip Op. at 9).

A dissenting opinion by Justice Clarence Thomas, joined by Justices Samuel Alito and Neil Gorsuch, pointed out that the balancing act the per curiam opinion crafted was not a remedy that either party had asked for. Further, this remedy raised immediate confusion: what exactly counts as a "bona fide" relationship? The per curiam opinion did not rigorously define this class of persons. This decision seemed to make the entry of some individuals subject to idiosyncratic decisions by lower officials. The limited scope of the Court's reasoning seemed destined to confound those who would try to defer to the Court's judgment.

If travelers with similar circumstances gain or fail to gain entry to the country arbitrarily, based on this vague rationale, would this outcome represent a just resolution? Is resolving the uncertainty about the travel ban's constitutionality worth the price of issuing a judgment without a fully fleshed out reason? Should the Supreme Court have stayed on the sidelines, letting the other branches of government make policy in this fraught arena?

The United States government exercises authority over citizens' lives and property through the judicial system. The Supreme Court, as just one example, holds the power of life or death over every inmate facing capital punishment. The justices enjoy extraordinary authority, vested, proverbially, in their marble palace in the District of Columbia. They may remain on the Court for life if they so choose. The voting public has no direct say in who ascends to the Court, nor can the public remove a justice via the ballot box. How can this independence and authority be justified?

When we consider whether this Court is performing adequately or not, it is easy to recall decisions it has made that could be viewed as inappropriate or exemplary. Surely the Court's preliminary judgment in *Trump v. International Refugee Assistance Project* angered some observers and pleased others. It is depressingly typical to hear that the Court behaves in far too liberal or too conservative a manner.

This book, however, is not concerned with whether Democrats and Republicans are happy with the ideology of the Supreme Court's decisions. Instead, consider what a definition of a well-functioning constitutional court, ideology aside, might entail. Then, compare the Supreme Court to that definition. Any such definition must arguably contain at least two elements: first, decisiveness, and, second, consistency.

The Supreme Court exists, in large part, to say "what the law is." That is, when conflict or confusion arises about whether a law or an action violates the Constitution, the Supreme Court steps in to settle things. Without this national arbiter, disagreements between lower courts could not be satisfactorily resolved, and perhaps the elected, majoritarian branches would exert more influence over law and policy than they presently do. Therefore, under our separation of powers system, the Court ought to exercise decisiveness in resolving disputes and conflicts.

In addition to resolving disputes, however, judicial bodies also ought to provide consistent rationales for their judgments. Consistency means that the outcome of a dispute is supported by reasoning, which itself is supported by a majority of judges on a collegial court. A judgment without a collective rationale, conversely, is an *unreasoned judgment*. In such a judgment, the Court collectively tells the nation, in essence: "Here's what we did. We (as a Court) can't tell you why."

Take *Trump v. International Refugee Assistance Project*. The Court ruled that the travel ban could go into limited effect immediately. Why? Because the Court said so. As lower judges, legislators, and citizens must interpret and obey legal doctrine proclaimed by the Court, the comprehensibility and coherence of that doctrine remains paramount. Therefore, the Court ought to resolve disputes with consistent sets of of opinions to the maximal extent possible.

Unfortunately, these goals of decisiveness and consistency seem to exist in direct conflict. A court that prioritizes decisiveness will generate more unreasoned outcomes as it resolves to tackle complex but important cases. And a court that maximizes the logical consistency of its opinions will inevitably avoid (if their rules allow it) some of these complex but important cases. It seems unlikely or even impossible to design a constitutional court that could simultaneously prioritize these two goals.

Some claim that resolving fundamental questions of life, liberty, and property in an inconsistent manner lacks legitimacy due to the absence of collective reasons given for the exercise of authority. Others contend that inconsistency in and of itself does not represent grounds for criticism—some inconsistency may be required for a large and diverse society to make progress on issues involving passionate and divergent preferences. Still others criticize courts for failing to resolve important conflicts between lower bodies, arguing that leaving the law unsettled makes for arbitrary and unpredictable outcomes for everyday people and businesses.

How can we adjudicate between these criticisms? If a consequence of decisiveness is the production of unreasoned judgments then it is essential to understand these judgments in particular. In the following pages, I analyze the properties of unreasoned judgments, and then turn attention to the impact of these judgments in the legal system and society.

Some might believe that unreasoned judgment is an esoteric phenomenon of primarily academic interest. Yet I find over five hundred such judgments in the Court's output between 1946–2010. My analysis shows that unreasoned judgments arise with unsettling frequency in politically salient cases and in exercises of judicial review. Further, it appears that the Court may not resolve conflicts between lower courts when such resolution would generate an unreasoned judgment.

Probing the mechanics of this phenomenon, I then show that the frequency of unreasoned judgments fell considerably after 1988, when the Supreme Court gained virtually total discretion to set its agenda. Thus, stability-enhancing institutions for legislative committees, like agenda control, can also improve the consistency of a collegial court's output. Yet while these reforms improved the consistency of the Court's output, they simultaneously reduced the amount of conflicts the Court resolves on an annual basis. Therefore, in the modern era, the Supreme Court evolved from an institution that prioritized decisiveness to one that appears to prioritize consistency.

Was this evolution positive? Turning to the impact of inconsistency, I show that unreasoned judgments receive little deference and fewer citations in the lower levels of the federal judicial hierarchy. Thus, an unreasoned judgment arguably wastes the time and resources of the Supreme Court.

From the perspective of the judicial system, then, unreasoned judgments are hardly a welcome sight. However, I show that Congress does not appear to be bothered by unreasoned judgments with any unusual intensity. Finally, I show that exposure to an inconsistent opinion does not reduce diffuse support for the Court among ordinary citizens. These latter two findings mitigate somewhat against the existential threat some argue inconsistency poses. Thus, relative to inconsistency, the broader consequences of indecision seem likely greater, as unreasoned judgments carry few consequences outside of the judicial hierarchy. The Court's evolution toward consistency and away from decisiveness appears to serve the Court's needs while impeding societal progress.

CHAPTER I

Introduction

> It not uncommonly happens, that there are two statutes existing at one time, clashing in whole or in part with each other, and neither of them containing any repealing clause or expression. In such a case, it is the province of the courts to liquidate and fix their meaning and operation.
>
> —Alexander Hamilton, "Federalist No. 78"

> The state is a necessary institution and it necessarily has a power of interfering with people...how is its power of interference to be made non-arbitrary?
>
> —Philip Pettit, "Deliberative Democracy and the Discursive Dilemma"

Five times. Criminals broke into Otis McDonald's home five separate times. He'd had enough. He resolved to protect himself and his home by whatever means necessary. Mr. McDonald, retired maintenance engineer, watched the neighborhood around his home deteriorate as the years passed, and he was fed up. Yet Mr. McDonald lived in Chicago, which at the time banned the personal ownership of handguns.

The Second Amendment to the United States Constitution reads, in full, "A well regulated Militia, being necessary to the security of a free State, the right of the people to keep and bear Arms, shall not be infringed." Yet it wasn't until 2008 that the Supreme Court interpreted this amendment to mean that an *individual's* right to own firearms was protected, as opposed to the right to own firearms related to militia service.[1] Moreover, that ruling did not incorporate the Second Amendment, meaning that as of 2008, this constitutional protection of the individual right to keep and bear arms did not apply to state and municipal laws.*

So, Mr. McDonald, along with several other frustrated citizens, filed a lawsuit against the city. They lost their case and a subsequent appeal. The Supreme Court then took the case. In *McDonald v. Chicago* (561 U.S. 742 [2010]), the Court produced a puzzling outcome (Cohen and Stearns 2010). The Court's judgment did incorporate the Second Amendment, invalidating Chicago's handgun ban. What reason did the Court provide for this substantial change in law and public policy? The City's brief pointed out that handguns in Chicago were routinely being used in the commission of the same violent acts that so frustrated Mr. McDonald. The ban was an effort to stem this tide (Brief For Respondents City of Chicago and Village of Oak Park, Otis McDonald et al. v. City of Chicago 2010).

Four of the nine justices participating subscribed to the rationale that the Second Amendment should be incorporated based upon the due process clause of the Fourteenth Amendment. Justice Clarence Thomas subscribed to the rationale that the Second Amendment should be incorporated based upon the privileges or immunities clause of the Fourteenth Amendment and rejected the due process rationale. The four justices subscribing to the due process rationale also explicitly rejected Justice Thomas's rationale. Thus, five of nine justices held that the Second Amendment should *not* be incorporated based on the due process rationale, and eight of nine justices held that the Second Amendment should *not* be incorporated based on the privileges or immunities rationale. Table 1.1 shows the voting coalitions in *McDonald*.

Despite these fractured coalitions over rationales, the Court incorporated the Second Amendment, and handguns are no longer banned in Chicago.

TABLE 1.1. Unreasoned Judgment in *McDonald*

	Premise (1) Due process	Premise (2) Privileges or immunities	Judgment
Thomas	N	Y	R
Scalia	Y	N	R
Roberts	Y	N	R
Alito	Y	N	R
Kennedy	Y	N	R
Breyer	N	N	A
Ginsburg	N	N	A
Sotomayor	N	N	A
Stevens	N	N	A
Court	*N*	*N*	*R*

Note: Either premise 1 or 2 must have majority support for a reversal to exhibit consistency.

Although a majority of justices preferred the outcome of incorporation, neither rationale provided for this judgment carried majority support; hence, *McDonald* was a judgment without a reason—an *unreasoned judgment* (Cohen and Stearns 2010).

Scholars variously refer to this phenomenon as a "doctrinal paradox" (Kornhauser and Sager 1986) or "discursive dilemma" (List and Pettit 2002; Pettit 2001). Yet the idea of a judgment without a collective reason extends beyond the specific formal definition of the doctrinal paradox. For example, the Court similarly fails to give a collective reason for its judgments in many of its opinions issued per curiam (by the Court). In such a decision, the justices announce a judgment with a short, unsigned opinion; this behavior also appears to constitute unreasoned judgment in certain circumstances.

Further, Kornhauser and Sager (1986) were not the first to apply social choice principles to the Court. Easterbrook (1982) notes that Arrow's (1951) impossibility theorem implies that the Court cannot guarantee its decisions always will exhibit logical consistency. This argument suggests that the Court's reasons may not coincide with its judgments in a wider array of instances than previous scholars have shown.

This phenomenon of unreasoned judgment happens whenever the judgment of the Court is issued without accompanying reasoning that is itself supported by a majority of the justices. In essence, the Court said in *McDonald* that Chicago's handgun ban was invalid, but it could not collectively provide a reason why.

The Purpose of a Supreme Court

The Constitution grants great independence to the Supreme Court. The justices serve for life and are never directly subjected to the electoral process. In ceding some of the authority of the state to an unelected, life-tenured body, clearly the framers who supported Article III intended to get something valuable from this court in return. In "Federalist No. 78," Alexander Hamilton discusses the need for an independent judiciary that is capable of resolving conflicts between different statutes. Hamilton also envisioned a judiciary capable of determining whether a given statute violated the Constitution. Thus, the framers' empowerment of this Supreme Court with its tremendous independence happened at least in part out of a desire for decisive resolution of conflicts over what the Constitution means.

In addition to decisiveness, the norms of just republican governance require that judicial bodies provide a reason for their actions. The Supreme

Court lacks an electoral mandate and famously enjoys the power of neither the purse nor the sword (Hamilton, Madison, and Jay 2008). Therefore, its explanations for why it exercised its authority as it did are paramount.

States exercise authority over citizens' lives and property through the judicial system. In the United States, the Supreme Court sits at the apex of the judiciary, resolving fundamental questions about life, liberty, property, and the allocation of political power. In principle, judicial bodies ought to justify this responsibility by providing consistent rationales for their judgments. Consistency means that the outcome of a dispute is supported by reasoning that itself is supported by a majority of judges on a collegial court. Yet without strong assumptions, collective decision making in collegial courts and other bodies is susceptible to inconsistency.

Because the Court lacks the legitimacy conferred by democratic accountability, it instead must protect its institutional legitimacy in part through the quality of its reasoning. Because the Court relies on other institutions to enforce its rulings, the quality of its reasoning is therefore integral to its efficacy as an institution. A loss of legitimacy in the eyes of the other branches could carry potentially dire consequences for the Court and the rule of law in America generally.

Avoiding inconsistencies between the Court's judgments and its rationales is perhaps the lowest objective standard for high-quality reasoning. If a decision of the Court is unreasoned, then the Court exercises its authority without providing a reason for its actions at the collective level. Pettit (2001) emphasizes that the minimum threshold for the legitimate exercise of government authority requires providing reasons. He writes:

> How are people to be empowered in relation to democratic majorities and democratic elites? How are they to be given a power of contestation against them. Whatever else is necessary, it seems clear that they must be able to ask after the reasons that support the decisions...it must be possible...to challenge such decisions on the grounds that the reasons quoted are not sound. (Pettit 2001, 282)

Resolving fundamental questions of life, liberty, and property in an inconsistent manner arguably lacks legitimacy due to the absence of reasons given.[2] The Court's reasoning can hardly appear persuasive to others when a majority of the justices oppose all suggested rationales for its judgment.

The term "legitimacy" used here should not be taken as synonymous with the concept of judicial legitimacy or diffuse support in the mass public (Caldeira and Gibson 1992). I make no claim that inconsistent decisions directly undermine public confidence in the Court. Rather, "illegitimacy" here should be taken to mean that the decision lacks the established normative features of legitimate republican governance. Chapter 7 explores the question of whether unreasoned judgments undermine both diffuse and specific support for the Court in the mass public; the evidence suggests they do not.

The Fundamental Irreconcilability of Decisiveness and Consistency

So, it is imperative that the Supreme Court resolve important conflicts while providing consistent reasoning for its judgments. These imperatives, however, stand in opposition to each other. Frequently, the sorts of questions that contain sufficient complexity and controversy to demand resolution by the Court will, due to this very same complexity and controversy, be nearly impossible to resolve with a consistent judgment and rationale.[3]

Indeed, as Sunstein (2007) points out, it is often difficult for a group of people to agree on an underpinning theory for a constitutional judgment while simultaneously agreeing on a proper resolution to a specific conflict. Sunstein advises "incomplete theorization" as a remedy to this problem: essentially, allow the group to reach a judgment that a majority can support, even if their underpinning rationales vary. Sunstein, in so arguing, prioritizes the necessity of decisiveness over complete consistency between judgments and rationales.

As an example of this dynamic, consider the experience of Justice Stephen Breyer, who, prior to joining the Court, served on the United States Sentencing Commission. With his colleagues, Mr. Breyer was tasked with writing new federal sentencing guidelines. These guidelines would instruct federal judges on the proper range of punishments for various crimes. Federal judges would be allowed to depart from this range but they would have to give an explanation (Breyer 1988).

The commission's collective judgments about how much prison time the various crimes in the federal code should require rested on a wide range of theories of punishment as well as practical rationales. For instance, Breyer recalls that some people wanted the commission to follow a "just desserts" theory of punishment (Breyer 1988, 15). This approach would rank-order crimes in terms of severity and then scale the punishments accordingly.

However, the problems associated with collectively applying this seemingly commonsense approach rapidly became apparent: "The difficulty that arises in applying this approach is that different Commissioners have different views about the correct rank order of the seriousness of different crimes." (Breyer 1988, 15) That is, because of underlying abstract disagreements about the relative severity of, say, embezzlement, pollution, and theft, the commissioners could not arrive at a concrete collective judgment about how much prison time each crime warranted.

Instead, the commission abdicated on the question of what theory of punishment to apply. They simply "decided to base the Guidelines primarily upon typical, or average, actual past practice" (Breyer 1988, 17) Faced with a congressional mandate to produce the guidelines, the commission ultimately made judgments about how much prison time various crimes warranted without coalescing around a supporting reason or theory. The commission (by necessity) prioritized decisiveness, producing the guidelines without resolving the question of *why* certain crimes deserved more or less punishment.

At the Supreme Court, the justices typically choose which cases to hear and which to ignore. If the Court resolved to hear as many important conflicts as it could handle, thus prioritizing decisiveness, it would inevitably end up promulgating unreasoned judgments. I explore an example of this dynamic in the following section.

Conversely, the Court could protect the logical consistency and quality of its opinions by ignoring complex and multifaceted cases. It could allow a thorny conflict to "percolate" in the lower courts for years in hopes of seeing the complexity of the problem reduced (Clark and Kastellec 2013). Of course, not all of these conflicts will "percolate" sufficiently to allow for a clean, consistent set of opinions. Therefore, prioritizing consistency means that the Court will leave numerous important questions and conflicts unresolved (Hellman 1995).

The Supreme Court's workload exhibits wide variation over time. Figure 1.1 shows the number of cases argued in the Court during the modern era, 1946–2010. The volume of cases before the Court varies considerably over time but appears to be on a clear downward trajectory. These workload data, along with a trove of other useful information on the Court, can be found in Epstein et al. (2012).

Owens and Simon (2012) considered a variety of causes for this decline. They expressed some surprise in finding a durable effect of an institutional change on the Court's workload; the Supreme Court Case Selections Act of 1988 is robustly associated with a decline in the number of cases heard. This act, lobbied for by all nine sitting justices at the time, allowed the Court greater discretion over its docket. Essentially, this act gave the justices almost total freedom to opt *not* to decide most disputes. As such, whether

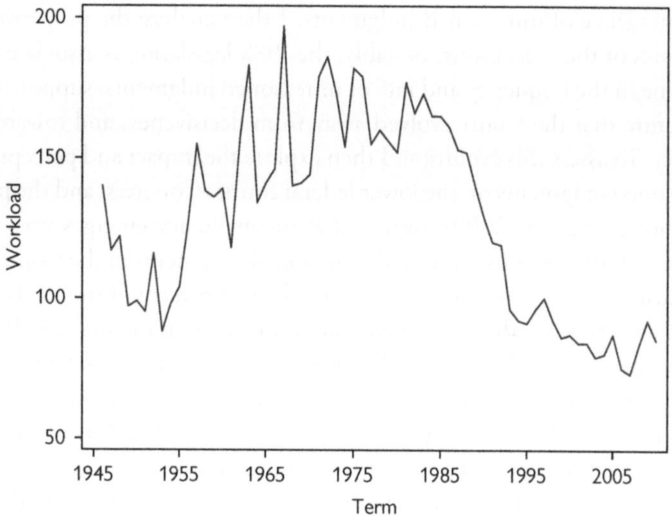

Fig. 1.1. Workload of the Supreme Court 1946–2010

consciously or not, the modern Supreme Court actively evolved away from decisiveness.

The justices respond to multiple audiences and seek to satisfy multiple goals (Baum 2006; Epstein and Knight 2013). Other judges, lawyers, and law professors consume and respond to the opinions of the Court. Unreasoned judgments can strike these elite legal audiences as especially incoherent and difficult to follow (Leonard 1984; McAleer 2013; Post and Salop 1992). As such, sensitivity to this criticism and a desire to produce "good" (consistent) law may induce the justices to prioritize consistency over decisiveness. Indeed, the justices express a desire for consistent law in their own private deliberations, as I will demonstrate below.

A single constitutional court cannot maximize both decisiveness and consistency. Certainly the modern Supreme Court has taken no steps toward *increasing* the number of disputes it resolves and indeed appears to have moved in the opposite direction.

Is the movement a good thing? Is the Court fulfilling its purpose as Hamilton and other like-minded framers intended? A confident empirical answer to such a large and normatively loaded question will likely eternally evade researchers. However, no progress at all can be made until the properties and consequences of unreasoned judgments are better understood.

This book's purpose is the systematic study of unreasoned judgments, aimed at contributing to that understanding. I offer a new theory predicting the emergence of unreasoned judgments. I then analyze the properties and dynamics of these decisions. Notably, the 1988 legislation is associated with a decline in the frequency and rate of unreasoned judgments, supporting the conjecture that the Court evolved away from decisiveness and toward consistency. To assess this evolution, I then explore the impact and perception of unreasoned judgments on the lower federal courts, Congress, and the public.

Scholars (Stearns 2000) assume that inconsistency emerges very rarely. Yet I have found over five hundred unreasoned judgments in the Court's output during 1946–2010, composing as much as 15 percent of the total output in certain terms. Further, precedents stemming from unreasoned judgments are less useful to the lower federal courts than consistent precedents. Unreasoned judgments occur more frequently in important or politically salient cases and when the Court exercises its power to invalidate Acts of Congress.

Moreover, it appears the Court may not resolve circuit conflicts when such resolution would generate an unreasoned judgment. Interestingly, however, neither Congress nor the mass public appears to mind an unreasoned judgment any more than they would a consistent, but ideologically displeasing, judgment. The evidence suggests that unreasoned judgments are viewed negatively by legal audiences, but not necessarily by legislative or mass public audiences.

It appears, then, that some amount of inconsistency may represent an unavoidable phenomenon that, while not innocuous, is likely acceptable from a societal viewpoint. Therefore, on balance, the modern Court's resolution of this difficulty may actually represent a less desirable arrangement than one that prioritized decisiveness. To support this argument, I continue with a theory for the emergence of unreasoned judgment at the Court that will be tested empirically in subsequent chapters.

Motivating a Theory of Unreasoned Judgment

The Supreme Court issues unreasoned judgments reluctantly. The justices themselves appear to know that these inconsistencies are undesirable and often prioritize securing a consistent majority opinion (Epstein and Knight 1998). However, under certain conditions, unreasoned judgments emerge. To give an example of these conditions and to demonstrate that the justices dislike inconsistency, consider the case of *Burson v. Freeman* (504 U.S. 191 [1992]).[4]

In this case, a campaign treasurer for a candidate for city council (Mary Rebecca Freeman) challenged a Tennessee statute that created a campaign-free zone within one hundred feet of a polling place. Freeman's challenge rested on the fact that the statute restricted political speech in a content-based manner. The Tennessee Supreme Court agreed with Freeman, invalidating the statute. The state of Tennessee filed a writ of certiorari, granted by the Supreme Court.

The dispute's resolution would impact similar election laws in every state. Further, the dispute implicated the limits of the government's ability to regulate political speech, a core component of individual liberty in the United States. In a preliminary memorandum to the justices regarding the petition for a writ of certiorari (i.e., an analysis of the case before the Court agrees to hear it), the law clerk writing to the justices stated, "This case is one of national significance...there are obviously a variety of interests implicated in this case."[5]

The Court's decision on the constitutionality of the Tennessee statute turned on three issues: whether the area within one hundred feet of a polling place constitute a public forum (as political speech in public forums is subject to strenuous constitutional protection), the level of scrutiny for content-based restrictions on political speech (Schurr 1994, 873), and whether the historical tradition of restrictive zones around polling places was a sufficient reason for upholding the statute.

Of the eight participating justices, three agreed that the Tennessee Supreme Court was correct, and the statute was unconstitutional. Five, a majority, thought the statute was constitutional. Four justices, the plurality of this majority, believed that the streets and sidewalks near polling places constitute a public forum. These justices then subjected the statute to strict scrutiny (the highest legal standard of scrutiny). However, they concluded that the statute survived strict scrutiny. They stated in their opinion that this content-specific regulation of speech survived strict scrutiny because states should not have to restrict other forms of speech that do not create the evils the state wishes to curtail (Schurr 1994, 878).

The fifth justice who believed the Tennessee law was constitutional, Antonin Scalia, disagreed. Justice Scalia believed that streets and sidewalks were not public forums. Therefore, he argued, the plurality's standard of strict scrutiny for laws of this type was inappropriate. Justice Scalia contended instead that laws creating restricted zones around polling places had existed for over one hundred years. Therefore, based on this historical tradition, these laws should not be overridden by a right to freedom of speech on streets and sidewalks. While the plurality acknowledged the historical background of laws like the Tennessee statute, they did not concur with this historical justification.

They concluded that the law survived strict scrutiny due to the state's compelling interest in providing free and fair elections. Table 1.2 shows the

TABLE 1.2. Unreasoned Judgment in *Burson*

	Premise (1) Public forum	Premise (2) Strict scrutiny appropriate	Premise (3) Tradition	Judgment
Blackmun	Y	Y	N	R
Rehnquist	Y	Y	N	R
Kennedy	Y	Y	N	R
White	Y	Y	N	R
Scalia	N	N	Y	R
O'Connor	N	N	N	A
Stevens	N	N	N	A
Souter	N	N	N	A
Court	*N*	*N*	*N*	*R*

Note: A = affirm, R = reverse.
Either premises 1 and 2 or premise 3 must have majority support for a reversal to exhibit consistency.

final voting coalitions in this case. Table 1.2 demonstrates that no rationale for the Court's judgment is supported by a majority—*Burson* is an unreasoned judgment.

As Justice Blackmun drafted what would ultimately be the plurality opinion, he expressed a desire instead for a consistent majority rationale. He courted Justice Scalia's endorsement of his draft rationale to this end. Justice Blackmun wrote to Justice Scalia, "With the campaign-free zones of forty-seven states on the line and two more First Amendment, public forum cases on our March calendar, I think that it is especially important for us to try to have a majority opinion in *Burson.*"[6]

After a series of revisions, Scalia responded to Blackmun. His response also demonstrated a distaste for an unreasoned judgment. Justice Scalia indicated his mutual desire for a majority rationale: "My preferred basis for deciding this case is that this is not a public forum and therefore strict scrutiny does not apply. I have extended myself to make a court [a majority opinion] on the theory that, in this case, this arrangement meets strict scrutiny, principally because history says it does."[7] However, Scalia reveals his motivation for leaving Blackmun's opinion and creating an unreasoned judgment, however distasteful, later in the same memo: "But I am very much unwilling to generalize from this case to others. I do not think that...the last two sentences of your latest proposal accord with our strict-scrutiny principles."

Blackmun responded a few days later:

> "While I appreciate your having extended yourself to make a Court in *Burson*, I am unwilling to remove the two sentences you object to...The principle that the 'First Amendment does not require States to regulate for problems that

> do not exist' is implicit in our decision...quite frankly, I am more comfortable with this general proposition than the one you offer, *i.e.*, that a law can pass strict scrutiny 'because history says it does.'[8]

These memos show that both Justices Scalia and Blackmun wanted the Tennessee statute to survive. Additionally, Justices Scalia and Blackmun both expressed a distaste for a fractious, inconsistent set of opinions. If obtaining a majority opinion was so important to Blackmun, why did he hold out and allow an inconsistency to emerge based on two sentences? And why did Scalia refuse to join the plurality opinion?

The answer, for both justices, was that the doctrinal implications of the decision for other pending cases and for the laws in other states were more important than avoiding inconsistency in this instance. Scalia, as his memos indicated, feared subjecting similar statutes to strict scrutiny, as the plurality opinion would have suggested. Conversely, Blackmun sought to avoid any constitutional argument that rested on a purely historical analysis, as Scalia's proposed rationale did. Indeed, "the more far-reaching a judge believes a particular case to be, the greater will be the desire to set out any disagreements in detail, often in the hope of offering some limitations on the scope of that decision" (Leonard 1984, 316).

The import of these doctrinal concerns shows through in private memos from one of Blackmun's clerks to the justice. This clerk, who was responsible for the opinion draft, signed her memos with only the name "Steff."[9] She wrote to Blackmun:

> "I'm the last person in the world who wants to see general principles come out of *Burson.* Like you, I fear that the only general principles that will come from this case are those that will haunt you...while AS' [Antonin Scalia's] vote would give you a majority opinion, it may also result in his citing *Burson* for the proposition that the scope of fundamental liberties depends on 'tradition'—a proposition you rejected in your *Bowers* dissent, and one that could come back to haunt you in *Casey*."[10]

The *Casey* case that "Steff" refers to is almost certainly *Planned Parenthood v. Casey* (505 U.S. 833 [1992]), a landmark decision that upheld the right to abortion but allowed more stringent restrictions on the practice. Justice Blackmun and his clerk apparently feared establishing a precedent allowing historical analysis to serve as the rationale for an argument that the right to an abortion is not, in fact, a fundamental liberty.

Burson resulted in an unreasoned judgment for four reasons. First, the case was of broad national importance, touching on election laws in every state, and the justices perhaps felt compelled to resolve it. Second, the majority of justices who favored reversal did so for different reasons, along different dimensions (or legal issues). Third, the justices' preferences were such that no single rationale was supported by a majority of justices. Fourth, the broader doctrinal concerns of these justices were more important to them than producing a consistent majority opinion in the instant case. Thus, while an unreasoned judgment represents an undesirable outcome for the justices, one resulted nonetheless in *Burson*. These internal deliberations offer clues as to why the Court produces inconsistencies and motivate a more general theory for the emergence of unreasoned judgment.

I now present a simple theory that offers testable predictions regarding the emergence of unreasoned judgments. The motivation for this theory arises from the formal literature on inconsistency as a general phenomenon, as well as qualitative analysis of the Court's internal deliberations.

A Theory of Inconsistency

Unreasoned judgments can arise when the Court faces a dispute that meets several necessary conditions; as the example of *Burson* illustrates, the justices would rather avoid producing an inconsistency if it can be helped. As such, when the justices are faced with disputes that can be resolved in other ways, that tends to be their preference. Consistent decisions might be seen as more praiseworthy by the elite intellectual peers of the justices—a critical audience (Baum 2006). Further, consistent decisions are likely easier for lower courts to apply, increasing the policy influence of the doctrine promulgated (Hitt 2016).

The literature on inconsistency and analysis of the internal deliberations of the justices themselves suggest these necessary conditions for inconsistency. A case that satisfies the first three conditions discussed below will theoretically result in an unreasoned judgment in some form. A case that also satisfies the fourth condition will result in a doctrinal paradox, a particularly visible form of unreasoned judgment.

Jurisdiction Condition

The Supreme Court enjoys considerable discretion to determine which cases it will hear. This discretion increased in 1988, when an Act of Congress gave the Court even more latitude to determine its agenda. As a result of greater agenda control, the Court decides considerably fewer cases today compared with earlier years (Owens and Simon 2012). Almost every case the Court now decides arises from the Court's discretionary jurisdiction. For the Court to hear a case, at least four justices must vote to grant certiorari.

The justices vote strategically on these cert petitions (Black and Owens 2009; Caldeira, Wright, and Zorn 1999; Kleiner and Moldovanu 2017). That is, the justices anticipate what the final outcome of a case might be if cert were granted. Given this anticipation, they vote at the agenda stage to attain their best possible final outcome. As the internal memos of the Court show, the justices dislike inconsistent decisions. As such, if the justices anticipate that a case may result in an inconsistency, they might prefer to avoid that case altogether by denying cert.

For a case to result in an unreasoned judgment, therefore, it must satisfy a jurisdiction condition (C1). The jurisdiction condition can be satisfied in one of two ways. First, a particular case could be of such importance that resolving the case, even with an inconsistency, is preferable to the justices compared with leaving the dispute unresolved (C1a). *Burson*, for example, satisfies C1a—the law clerk writing the cert memorandum noted the broad significance of the dispute and the issues involved.

Interestingly, this clerk also recommended a denial of cert despite the importance of the issue—perhaps recognizing the eventual difficulties the justices would face. Or alternatively, the clerk might have simply been exercising caution; clerks tend to be more conservative in recommending cert than the justices themselves (Blake, Hacker, and Hopwood 2015).

Other cases satisfy the jurisdiction condition in this way as well. Any case for which the immediate judgment in the case, as opposed to the issues involved, is of such importance that the justices prefer to resolve the case, even inconsistently, satisfies this condition. *Bush v. Gore* (531 U.S. 98 [2000]) satisfies C1a due to the importance of the immediate judgment, for example.

Cases can satisfy the jurisdiction condition in a second way. For certain classes of disputes, the Court has mandatory jurisdiction. That is, the Court is obliged to consider the case and issue a ruling, irrespective of what the the justices prefer.

Justices dislike these mandatory cases. In the 1920s and again in the 1980s, the justices successfully lobbied Congress to eliminate some classes of disputes that fell under mandatory jurisdiction. The elimination of these classes of mandatory jurisdiction cases increased the Court's discretion (and leisure time), while deprioritizing decisiveness. As of 2019, however, some disputes remain mandatory. As such, any case arising under the Court's mandatory jurisdiction satisfies the jurisdiction condition by definition (C1b).

As of this writing, the types of disputes that still fall under mandatory jurisdiction are appeals of final decisions of three-judge district court panels in select areas. In particular, appeals to decisions related to reapportionment cases, cases arising under the Voting Rights Act and Civil Rights Act, and cases arising under the Presidential Election Campaign Fund Act remain subject to a mandatory appeal.

Similarly, Congress cannot alter the Court's original jurisdiction, though it can extend concurrent jurisdiction in such matters to other courts. The Court's original jurisdiction is stipulated in Article III of the Constitution. These cases, in which the Supreme Court is the first court to hear a case, arise rarely today. Original jurisdiction covers disputes between two or more states (usually over boundary disputes), state(s) and the federal government, a lawsuit brought by a state against a citizen of a different state, and actions to which ambassadors and other public ministers are parties. Such original jurisdiction cases naturally also satisfy the jurisdiction condition.

Case Characteristics Condition

The formal work on discursive dilemmas and doctrinal paradoxes (a subset of unreasoned judgments) shows that disputes must have more than one dimension of conflict to result in an inconsistency (Pauly and Van Hees 2006). The median voter theorem (Black 1948) maintains that on a single-dimension conflict, a stable equilibrium results, centered on the preferences of the median actor. Similarly, if there is only one legal issue or question at stake, then it follows that a majority of justices have to support both the judgment and the rationale in order to resolve the case.

That is, a case with only one issue or question is in effect a dispute with a single dimension. Unidimensional decision problems are not subject to inconsistency. As such, no inconsistency can possibly occur for cases with only one dimension of conflict. A case that is sufficiently complex to include at least two dimensions of conflict (i.e., contains multiple legal issues) therefore satisfies the case characteristics condition (C2).

Preference Condition

Stearns (2000) shows that a multidimensional dispute, in and of itself, will not necessarily generate an inconsistency. Stearns points out that if the preferences of the justices can be arranged from left to right on every dimension of conflict, then the result is not paradoxical. List (2003) and Dietrich

(2006) show formally that if the actors making a collective judgment can be ordered from right to left on every proposition (both the legal rationales and the judgment itself), then the doctrinal paradox is not possible.

This requirement is quite similar to the single-peakedness assumption of spatial models of voting (e.g., (Black 1948)). Thus, if the preferences of the justices cannot be aligned on a left-to-right spectrum on every proposition in a dispute, then that dispute satisfies the preference condition (C3) and may result in an unreasoned judgment.

Doctrinal Condition

Any dispute that satisfies C1, C2, and C3 satisfies necessary conditions for unreasoned judgment. As I elaborate on in chapter 2, unreasoned judgment arises in several different ways. The most visible of these manifestations, doctrinal paradoxes (which appear as plurality decisions), satisfy one final condition.

As the discussion of *Burson* showed, these paradoxes may occur when the justices' preferences over long-run doctrine outweigh their concerns over the consistency of the immediate judgment. As such, justices sacrifice consistency in the immediate case to avoid creating a clear and consistent precedent they disfavor (Leonard 1984). Indeed, it may be the case that individual justices cultivate unreasoned judgment in certain instances in order to sabotage the doctrinal position of the plurality.

That is, at times certain justices seem to prefer making a ruling that is difficult or impossible for lower courts to apply consistently than to promulgate a coherent doctrine they disagree with. As such, whenever long-run doctrine matters more to the justices who favor the majority's judgment, a doctrinal paradox will result if the other three conditions are also met, along with this doctrinal condition (C4).

When the first three conditions are met but the doctrinal condition is unmet, that means that a potentially inconsistent case is before the Court, and the justices are more concerned about the judgment than the long-run doctrinal implications of their rulings. Cases for which the judgment matters more than the long-run doctrine raise the possibility of poor opinion quality (Carrubba et al. 2012). In these instances, the justices may be willing to compromise on doctrine by issuing a less transparent form of unreasoned judgment.

These less visible types of unreasoned judgment, discussed in detail in chapter 2, can appear in at least two forms. First, the justices may agree to issue an opinion per curiam. In this manner, the Court presents a unified front for its judgment without committing itself to doctrine some justices disagree with. Second, justices may subordinate their preferences regarding long-run doctrine to secure the judgment desired in the instant case. When a case meets conditions C1, C2, and C3, but not C4, then a different, less visible form of unreasoned judgment results. This judgment can manifest observably as an opinion per curiam or unobservably as an instance of preference subordination—in which some justices join opinions contrary to their sincere preference on issues of legal doctrine in order to secure a majority opinion.

For instance, in *National Federation of Independent Business v. Sebelius* (132 S. Ct. 2566 [2012]), the Court upheld the individual mandate portion of the Affordable Care Act (ACA). Four traditionally liberal justices wrote a lengthy opinion that would have upheld the ACA based on the commerce clause powers of Congress. Four traditionally conservative justices wrote a lengthy opinion to overturn the mandate, as well as other portions of the law. Chief Justice Roberts wrote an opinion, which would become the opinion of the Court, in which he ruled that the individual mandate to purchase health insurance was constitutional under the taxation powers of Congress. Justice Roberts disagreed with the liberals' rationale regarding the commerce clause. In some circumstances, the four concurring justices (Ginsburg, Breyer, Kagan, and Sotomayor) might have simply concurred in the judgment and created a plurality opinion (and a doctrinal paradox) upholding the law. However, in this case, the four liberals added two sentences at the end of their opinion endorsing and joining Roberts's taxation rationale.

It is (unfortunately) likely impossible to distinguish between preference subordination and genuine doctrinal agreement in consistent decisions. The Court's earlier norms of consensus almost certainly masked a great deal of inconsistency (Epstein, Segal, and Spaeth 2001; Leonard 1984). Therefore, this class of unreasoned judgment is currently unobservable. But the probable existence of such cases (e.g., *Sebelius*) implies that this research does not encompass all forms of unreasoned judgment, only those that may be uncovered using observable information.

Unreasoned judgment would best be thought of as a common latent phenomenon that arises in diverse ways. These manifestations vary in their observability and amenableness to measurement. This research focuses on the most visible manifestations of unreasoned judgment, but future theoretical or case study research could and should explore the emergence of inconsistency in less easily observable forms.

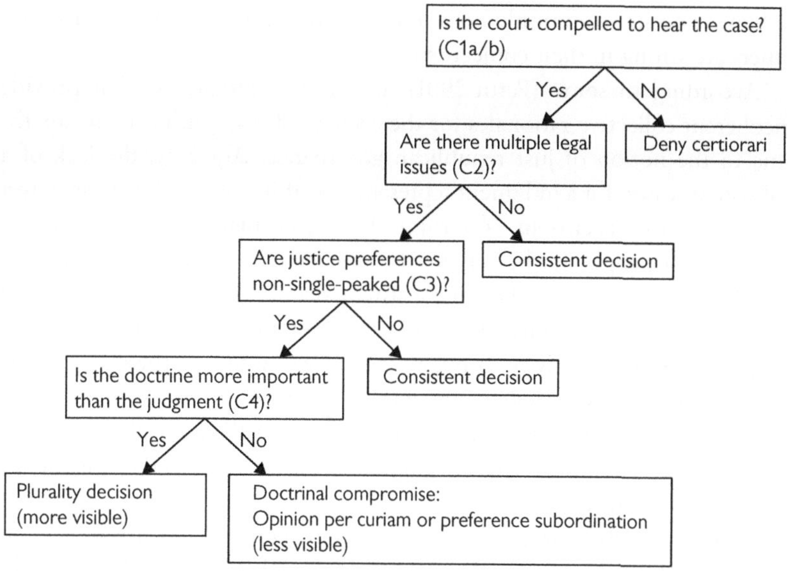

Fig. 1.2. Flow Chart of the Emergence of Unreasoned Judgment

Figure 1.2 combines the four conditions of this theory to show the possible outcomes of disputes brought to the Court, according to which conditions are met. Chapter 3 will test some of the implications of this theory. Note that the justices prefer at every turn to avoid unreasoned judgment when feasible, either by denying cert or by resolving cases consistently. As the justices' internal communications show, they dislike producing inconsistencies—a sensible perspective given their audience of legal elites (Baum 2006). Yet at times they cannot avoid it (Easterbrook 1982). As the following chapters will show, this dislike for inconsistency may be well placed—inconsistencies negatively affect the American judicial hierarchy. But this focus on legal audiences and therefore consistency carries a cost in terms of decisiveness, which may be more prized by nonlegal audiences.

Looking Forward

While troubling in theory, empirical evidence for the frequency and impact of unreasoned judgment is lacking. Thus far, scholars (Stearns 2000) presume that inconsistency must be a very rare and esoteric phenomenon. My conception of unreasoned judgment is broader than Stearns's (2000) discussion of the doctrinal paradox. Therefore, a demonstration that unreasoned judgment occurs commonly does not constitute evidence that Stearns and others are wrong in their conjectures.

According to some (Pettit 2001), unreasoned judgments that provide incoherent collective rationales for the exercise of state authority are anathema to the notion of just republican governance. Arguably, the lack of a consistent reason for a judgment represents an arbitrary exercise of the power of the state over its citizens. If nothing else, the normative concept of justice requires that people not be subjected to coercion and violence for random or arbitrary reasons. Further, inconsistent decisions cause confusion and volatility in the lower courts (Leonard 1984; Post and Salop 1992), cascading illegitimate judicial activity throughout the legal system. If these arguments are true, unreasoned judgments may therefore pose a threat to the just rule of law in the United States, particularly because it is theoretically impossible to design a system for aggregating judgments that guarantees the consistency of judgments and rationales.

Of course, others argue that inconsistency alone should not be viewed as grounds for criticizing a decision (Easterbrook 1982). And some, taking a societal perspective, may indeed view inconsistency as a necessary phenomenon if difficult and fractious disputes are to be resolved at all (Sunstein 2007). This book focuses on providing empirical verification for the opposing sides of this debate.

The guiding question of this book asks, how well is the Supreme Court functioning? Given that a court cannot maximize decisiveness and consistency simultaneously, which of the two is more desirable? Addressing this broader theme requires an in-depth study of the properties and dynamics of unreasoned judgments. The first question is empirical—how common is this phenomenon, and how ought we measure it? Second, drawing motivation from the theory advanced above, what kinds of disputes end up being resolved inconsistently? Third, what are the dynamics of unreasoned judgment—is this phenomenon becoming more or less common, and why? Fourth, what effect do these decisions have on the American legal system? Fifth, do the other branches of government—namely, Congress—view unreasoned judgments negatively? Sixth, do ordinary people view this phenomenon as less legitimate than other Supreme Court decisions? Finally, what is the implied health of the American judiciary? Should the Court reverse its evolutionary trend and reprioritize decisiveness over consistency? Or should even more severe reforms be considered to further minimize inconsistency?

To address these points, I begin with a simple empirical question: how should this phenomenon be measured in the aggregate? How common is the phenomenon, and what are its dynamics over time? Chapter 2 explores this theme. Chapter 3 goes on to explore the case-level factors that are associated with unreasoned judgments. Chapter 4 then investigates how institutional changes at the Court influence the emergence of unreasoned judgments. Chapter 4 provides primary evidence for the claim that the Court has evolved toward consistency at the cost of decisiveness.

After exploring the correlates and dynamics of unreasoned judgment, the second half of the book analyzes the consequences of this phenomenon in American society. Chapter 5 examines the broader impact of the unreasoned judgments as precedent on the American judicial hierarchy. After defining a new method for measuring the legal influence of Supreme Court precedent, chapter 5 shows that unreasoned judgments are followed and cited significantly less in the lower levels of the federal judicial hierarchy, indicating that inconsistent precedents are of little use to the legal system.

I then turn to the effect of inconsistency in American society more generally. Chapter 6 analyzes the response of Congress to unreasoned judgments at the Court. Applying Clark's (2009) and Elliott's (1958) framework of "Court-curbing", I show that the introduction of legislation meant to punish the Court is not a function of the rate of unreasoned judgments being produced. Moreover, even though the Court does at times exercise judicial review over Congress with unreasoned judgments, even this practice does not appear to provoke congressional wrath any more so than usual. Moving to the mass public, chapter 7 presents the results of an experiment: a nationally representative random sample of American adults was presented with a stylized version of a Court decision. Subjects were randomly assigned to read a hypothetical decision that was either unreasoned or consistent. The results show that unreasoned judgments are not viewed as less legitimate than consistent decisions nor do they reduce diffuse support for the Court. Chapter 8 then considers the current implied health of the American judicial system and concludes. On balance, while the Court's evolution toward consistency proves worthwhile for legal audiences, it is likely not a desirable trade-off from a societal perspective.

CHAPTER 2

Measuring Unreasoned Judgments

> The comprehensive deliberative account proposes two demands to prevent majority tyranny or unreasoned majority decisions and to enhance democratic legitimacy. First, collective decisions should be supported by publicly decided reasons; second, the overall system of collectively decided reasons and outcomes should be coherent.
>
> —Christian List, "The Discursive Dilemma and Public Reason"

Sandra Lockett drove the getaway car, but she never stepped foot in the pawnshop. She didn't kill Sydney Cohen. But, in aiding in the commission of a felony that ended in a murder by her accomplices, she was subject to capital charges. The state of Ohio sentenced Sandra Lockett to death for her participation in the crime. Her guilt as an accessory was not in doubt. However, was death a just punishment for this crime? Ms. Lockett tried to introduce evidence at the punishment phase of her trial showing that she had strong prospects for rehabilitation and that her I.Q. was low enough to potentially constitute an intellectual disability (Hertz and Weisberg 1981).

Her sentence, however, came under an Ohio statute that allowed judges in capital cases to consider only three specific mitigating circumstances: victim inducement; duress, coercion, or provocation; or psychosis (Hertz and Weisberg 1981, 324). If none of these circumstances were present, the judge was required to sentence the defendant to death. Ms. Lockett's mitigating circumstances were therefore not admissible as evidence. She appealed her sentence. The Sixth Circuit Court of Appeals affirmed her death sentence. She appealed once more, and the Supreme Court heard the case in January 1978.

After oral arguments, Chief Justice Warren Burger circulated a memo to his colleagues, writing:

> Although I did not agree with the views of the plurality in our preceding cases [on the death penalty], I am now prepared to yield with the hope that there can be a majority opinion here. With deference, I feel that our plurality opinions on the death penalty have created uncertainty and instability in an area which deserves the greatest certainty and stability that can be provided, and this calls for a Court opinion....If there is a possibility that four others could yield their individual views, as I would be yielding mine, and join in an opinion based generally on my proposal, then there is hope that we can produce the first majority opinion on this issue since we stirred up the subject.[1]

Chief Justice Burger recognized the importance of consistency of judgment and rationales for the sake of stability and certainty in lower courts. He further offered to subordinate some of his personal views in order to obtain a consistent decision. Burger would later circulate draft opinions to the other justices that, in part, struck down Ohio's statute for violating the Eightth and Fourteenth Amendments, stating that judges or juries cannot be precluded from considering as a mitigating factor any aspect of the defendant's record, character, or circumstances of the offense.

Internal negotiations over various draft opinions continued for several months. In June 1978, Chief Justice Burger recognized that the consistent outcome he craved at the outset was not forthcoming. He circulated a second memo stating, "Absent a Court in support of something along the enclosed lines, I have concluded that a terse per curiam reversing is in order with the less said the better."[2] Burger recognized that while a majority of the Court supported a judgment reversing Lockett's death sentence, a majority would not coalesce on a rationale. This memo demonstrates that at times the Court considers the per curiam option when faced with a potential inconsistency of judgment and rationale.

Yet the terse per curiam was not the outcome in this case. The Court issued a plurality opinion instead. Justice Byron White created this dilemma by agreeing with the judgment reversing Lockett's death sentence. However, he based his agreement upon an entirely separate rationale relative to the constitutional reasoning found in Justice Burger's plurality opinion.[3] Under Justice White's rationale, the Ohio statute would not be found unconstitutional. Justice White explained to his colleagues that he wrote separately because,

> ...vesting in the jury unlimited authority to consider mitigating circumstances is to enhance its power to dispense at will its own brand of justice in an essentially standardless manner. In the long run, imposing the death penalty under such a mandate would revert to that which in my view was an unacceptably erratic system that could not be relied upon to contribute to any of the ends of criminal punishment.[4]

Justice White created this logically inconsistent outcome because he favored a judgment reversing Lockett's death sentence, but he could not subscribe to the rationale for this reversal offered in Justice Burger's opinion. Justice White placed his preferences over broader legal doctrine above any preferences he might have had for a clear, stable, and consistent outcome in the instant case. Indeed, the memo suggests that the last thing Justice White wanted in this case was a clear standard for lower courts to follow, as the standard offered by Justice Burger's opinion was one that Justice White considered to be wrong (Leonard 1984).

The goal of this brief vignette was to illustrate the common latent underpinnings of various types of unreasoned judgment. Both a doctrinal paradox/plurality opinion and a terse per curiam opinion were possible in this case, which was ultimately resolved with a doctrinal paradox. This resolution almost certainly failed to clear up the instability and uncertainty in the lower courts on the issue of the death penalty referred to by the Chief Justice.

The story of the *Lockett* decision emphasizes that regardless of what the final public explanation of the judgment looked like, a rationale that a majority could support for overturning her death sentence did not exist. Yet a majority of justices supported the outcome of overturning her sentence. Therefore, measuring unreasoned judgment requires acknowledging there exist multiple potential manifestations of this phenomenon.

Resolving the seemingly simple question of measurement allows us to begin an empirical inquiry into the scope of this phenomenon—until now such understanding remained anecdotal and theoretical. Should the prevalence of unreasoned judgments motivate substantial institutional changes at the Court, as Pettit (2001) contends? Obviously, knowing the prevalence of unreasoned judgments to begin with is the proper starting place to start addressing that question.

I now endeavor to resolve this measurement problem. I begin with a theoretical definition of unreasoned judgment. I then argue that two seemingly different decisional outcomes at the Court actually both fit this theoretical definition—plurality decisions and (some) opinions per curiam. In both instances, the Court issues an opinion or set of opinions that demonstrate that a majority of the justices are unwilling to express agreement with a singular rationale for the Court's judgment. I then explore some basic properties of unreasoned judgments, showing their frequency over time, their correlation with various policy areas, and their emergence in politically salient disputes. Ultimately, unreasoned judgments emerged more than five hundred times between 1946 and 2010, demonstrating that this phenomenon is hardly a rare academic curiosity but an empirical regularity worthy of systematic inquiry.

Unreasoned Judgment: Formal Definition

The concept of consistency between judgments and rationales stems from a rich theoretical literature across several disciplines; here I define consistency as it is typically discussed (List and Pettit 2002; List 2012).[5]

The abstractness of these definitions should underscore that while I discuss unreasoned judgment in specific reference to collegial courts, this phenomenon remains possible whenever a group of individuals must come to a collective judgment based on underlying reasons. Examples of unreasoned judgments abound across economics (Claussen and Roisland 2010), psychology (Bonnefon 2011), and international law (Chilton and Tingley 2012).[6]

A finite group of *actors*, at least two, must make judgments over a set of *propositions*. Both atomic propositions, which are individual statements, and their logical connectives (i.e., conjunctions to make compound propositions: not, and, or, implies) are contained in this set of propositions. In the instance of collegial courts, the actors are judges, and the set of propositions contains both premises for a judgment (e.g., the Fourth Amendment bars searches of this type), as well as conclusive judgments in cases (e.g., find for the plaintiff).

The *agenda*, a subset of the set of propositions, contains every proposition over which actors must make judgments. Since it must be possible for actors both to affirm or to reject a proposition, the negation of every proposition is also contained in the agenda.

Individuals make judgments, either affirming or negating each proposition on the agenda; these judgments combine into each individual's *judgment set*. Individuals must affirm or negate each proposition on the agenda *(completeness)* and may not simultaneously affirm and negate any proposition *(consistency)*.

Logical entailment distinguishes work on judgment aggregation from the preference aggregation literature (Arrow 1951). List and Pettit (2004) discuss the connection between Arrow's impossibility theorem and the discursive dilemma in detail, highlighting this distinction. A set of judgments *logically entails* some proposition if accepting the negation of that proposition makes the set of judgments inconsistent. For instance, if an individual's personal judgment set includes two propositions, call them "p" and "q," then the compound proposition "both p *and* q" is logically entailed.

Concretely, if one person sues another for breach of an oral contract, a judge might consider two propositions. First, whether there was in fact a binding contract between the two parties. Second, whether the defendant's conduct violated the terms of contract. If the judge independently affirms both propositions (there was a contract, and it was violated), then a finding for the plaintiff is *logically entailed* by the judgments on these atomic premises. If the judge ruled for the defendant, then the judge would simultaneously hold the positions that there was a contract, the defendant's behavior violated that contract, but the defendant is not liable for a breach of contract. This combination of judgments violates *consistency*.

A *judgment aggregation rule* maps individual judgment sets into one *collective judgment set*—a set of the propositions accepted by the entire group. The judgment aggregation rule, then, is the mechanism the group uses to determine the outcome of a decision problem.

Majority voting is one such aggregation rule. Under majority voting, each proposition is collectively accepted if and only if it is accepted by a specified majority of individuals. That is, only propositions in the individual judgment sets of more than half of the individuals are accepted by the group. Under pure majority voting, every proposition, whether a premise or a conclusion, receives the same treatment. The proposition receives a vote, and if it carries a majority, the group accepts it. Some alternatives to pure majority voting differ by weighing some propositions more heavily than others.

A *premise-based judgment aggregation rule* is a rule that determines the set of collective judgments by applying majority voting (or some other method) to a privileged subset of propositions (premises), then accepting the logical entailment of the results. Under this rule, the group chooses some premises, votes only on these, and commits to accept whatever other judgments are *logically entailed* by the result.

A *conclusion-based judgment aggregation rule* also privileges a subset of propositions (conclusions) and comes to a judgment based on votes only over these privileged propositions, but does not require logical closure of the resulting judgments. Under the conclusion-based approach, there is no notion of logical entailment; rather, the collective makes its judgments based upon the aggregation of individual judgments over a subset of privileged propositions, independent of whether the final outcome is consistent.[7]

Reasoned Judgment is obtained when the final collective judgment set is *consistent*—which means that every proposition included in the final outcome set is logically entailed by the group's judgments on all the other propositions. If the final collective judgment set obtained under a conclusion-based aggregation rule is the same as the set of judgments obtained with a premise-based voting rule, then the set of judgments obtained under the conclusion-based rule does not violate *consistency*, and thus the outcome exhibits *consistency* (Pettit 2001). If, however, the collective outcome reached by a premise-based rule conflicts with the outcome that might be reached by a conclusion-based rule, the combination of group-level judgments violates *consistency*. That is, in such a scenario, the group accepts a conclusion that its collective judgment on the premises would reject, or vice versa. This outcome is an *unreasoned judgment*.

Unless some propositions on the agenda are privileged (which both premise-based and conclusion-based rules require), neither majority voting nor any other method of aggregating judgments guarantees reasoned judgment (List and Pettit 2002). List and Pettit's (2002) key insight is that even if every actor in a collective decision-making body makes their individual judgments consistently, the *group-level* judgment cannot be assured to be consistent.

Unreasoned Judgments Vary in Visibility

A doctrinal paradox, observed as a plurality decision (as I discuss in detail below), is a particularly visible manifestation of unreasoned judgment found at the Supreme Court. But it is not the only manifestation. The definition of reasoned judgment requires only that every proposition included in the final outcome set (the judgment itself) is logically entailed by the group's judgments on all the other propositions (the various underlying legal rationales). This definition implies that other categories of decisions at the Court can fail to satisfy this definition and therefore represent a manifestation of unreasoned judgment.

Unreasoned judgment can be conceived of as a spectrum of related phenomena. The poles of this spectrum are defined by their transparency. At times, a simple reading of the Court's opinions, taken together, reveals the underlying inconsistency (as in a doctrinal paradox). Alternatively, when the Court's reasoning accompanying a judgment is brief, opaque, or fails to touch on important and complex legal questions presented in a case, it is impossible to discern whether the rationale for the judgment carries a majority, as the rationale itself is unclear. Opinions issued per curiam fit the description of brief and opaque reasoning quite well. In such an opinion, the Court announces a judgment with a very short, unsigned opinion. The brevity of the reasoning in these cases makes it difficult to ascertain what legal rationale was applied in the case and how lower courts ought to deal with similar disputes.

Opinions per curiam may result when the justices cannot reach an agreement over both legal rationales and the outcome judgment in a case as a compromise of sorts. Consider, for instance, the Court's March 2016 decision in *Friedrichs v. California Teachers Association*, 578 U.S. ___ (Slip Op.). This case dealt with the right of public sector unions to extract dues from nonmembers, an issue of considerable interest and controversy. Scores of individuals, governments, and interest groups filed briefs amicus curiae in the case. The Opinion of the Court reads, in its entirety, "PER CURIAM. The judgment is affirmed by an equally divided Court." It is unlikely that this opinion offers much guidance to the lower courts, and the brevity of this opinion makes it impossible to know what legal rationale supports this limited affirmance or whether any of the possible rationales for this judgment were supported by at least half of the evenly divided Court. As a sidebar, in the contemporary political climate, where the Senate would not even hold a hearing for a Supreme Court nominee (Merrick Garland) from a president (Barack Obama) of the opposing party, this form of unreasoned judgment may occur even more frequently going forward following future vacancies at the Court (Lyall 2017).

Finally, a third potential manifestation of unreasoned judgment arguably occurs if and when justices subordinate their preferences over rationales in order to avoid the doctrinal paradox. That is, justices may at times join opinions containing reasoning they disagree with when those opinions support a desired outcome. The justices might engage in this behavior to strengthen a preferred judgment by giving it the appearance of consistency.

National Federation of Independent Business v. Sebelius (132 S.Ct. 2566) (the "Obamacare" decision) may be an example of such a case. Inconsistencies manifested as preference subordination are likely impossible to measure due to their observational equivalence with consistent decisions. Modern justices may only engage in this behavior in rare cases of extraordinary political salience in which both the immediate judgment

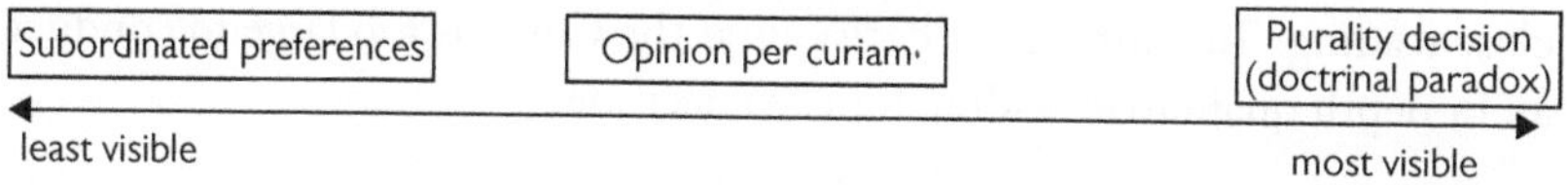

Fig. 2.1. The Visibility of Unreasoned Judgments

and the public appearance of consistent reasoning outweigh doctrinal preferences.

Figure 2.1 aligns these three manifestations along the dimension of transparency. The doctrinal paradox represents the most visible manifestation of this phenomenon. These paradoxical decisions appear to trouble many scholars in law and philosophy (Leonard 1984; Pettit 2001; Stearns 2000).

Conversely, the least visible manifestation in figure 2.1 is subordinated preferences. Such outcomes seem quite inconsistent from the perspective of sincerity—the visible consistency obtained in such circumstances is not genuine. These outcomes mask underlying disagreements about legal doctrine, perhaps inhibiting progress on important and controversial issues (Leonard 1984; Epstein, Segal, and Spaeth 2001; Sunstein 2007).

However, it is less clear that these decisions would be as unacceptable as a doctrinal paradox from the perspective of legitimate republican governance. The Court does provide a facially consistent rationale for its judgment in these instances, but this visible support may mask insincere motivations on the part of some or all of the justices. Much scholarly attention is given to insincere voting in a variety of political contexts (Abramson et al. 1992; Caldeira, Wright, and Zorn 1999; Gibbard 1973; Kleiner and Moldovanu 2017; Satterthwaite 1975). As such, the existence of this least transparent form of inconsistency may be normatively troubling to some scholars as well. This form of unreasoned judgment may defy reliable measurement due to the ambiguities associated with distinguishing sincere versus revealed preferences with observational data. Therefore, I do not undertake to measure preference subordination in this book. Perhaps future generations of scholars can resolve the seeming intractability of measuring subordinated preferences at the Court reliably in a large sample of decisions.

Figure 2.1 presents three discrete manifestations of unreasoned judgment residing on a spectrum. These manifestations should not be thought of as exhaustive. Certainly legally trained experts could find points of disagreement or ambiguity in many sets of opinions the Court produces in complex, multifaceted areas of the law. I use the terms "consistent" and "inconsistent" throughout this book. I do not, however, claim that all decisions of the Court not identified as one of the manifestations of inconsistency studied here therefore must automatically satisfy the principle of consistency upon close reading. The universe of decisions at the Court is too large to conduct an in-depth qualitative reading for each decision.

Plurality Decisions as Doctrinal Paradoxes

The doctrinal paradox (Kornhauser and Sager 1986) represents one visible manifestation of unreasoned judgment. If a decision is a doctrinal paradox, it is also an unreasoned judgment. Therefore, counting these paradoxes is a crucial element in measuring unreasoned judgment more generally.

Identifying the doctrinal paradox, however, is somewhat complicated. Dispositive identification of a paradox requires intensive analysis of the case's opinions and briefs and constructing the voting coalitions associated with each premise (Leonard 1984; Nash 2003; Post and Salop 1992; Stearns 1999, 2000). Doing such work for a large enough random sample of cases for statistical precision is infeasible.

Instead, I use existing theory as a guide to define an observable proxy for the underlying phenomenon of the doctrinal paradox. A subset of cases that exhibit this proxy were then hand-coded for verification of the existence of the paradox by third-year law student research assistants. Theoretical works (List and Pettit 2002; List and Pettit 2004; List 2003, 2005; Dietrich 2006; Bovens and Rabinowicz 2006; Brennan 2001; Kornhauser and Sager 2004; Chapman 1998) suggest possible proxies for doctrinal paradoxes, as some (Bovens and Rabinowicz 2006; List 2003; Dietrich 2006; Pigozzi 2006; Lax and Landa 2009) identify conditions under which the doctrinal paradox can occur. One particular type of decision at the Court seems to fit these theoretical conditions for unreasoned judgment very well.

In a plurality decision, a majority of justices agree on a judgment but write several separate opinions, none of which carries a majority. A plurality decision entails at least one special concurrence (a concurrence in the judgment only). A plurality outcome is therefore a strong indicator that a decision may be a doctrinal paradox. Stras and Spriggs (2010) and Corley (2009) remark that the lack of a clear majority rationale in plurality outcomes leads to volatility in the lower courts, just as others (Post and Salop 1992) note that doctrinal paradoxes cause the same issues. Thus, plurality opinions serve as the key proxy for the doctrinal paradox. The data on plurality decisions are catalogued in Spaeth's Supreme Court Database for all cases from 1946–2010.

Does this coding of plurality decisions accurately track genuine disagreement with the rationale provided in the Opinion of the Court? There are two distinct kinds of concurring opinions at the Court—regular concurrences and "special" concurrences. A plurality opinion must be supported by an Opinion of the Court, plus at least one special concurrence—a concurrence in the judgment. To ensure that special concurrences (typically denoted: Justice (blank), concurring in the judgment) are in fact instances where a justice disagrees with one or more of the reasons given by the majority for the decision but concludes for different reasons that the majority's decision is correct, I randomly sampled twenty cases from the data that Spaeth coded as regular concurrences and twenty cases Spaeth coded as special concurrences.[8]

A pithy distinction between regular and special concurrences is that regular concurrences are of the "yes, and..." variety, and special concurrences are of the "yes, but..." variety. Of the twenty randomly sampled cases with regular concurrences, nineteen of the concurring opinions do not feature justices disagreeing with the underlying reasons or premises of the majority opinion. A good example is Justice Scalia's concurrence in *Lockhart v. United States* (546 U.S. 142 [2005]): "I join the opinion of the Court, because it does not imply that the requirement is binding. *I would go further* (emphasis added), however, and say that it is not."

The case that did not meet the neat "yes, and..." description in the sample (*Alderman v. United States*, 394 U.S. 165 [1968]) seems likely miscoded by Spaeth; it has two separate opinions along with the majority opinion, both of which concur in part and dissent in part. Spaeth codes the case as containing one regular concurrence, one special concurrence, and one dissent. Still, 95 percent of the sample of cases coded as containing regular concurrences have opinions that do not directly disagree with the reasons of the majority.

The sample of cases with special concurrences exhibits a different pattern. Justices writing opinions concurring in the judgment took issue with a reason or logical pathway the majority took to reach their decision. Justice Stewart's special concurrence in *United Parcel Service, Inc. v. Mitchell* (451 U.S. 56 [1981]) is an apt example: "The Court believes itself obligated by Auto Workers v. Hoosier Cardinal Corp., 383 U. S. 696, to determine the applicable statute of limitations in this case 'as a matter of federal law, by reference to the appropriate state statute of limitations.' I do not believe, however, that we are so constrained by Hoosier."

Similar disagreements with majority logic or reasons were found in seventeen of the twenty cases sampled. The three remaining cases, which could not be classified, were cases decided per curiam, for which there was only a footnote: "Justice [blank], concurring in the judgement." No written opinions could be found to clarify the substance of these special concurrences.

These three cases suggest that opinions per curiam could indeed also represent a manifestation of unreasoned judgment. That is, for over 97 percent of this sample, the distinction between regular and special concurrences appears valid, and the potential errors in classification are due to acceptable random measurement error. This exercise provides confidence that using plurality opinions, marked as they are by special concurrences, seems to capture the phenomenon of unreasoned judgment with considerable validity.

From 1946–2010, 228 of 8,353 decisions at the Court were supported by plurality opinions. These decisions are thus likely to be instances of the most visible form of unreasoned judgment (the doctrinal paradox). Other cases previously identified by other scholars (Stearns 1999, 2000) as doctrinal paradoxes are identified as doctrinal paradoxes under this coding scheme.[9]

To buttress the validity of this coding scheme, I employed third-year law student coders to verify the existence of a doctrinal paradox in these cases. The coders were instructed to read the opinion of the Court and all concurring opinions in each case, then determine whether those concurring in the judgment also supported the reasoning contained in the opinion of the Court, or vice versa. Ninety-six percent of cases coded exhibited the doctrinal paradox in the judgment of these coders (that is, the coders verified that no rationale for the Court's judgment carried a majority), indicating a high level of construct validity.[10]

These coders read the cases in question and constructed tables of each issue area and where the justices stood on those issues for each case. The two coders overlapped with 100 percent agreement on the presence of unreasoned judgment on an overlapping sample of six cases.[11]

Figure 2.2 shows the overall frequency of plurality decisions over time. The frequency of these outcomes varies considerably; in some terms (1970) as many as fifteen plurality decisions were rendered by the Court. The overall frequency of these outcomes appears to be on the decline; however, this result could easily be a function of the Court's overall declining workload. As we will see later, it is crucial to account not only for the raw count of unreasoned judgments but also the rate of such judgments over time.

Opinions Per Curiam as Unreasoned Judgments

Importantly, as an alternative to the issuance of a plurality decision or of the subordination of preferences, judges may choose to issue per curiam opinions when they cannot agree on both premises and judgment. This format papers over inconsistencies by eschewing premises but reaching a desired outcome.

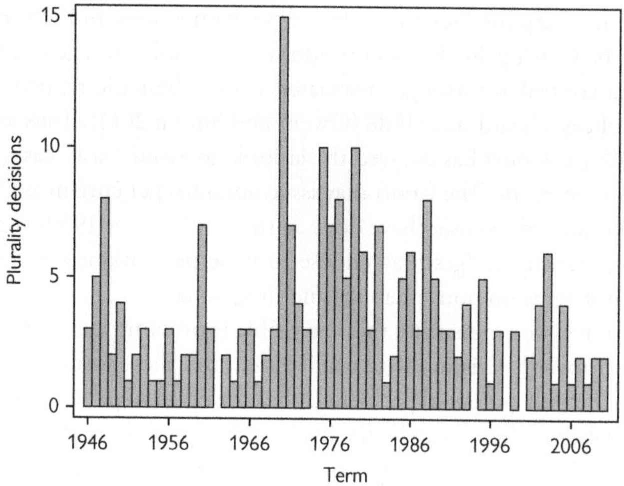

Fig. 2.2. Unreasoned Judgments in Plurality Decisions, 1946–2010

For instance, while on the U.S. Court of Appeals, then judge Sotomayor joined a per curiam judgment in a controversial case in which white firefighters alleged reverse discrimination in New Haven, Connecticut. Some have argued that the per curiam opinion was the result of a deal among the judges to preserve the desired outcome without exposing underlying disagreement on the premises (Flanders 2009). Indeed, tension between preferences over judgments and preferences over premises is a feature of many controversial cases (Carrubba et al. 2012). On close analysis, the per curiam opinion in *Bush v. Gore* appears unreasoned (Abramowicz and Stearns 2001). Indeed, controversial cases can easily result in opinions per curiam.

The preceding sections establish that certain opinions per curiam represent a less visible manifestation of unreasoned judgment. The per curiam opinion first emerged in the nineteenth century as a housekeeping device (Ray 2000). It was not until the 1930s that separate opinions began to be associated with per curiam opinions (Ray 2000). This shift, however, indicates that opinions per curiam began to be used to resolve issues of genuine controversy.

To be sure, some per curiam opinions allow the Court to dispose of unimportant or noncontroversial cases. Chief Justice Warren, for instance, utilized the per curiam opinion to exercise some of the Court's summary judgments. These summary judgments typically grant, vacate, and remand a lower court decision to reconsider in light of a (usually recently announced) Supreme Court precedent (Gizzi and Wasby 2012).

But housekeeping does not explain all such outcomes. In 1925, and again in 1988, the Court gained greater freedom to determine its agenda. Changes in agenda control are strongly associated with a dramatic reduction in the number of cases heard since 1988 (Owens and Simon 2012). Thus, especially after 1988, the Court has enjoyed the latitude to avoid "easy" cases without per curiam opinions. The Court may issue opinions per curiam as a strategic device and indeed seems to have done so since at least the 1950s (Ray 2000, 538). Importantly, judges may choose to issue per curiam opinions when they cannot agree on both premises and judgment.

My strategy for measuring this less visible form of unreasoned judgment is straightforward. Existing data readily identifies these instances of inconsistency. The only potential problem is that the opinion per curiam could be used as a labor-saving device by the justices, discussed above, rather than as a strategic device intended to preserve a desired judgment when the justices fail to come to a consensus over legal rationales (Ray 2000). Fortunately, there is a way to distinguish between "easy" cases and cases with genuine controversy. Some per curiam opinions are preceded by oral arguments, while others are issued based only on the certiorari documents. The latter cases are "easy"; the former almost always involve genuine controversy. Further, some per curiam opinions are accompanied by separate concurring or dissenting opinions; these are unlikely to be examples of housekeeping. In the analysis to follow, *I consider only opinions per curiam issued after oral argument and accompanied by at least one separate opinion as unreasoned judgments.* This strategy discriminates further between "easy" cases and more genuine controversies.

Spaeth's Supreme Court Database (scdb.wustl.edu/index.php) permits identification of these variables—thus, any case resolved with an opinion per curiam that both follows an oral argument and is accompanied by at least one separate opinion is considered an instance of the opaque manifestation of unreasoned judgment. Of course, this measurement strategy relies on the assumption that there are significant differences in the likelihood of genuine controversy between argued and nonargued per curiams. I test this assumption in the following section.

Properties of Argued and Nonargued Per Curiams

The property "genuine controversy" seems unamenable to direct measurement. Several observable variables, however, should be related to this latent construct. Observable features of disputes that relate to genuine controversy might include indicators of interest from well-connected political organizations or political and social salience as a general matter. Further, genuine controversy as a doctrinal matter might be related to the amount of discussion a decision receives in subsequent judicial opinions; obviously examples of housekeeping would seem less likely to be invoked or followed than judgments that address issues of importance to judges.

Since orally argued opinions per curiam accompanied by at least one concurrence or dissent are treated as an opaque manifestation of inconsistency, these decisions should share more features with doctrinal paradoxes than other per curiam opinions. Chapter 1 theorized that several properties of individual cases should be associated with unreasoned judgment. If this measurement strategy enjoys any validity, these characteristics should be present to a greater degree in per curiam opinions counted as unreasoned judgments.

First, some per curiam opinions are supported by nonsingle-peaked voting coalitions, as measured by the ideology scores of Martin and Quinn (2002), while others are not, satisfying the preference condition of chapter 1's theory. If the voting coalition on every atomic proposition and the final judgment can be ordered unidimensionally (i.e., all those in favor are strictly to the left or right of all those opposed on every point), an unreasoned judgment is theoretically impossible (List and Pettit 2002; List 2003; Dietrich 2006). That is, if all the issues in a case align themselves on a single preference dimension (e.g., liberal to conservative) and the judgment itself, along with all the decision makers, fit on this spectrum, there is no room for a complex compromise that produces an unreasoned judgment. Instead, the median position on this dimension will prevail (Landa and Lax 2009). While it is difficult to observe voting coalitions on each premise, the coalition on the judgment is observable. If the actors are not aligned on a single anticipated dimension—a "disordered" coalition, per Edelman, Klein, and Lindquist (2008)—that is evidence of a second dimension in a case, and the doctrinal paradox remains a possibility. Using Martin and Quinn's (2002) data on justice ideology, I can pinpoint whenever a decisions's voting coalition deviates from its expected unidimensionality (i.e., *not* all justices to the right of the median vote against all those to the left of the median). I measure proportion of judgments supported by nonsingled-peaked voting coalitions using the data of Martin and Quinn (2002) as before.[12]

Second, decisions resolved by per curiam opinions vary in the number of substantive issues they contain, as reported in the Spaeth database, satisfying the case characteristics condition of chapter 1's theory.

To compare per curiams issued after oral argument and accompanied by at least one separate opinion to those with neither feature, I operationalize the notion of genuine controversy in several ways. First, to measure the attention of powerful groups in society, I compare the maximum eigenvector centrality score for interest groups participating amicus curiae in the dispute across the two categories of opinions per curiam (Box-Steffensmeier, Christenson, and Hitt 2013). These data, from Box-Steffensmeier, Christenson, and Hitt (2013), measure the highest level of connections to other powerful groups in society enjoyed by an interest group in a given case using network analytic methods.[13] This variable is undefined for the small minority of disputes in this subset of the data that did not generate an *amicus* brief from an organized interest group or business.

Second, to measure the political and social salience of a dispute generally, I compare the proportion of disputes reported on the front page of the following day's *New York Times* across the two categories of per curiam opinions (Epstein and Segal 2000).

Third, to measure the relevance of disputes to other judges, I compare the two categories of per curiam opinions in terms of their subsequent citation counts and positive citation counts in opinions by federal judges. As shown in Hitt (2016), these variables are based on the sum of three z-scores. Each score is the standardized count of citations or follows in the district, circuit, and Supreme Court a precedent receives, respectively. In brief, these citation/follow data were collected from *Shepard's* citation reports through LexisNexis for every Court precedent from 1946–2010. The counts of citations and follows at each level of the federal judicial hierarchy were extracted from these reports via the R programming language (R Core Team 2014).

Only one these many variables, the presence of multiple substantive issues, fails to exhibit a statistically significant difference between the categories of opinions per curiam. For interested readers, I present the full results of a test of these differences in appendix B. The results show that per curiam opinions issued after oral argument and accompanied by at least one separate opinion attract the participation of more powerful interest groups and national media attention more often, are cited and followed more in judicial opinions, and feature disordered voting coalitions with much greater frequency. Per curiam opinions vary in their likelihood of exhibiting genuine controversy. The measurement strategy employed here is obviously imperfect, but it does appear to capture a subset of opinions per curiam that share a number of features with complex and controversial disputes.

Figure 2.3 shows the dynamics of these more opaque unreasoned judgments over time. Similar to the dynamics of the plurality decisions shown in

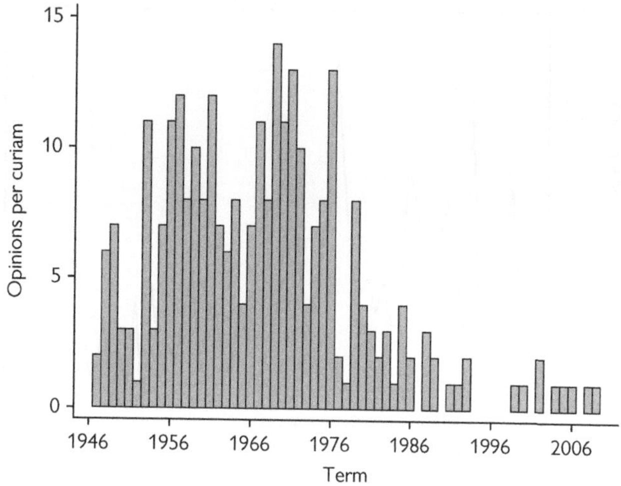

Fig. 2.3. Unreasoned Judgments in Opinions Per Curiam, 1946–2010

figure 2.2, opaque inconsistency waxes and wanes over time. It is not clear confined to any obvious era or chief justiceship. Figure 2.3 does indicate that opaque inconsistency is on the decline.

The Rate of Unreasoned Judgments

The declines in unreasoned judgments observed in figures 2.2 and 2.3 seem to indicate that unreasoned judgments are on the way out at the Supreme Court. Perhaps, as I investigate in chapter 4, we can explain these declines by understanding how the Court has changed during this time period as well. One such change is that the Supreme Court's workload is substantially smaller today than in previous decades. The Court decides, with oral argument, only about half as many cases today as it did during the 1970s and 1980s. As such, we should take the Court's overall workload into account when ascertaining whether unreasoned judgments are in fact on the decline.

Measuring the rate of unreasoned judgment is easily done: the rate in a given term is simply the sum total of plurality decisions and opinions per curiam divided by the total number of cases decided. Figure 2.4 shows this rate between 1946 and 2010.

Figure 2.4 shows that the overall rate of unreasoned judgment peaked in the 1970s. The rate is fairly volatile, especially in earlier years, as the large spikes indicate. The rate by 2010 is considerably lower than in previous decades. This dynamic shows that unreasoned judgments are indeed

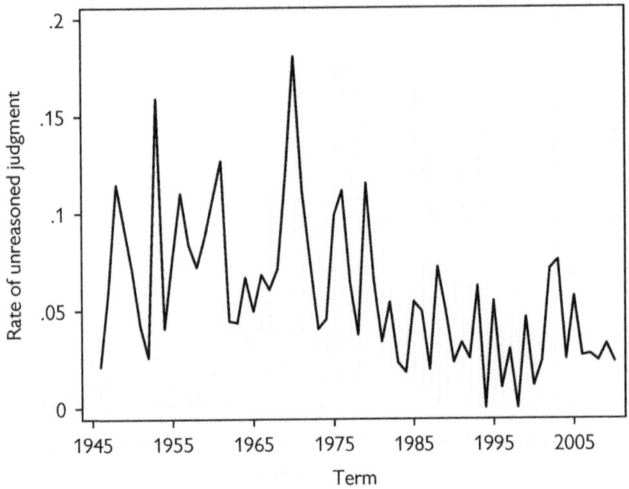

Fig. 2.4. Rate of Unreasoned Judgments, 1946–2010

less common today; the declines in frequency are not an artifact of a lower workload. I investigate what might be driving this decline in chapter 4.

Properties of Unreasoned Judgments

What sorts of cases are these unreasoned judgments? Are certain kinds of disputes more prone to this phenomenon than others? Spaeth's Supreme Court Database catalogues the primary substantive issue area for each dispute to allow for a basic comparison. Figure 2.5 shows the percentage of unreasoned judgments that fall into these issue categories. Plurality decisions and opinions per curiam are shown separately, as there are some worthwhile differences. Judicial power issues are most common for per curiam opinions, while criminal procedure cases make up the largest proportion of plurality decisions.

Moreover, figure 2.5 shows that the bulk of unreasoned judgments occur in cases dealing with civil right and liberties. Given the politically salient nature of these issues, it is perhaps unsurprising that the justices felt compelled to decide these cases, even if an unreasoned judgment would be the result.

To explore that conjecture, figure 2.6 shows the proportion of unreasoned judgments that are politically salient. As before, when a decision is covered on the front page of the *New York Times*, it is deemed salient (Epstein and Segal

(a)

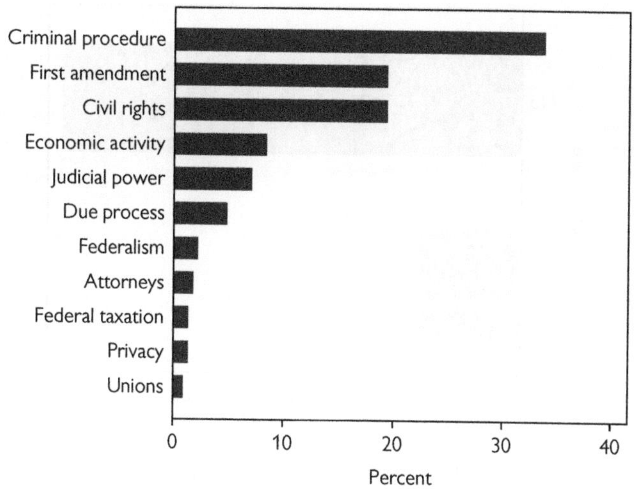

(a) Plurality Decisions by Issue Area

(b)

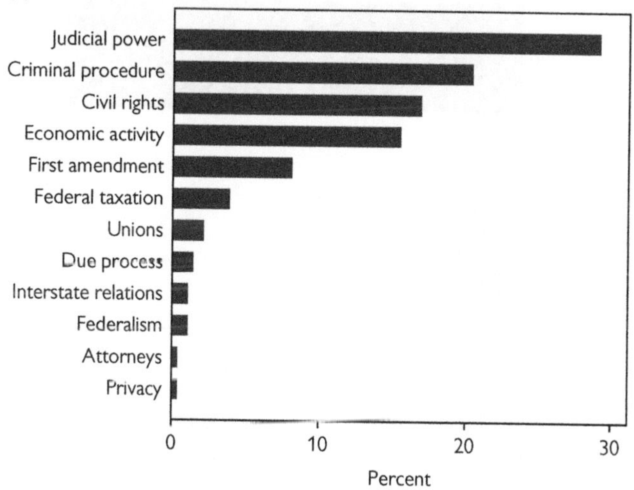

(b) Per Curiam Decisions by Issue Area

Fig. 2.5. Unreasoned Judgments by Issue Area

2000). Figure 2.6 contrasts this proportion with the proportion of salient cases among logically consistent (reasoned) decisions.

Figure 2.6 shows that unreasoned judgments are likelier to involve salient cases than consistent decisions. Indeed, about 18 percent of unreasoned judgments occur in a salient case compared to about 12 percent of consistent decisions. This difference is statistically significant at conventional levels.[14]

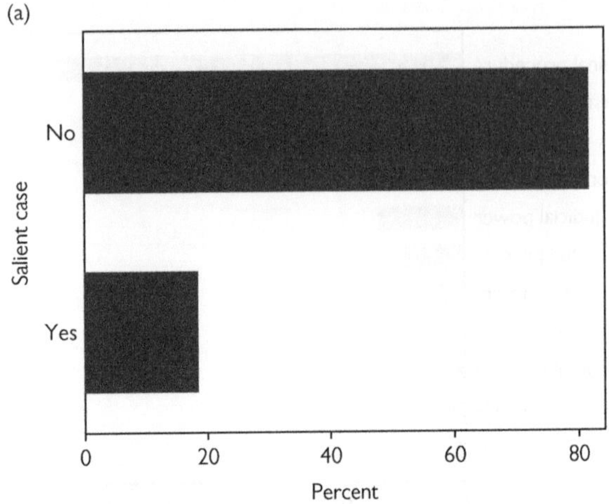

(a) Case Salience in Unreasoned Judgments

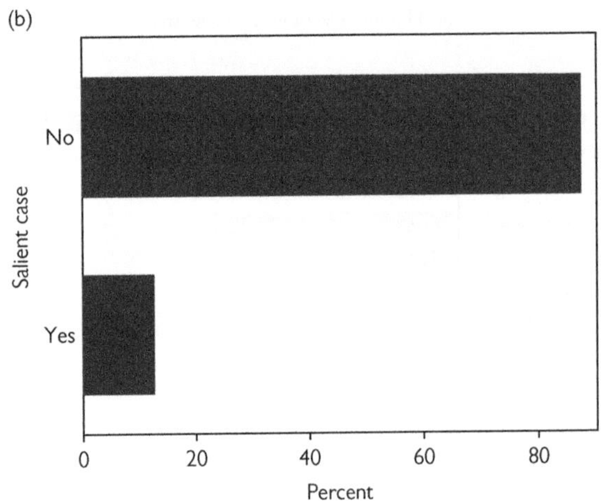

(b) Case Salience in Consistent Decisions

Fig. 2.6. Case Salience and Unreasoned Judgments

Conclusion

Unreasoned judgment represents a complex social phenomenon that may occur in one of several manifestations. Measurement of concepts like unreasoned judgment is a crucial element of social science research. While no measurement strategy is perfect, this chapter undertook a number of analyses aimed at ensuring the validity of the approach utilized in the remainder of this book.

In short, unreasoned judgment exists in two visible manifestations: plurality decisions and opinions per curiam. To verify the likely existence of unreasoned judgment, supplementary analyses were carried out. Third-year law student research assistants hand-verified the presence of unreasoned judgment in plurality decisions, with high construct validity and interrater agreement.

I limited the measurement of unreasoned judgment in opinions per curiam to only those issued after oral argument and with at least one separate opinion. A supplementary analysis indicated that this subset of per curiams dealt with significantly more complex (in terms of the number of issues) and salient (in terms of interest group activity and media coverage) cases than other opinions per curiam.

Using this measurement strategy, I then showed that unreasoned judgments have occurred over five hundred times at the Court between 1946 and 2010, over 6 percent of the total output during this time. In some terms, the rate of unreasoned judgments is as high as 15 percent of the total output. Moreover, it appears that unreasoned judgments occur regularly in politically salient cases. Taken together, these descriptive analyses demonstrate that while the consequences of unreasoned judgment may vary, their persistent presence in the Court's output is clear. While some work reasonably conjectures that unreasoned judgment occurs rarely (Stearns 2000), I show here that such outcomes emerge perhaps more frequently may have been anticipated. Most critically, this analysis demonstrates that if negative costs and consequences for the Court and American society accompany unreasoned judgments, then their frequency would likely be viewed as sufficiently common as to warrant major reforms aimed at limiting their emergence. Finally, I show that the frequency and rate of unreasoned judgment appears to be on the decline in recent decades.

I maintain this measurement strategy for unreasoned judgments throughout the remainder of the book. I now turn toward testing the theory laid out in chapter 1: why are only some cases resolved with an unreasoned judgment?

CHAPTER 3

The Emergence of Unreasoned Judgments in Individual Cases

> Great cases like hard cases make bad law. For great cases are called great, not by reason of their importance...but because of some accident of immediate overwhelming interest which appeals to the feelings and distorts the judgment.
>
> —Justice Oliver Wendall Holmes, opinion in *Northern Securities Co. v. United States*

Introduction

How often does a presidential election comes down to just nine votes? The Supreme Court probably wanted to avoid determining the winner of the 2000 election between Vice President Al Gore and Governor George W. Bush. Yet the tidal wave of history swept this responsibility to the doors of the Court's marble palace.

The peculiarity of America's system for choosing presidents can end up enshrining candidates who lose the popular vote in the White House. Moreover, the electoral college system thrusts particular states into the spotlight from time to time. Never did this peculiarity come more into focus than in the year 2000. Vice President Gore and Governor Bush engaged in a tight and fiercely contested campaign. Governor Bush led national likely voter polls by about 2.7 points in the weeks leading up to election day (Silver 2012).

The race proved even tighter than this polling margin. Vice President Gore went on to win the popular vote by approximately half of a percentage point. Ultimately, the winner of the election would be whichever candidate carried the state of Florida and its accompanying electoral college votes.

On election night, the major news networks variously called the election for both candidates at different points in the evening. The first official vote count in Florida gave the state, its electoral college votes, and the presidency to George W. Bush by just 1,784 votes (Hasen 2004). An automatic recount began, in accordance with Florida law. This first machine recount still gave the state to Bush, by an even narrower margin (Abramowicz and Stearns 2001, 1855).

That's where things got interesting. The Gore campaign noticed that far right Reform Party candidate Pat Buchanan received thousands more votes in heavily Democratic Palm Beach County than he received elsewhere in the state. Palm Beach County provided voters with an unusual "butterfly" ballot. This ballot featured a central column where voters would punch the appropriate hole for their chosen candidate. Candidates' names appeared on both the left and right sides of this ballot. Brady et al. (2001, 60) recount:

> One look at the ballot suggested that marking it correctly would be easy for Bush voters, who only had to match the first name on the ballot with the first punch-hole. But Gore voters, who had to match the second name on the left-hand side of the ballot with the third punch-hole in the center of the ballot, could easily mismark their ballots. If Gore voters mistakenly punched the second hole, they cast their vote for Pat Buchanan whose name was listed on the right hand side of the ballot, somewhat higher on the page than Al Gore's name but somewhat lower than George Bush's name.

As such, it seems at least plausible that many of these Buchanan voters in a heavily Jewish and African American county actually intended to vote for Gore. Indeed, careful statistical analysis indicated that Palm Beach County was an extreme outlier in terms of its support for Buchanan (Brady et al. 2001).

Further, over 19,000 ballots in Palm Beach County were voided for various errors. Usually, these voided ballots indicated multiple votes for president, which may also have been caused by the confusing butterfly ballot (Hasen 2004). As such, Vice President Gore sued for a manual recount of the ballots in Palm Beach County and three other counties. Because of the large amount of time needed to manually count these ballots, Mr. Gore also sued to extend the amount of time for a recount beyond the limits of Florida law (Hasen 2004).

The Florida Supreme Court ruled in favor of this extension, allowing the manual recounts to proceed. Uncertainty over the winner of the election reigned for days on end, and the country held its breath as various legal challenges between the campaigns were litigated in state and federal court.

After much back and forth, the legal question that pushed the U.S. Supreme Court into the fray involved whether these manual recounts could continue and indeed should proceed in every Floridian county. Election officials were to use a "clear intent of the voter" standard when deciding which candidate to award votes to (Hasen 2004). Governor Bush filed for certiorari, and the Court agreed to hear the case. The Supreme Court could have declined to get involved. But perhaps with so much at stake and so much uncertainty permeating the nation, the justices felt compelled to weigh in.

In a tremendous display of speed, the Court heard arguments on December 11, 2000, and issued an opinion the following night (Hasen 2004). The Court overturned the Florida Supreme Court, stopping all recounts and ultimately certifying George W. Bush as the forty-third president of the United States.[1]

The Court resolved the case of *Bush v. Gore* (531 U.S. 98 [2000]) with an opinion per curiam. That is, no justice signed their name to the Opinion of the Court: journalists were unsure of how many justices endorsed this ruling upon its issuance (Abramowicz and Stearns 2001, 1858). The per curiam opinion held that the Florida Supreme Court's ruling violated the Constitution's equal protection clause.

The unidentified author or authors of the per curiam opinion essentially admonished future judges to ignore their opinion as legal doctrine. "Our consideration is limited to the present circumstances, for the problem of equal protection in election processes generally presents many complexities" (per curiam opinion for the Court, *Bush v. Gore*, 531 U.S. at 109). That is, the justices responsible for this judgment explicitly *did not* want to simultaneously create lasting legal doctrine. Therefore, to this group of justices, the judgment itself, and not the underlying reasoning, seems clearly to have been of prime importance.

Abramowicz and Stearns (2001, 1866–1867) discuss the unreasoned nature of the Court's judgment. "It is beyond our scope to assess whether the majority's equal protection analysis was sound, let along correct, and we concede that one might well devise a persuasive justification. For our purposes it is sufficient to note that the Court plainly did not supply one." That is, the per curiam opinion overruled the Florida Supreme Court on equal protection grounds, but the Court did not discuss any line of precedent or doctrine that would imply such a conclusion, given the accepted facts of the case. Indeed, only later did legal scholars suggest possible doctrinal rationales, post hoc (Abramowicz and Stearns 2001, 1867).

Because no justification for the Court's judgment was supplied in the per curiam opinion, there simply is no reason underpinning the judgment at all. *Bush v. Gore* squarely meets the definition of opaque unreasoned judgment supplied in chapter 2. This opinion per curiam was issued following oral argument, accompanied by at least one separate opinion. While *Bush v. Gore* is an extraordinary case, it is nonetheless encouraging for the measurement strategy outlined in chapter 2 that this strategy correctly identified this decision as unreasoned, given that close legal analysis comes to the same conclusion (Abramowicz and Stearns 2001). Moreover, since *Bush v. Gore* is not a plurality opinion/doctrinal paradox, its status as a clearly unreasoned judgment underscores the importance of measuring this phenomenon according to multiple observable manifestations.

More than six hundred legal scholars vigorously attacked the Court's per curiam opinion (Hasen 2004). The Court acted with tremendous speed, hearing arguments and issuing an opinion within a two-day stretch. So, why did *Bush v. Gore* end up as an unreasoned judgment? More generally, why do some disputes end up being resolved with unreasoned judgments? It seems very unlikely all conflicts are equally vulnerable to this phenomenon.

In theory, unreasoned judgments in United States Supreme Court decisions violate norms of just republic governance. Certainly intervening dramatically in a presidential election without a doctrinal justification might qualify as a sufficiently troubling exercise of authority by the Court. Some argue for a wholesale reform of the Court as an institution (Pettit 2001; Kornhauser and Sager 2004) based on this theoretical issue, while others argue such concerns are overblown (Rogers 1991).

While isolated incidents like *Bush v. Gore* raise alarms, the first step toward understanding whether this theoretical issue warrants widespread concern requires a clearer and more systematic understanding of what sorts of cases generally become unreasoned judgments. Chapter 2 presented some descriptive evidence to that end, but more work remains to be done.

While inconsistency does not constitute a majority of the Court's output (Stearns 2000), understanding the correlates of inconsistency helps determine to what extent the Court was justified in evolving away from decisiveness to, in part, avoid inconsistency. Chapter 4 analyzes this evolution in detail. If inconsistency comprises only a small percentage of the Court's output, a scholar might conclude that the problem is not severe.

However, if unreasoned judgments tend to emerge with regularity in important constitutional disputes, then their overall frequency becomes a lesser concern. That is, if even just a few inconsistent decisions overturn Acts of Congress or settle key doctrinal issues, then concern may grow. Inconsistencies of that sort arguably represent failures of the Court to provide the rational, coherent judgments expected of them by the founders, in, for example, "Federalist No. 78" (Hamilton, Madison, and Jay 2008).

However, if unreasoned judgments tend to emerge in disputes of minimal relative interest or significance, then their existence would be of little consequence. This tension motivates an empirical analysis of the case-level factors associated with unreasoned judgment.

Moreover, theories of collective decision making rightly stay at a very abstract level. For instance, Arrow (1951) and Pettit (2002) discuss the impossibility of designing any system for preference (Arrow) or judgment (List and Pettit) aggregation that ensures transitivity (Arrow) or consistency (List and Pettit). The particular subject matter that returns a chaotic result is left unspecified in such theories.

These theories enjoy a very broad and general usefulness as a result. However, as a practical matter, the fact that we cannot guarantee consistency does not imply that all collective decisions are equally susceptible to inconsistency. Indeed, disputes likely vary considerably in their vulnerability to such results. However, empirical research regarding what sorts of disputes at the Court tend to yield inconsistent outcomes is lacking. This analysis speaks to these individual differences at the dispute level in the probability of inconsistency, thereby connecting the abstract, general theories of Arrow and List and Pettit to the day-to-day work of the Supreme Court.

In this chapter, I investigate these case-level correlates. In so doing, I provide an empirical test for the theory of inconsistency presented at the end of chapter 1. I further explore the kinds of disputes that are resolved inconsistently. Among other results, unreasoned judgments rarely emerge when the Court resolves a conflict between lower courts.

Perhaps most troubling, I show that doctrinal paradoxes, the more visible form of inconsistency, are significantly associated with exercises of judicial review by the Court over Acts of Congress and politically salient cases. This result demonstrates that inconsistencies do emerge in theoretically and politically salient contexts. The result underscores the threat that judgment–rationale inconsistency arguably poses to the health of the American legal system.

While I reserve extended discussion of the relative health of the American legal system for the concluding chapter, in brief, assessing the health of the legal system given the reality of unreasoned judgments requires carefully defined desiderata for the whole system. That is, what is the judicial system meant to accomplish to begin with? Inconsistency's inevitability (List and Pettit 2002) means that if society wants controversial topics addressed, courts may only be able to address these topics inconsistently. But if societies prefer logically consistent legal doctrine, then some conflict may never be addressed at all. Is the current balance of decisiveness and consistency at the Supreme Court optimal? Such a question can only begin to be answered with an empirical grounding of the correlates of unreasoned judgments.

Operationalizing the Case-Level Theory of Unreasoned Judgment

It is theoretically impossible to design a system for aggregating judgments (or preferences, for that matter) that guarantees consistency between judgments and rationales (List and Pettit 2002). In the abstract, any time a group of people must solve a collective decision problem, some form of inconsistency, intransitivity (Arrow 1951), or chaos (McKelvey 1976) may result. These results demonstrate that under very weak assumptions, it is mathematically impossible to guarantee consistent outcomes. Majority voting, for instance, the most basic and dominant method of preference or judgment aggregation, can easily result in collective decisions that exhibit inconsistency between the group's judgment and the underlying rationales underpinning that judgment.

Chapter 1 applied these insights to present a theory of unreasoned judgment at the U.S. Supreme Court. This theory, motivated by the social choice literature and scholarship on the Court, as well as qualitative analysis of the Court's own internal deliberations, suggests that inconsistent outcomes result from a combination of specific case-level factors. Each of these factors motivates a testable empirical hypothesis.

First, the justices might like to avoid complex and potentially fractious cases if they can. The justices seem to view inconsistencies as an undesirable outcome. Nonideological goals may motivate this avoidance (Epstein and Knight 2013). The legal elite community may be the important professional audience for the opinions of the Court (Baum 2006). This community directly consumes the Court's opinions and gives feedback freely. This audience dislikes inconsistent legal doctrine, as applying such doctrine proves challenging (McAleer 2013). Therefore, if a dispute features complicated, multidimensional issues that fracture the justices, the better option for satisfying elite audiences might simply be to avoid attempting to resolve the dispute in the first place.

Generally, the modern Court enjoys great discretion to hear only the disputes it so chooses. Yet some disputes, even if they can formally be ignored, may demand resolution based on external factors. Any dispute that the Court is compelled to decide satisfies the first condition, the jurisdiction condition, of chapter 1's theory. Disputes may satisfy this condition in two ways. First, some cases fall under the Court's mandatory jurisdiction, meaning that the Court is obligated to consider an appeal and issue a judgment. Congress eliminated most of the remaining mandatory caseload in 1988.[2]

The justices lobbied hard for this change, submitting a letter to the House Judiciary Committee, signed by all nine active justices, stating in part, "Unfortunately there is no correlation between the difficulty of the legal issues presented in a case and the importance of the issue to the general public. For this reason, the Court must often call for full briefing and oral argument in difficult issues which are of little significance."[3] The justices lobbied for increased agenda control out of a desire to avoid complex and difficult cases if such difficult issues could be avoided for lack of general relevance to the public. Indeed, agenda control is known to enhance stability in other elite political bodies that face similar problems of inconsistency, intransitivity, and chaos (Shepsle and Weingast 1981; Levmore 1989). Thus, the *mandatory jurisdiction hypothesis* states that cases arising under the Court's mandatory jurisdiction lack the escape valve of certiorari denial and may thus be associated with a higher probability of inconsistent outcomes.

Decision problems that may result in unreasoned judgments must contain more than one dimension of conflict as a necessary condition (Stearns 2000; Bovens and Rabinowicz 2006; Pauly and Van Hees 2006). If a dispute rests on only a single proposition, then it must be the case that majority voting could yield a judgment consistent with this rationale. That is, if the justices are individually rational, they will vote on the outcome in accordance with their beliefs on this single rationale. Therefore, the final majority on the outcome will be composed of justices who also agree on this single, outcome-determinative proposition as well.

Chapter 1 theorized that unreasoned judgments must therefore satisfy a case characteristics condition. That is, disputes must be multidimensional for an inconsistency to emerge. Spaeth's database measures the number of legal provisions (such as statutes to be interpreted) and legal authorities (such as the Court's supervisory power over the lower federal courts) invoked by the Court. Thus, the *multiple legal provisions hypothesis* conjectures that the probability of an inconsistency should rise with increases in the amount of legal provisions and authorities the Court considers in a case.

Stearns (2000), List (2003), and Dietrich (2006) show that inconsistency cannot occur, even in multiple dimensions, if the preferences of all the actors are single-peaked or unidimensionally aligned. That means if one could line up all the justices who agree on every proposition and the judgment on a left-to-right scale, with all the justices who disagree on the other side, then there will be a majority that agrees on every rationale as well as the final judgment, avoiding any inconsistency.

When we think of the justices as "liberal" or "conservative," we appeal to this single-peaked preference idea. The notion that a single continuum of liberalism to conservatism underpins much of the scholarship on judicial behavior (Segal and Spaeth 2002). Yet at times this single ideological dimension fails to capture the range of preferences expressed by the justices. Edelman, Klein, and Lindquist (2008, 2012) study what they term "disordered voting," by which they mean the extent to which voting coalitions deviate from an expected unidimensional alignment. The preference condition in chapter 1 stated that the justices must have nonsingle-peaked preferences for an inconsistency to emerge. Therefore, the *disordered coalition hypothesis* conjectures that whenever the final outcome voting coalition deviates from unidimensional alignment, an unreasoned judgment should be more likely to arise. For example, if the reliably "conservative" Justice Thomas joined with four "liberal" justices (such as Justices Ginsburg and Breyer) to form a majority opinion, then this coalition would be "disordered" according to Edelman, Klein, and Lindquist (2012).[4]

The last condition of chapter 1's theory of inconsistency, the doctrinal condition, applies only to doctrinal paradoxes/plurality opinions. It states that the justices only produce an inconsistency when they have stronger preferences over the long-run doctrine to be promulgated than the immediate judgment in the case. That is, the justices only produce a visible inconsistency when they are unwilling to compromise over doctrine to obtain a consistent outcome. Here we see how *Bush v. Gore* diverged from this theoretical pathway: the justices favoring the per curiam opinion emphatically did not want to create lasting doctrine. As such, the generation of the opaque per curiam opinion to support the judgment was a more sensible decision.

This condition, unlike the others, is more difficult to directly measure. As such, I operationalize this condition in four complementary, but distinct, ways. First, decisions considered salient by the media are likely to involve important constitutional issues that the justices are unlikely to want to compromise on (Corley et al. 2010). Epstein and Segal (2000) argue that decisions reported on the front page of the next day's *New York Times* are more salient than others. Further, they argue that this metric is not tainted by revisionist bias, unlike other metrics (such as expert surveys of important decisions). This lack of revisionist bias is important for testing the doctrinal condition. The condition applies to the justices at the moment they are deciding the case—the importance of the doctrine to the justices years after a case has been decided is irrelevant. Thus the *case salience hypothesis* states that decisions reported on the front page of the *New York Times* should have a higher probability of the doctrinal paradox.

The *New York Times* measure could arguably be endogenous to the political or ideological impact of the Court's rulings, and scholars have developed good alternatives in recent years (Black, Sorenson, and Johnson 2013; Clark, Lax, and Rice 2015; Collins and Cooper 2012). For these purposes, however, the *New York Times* measure suffices. As Spill and Oxley (2003, 27) show, even the print media rarely discuss the justices' justifications for a decision in the first place. If the media ever comment on the unreasoned nature of a judgment, such an event would be exceedingly rare. As such, we can confidently assume the *New York Times* measure is exogenous to the unreasoned property of judgments.

Second, different areas of law may vary in terms of how much the justices are willing to compromise on doctrine. Because civil liberties cases turn on salient and politically charged issues, justices may not be able to separate their preferences on the doctrine from their preferences on any other proposition (Braman 2006). This dynamic means that the justices will not compromise on doctrinal considerations in these cases. Thus, the *civil liberties hypothesis* conjectures that civil liberties cases should be more likely to be resolved with plurality opinions/doctrinal paradoxes.

Third, the power of the Court to invalidate laws enacted by the legislature represents the least democratic institution in the United States (Bickel 1962). Of course, the exercise of judicial review itself does not always mean the Court directly overrides the will of the majority in America (Dahl 1957; Whittington 2005). Indeed, the Court appears to behave in a majoritarian rather than counter-majoritarian manner much of the time (Hall and Ura 2015). That said, the subjection of congressional actions to review by an appointed judiciary represents one of the most controversial devices in American governance. The justices' doctrinal preferences seem likely to be quite intense when the Court considers its justification for exercising this authority, given its controversial nature.

In "Federalist No. 78", Hamilton wrote:

> "No legislative act, therefore, contrary to the Constitution, can be valid. To deny this, would be to affirm, that the deputy is greater than his principal; that the servant is above his master; that the representatives of the people

are superior to the people themselves; that men acting by virtue of powers, may do not only what their powers do not authorize, but what they forbid" (Hamilton, Madison, and Jay 2008).

On the same topic, anti-Federalist Brutus (Samuel Yates), wrote:

"When the courts will have a precedent before them of a court which extended its jurisdiction in opposition to an act of the legislature, is it not to be expected that they will extend theirs, especially when there is nothing in the constitution expressly against it? and they are authorised to construe its meaning, and are not under any control? This power in the judicial, will enable them to mould the government, into almost any shape they please" (Storing 2008).

The controversy over the power of the judiciary continues to this day. While there exists much theoretical work on the proposed counter-majoritarian difficulty of judicial review, Friedman (2002) encouraged scholars to focus attention instead on how well this institution works in the real world (257). To probe this question, figure 3.1 explores the extent to which the Court exercises its power of judicial review with inconsistent decisions. Figure 3.1 compares doctrinal paradoxes, the most visible form of inconsistency, with consistent decisions. Figure 3.1 presents a striking finding: less than 1 percent of consistent decisions exercise judicial review, while about 7 percent of doctrinal paradoxes exercise judicial review (over Congress). Of all Court decisions analyzed here (1946–2010), about 1 percent represent an exercise of judicial review. Of these, about 12 percent of these decisions are doctrinal paradoxes. That is, for every instance of judicial review (of Congress) 1946–2010, the Court exercised this power inconsistently a little more than once out of every ten occurrences. Conversely, only about 2.5 percent of decisions that do not exercise judicial review are doctrinal paradoxes. The χ^2 value of this comparison is 26.91, $p =< 0.001$.

Figure 3.1 shows that when the Court exercises its most controversial power, it fails to present a consistent rationale for its actions at a much higher rate than in its other decisions. Some might argue that it is normatively troubling that the Court would ever produce an unreasoned judgment when exercising its most anti-democratic power. Certainly critics of judicial review (Waldron 2006) would seem unlikely to view such behavior positively. While strong arguments exist for the institution of judicial review (e.g., "Federalist No. 78"), these arguments must be undercut somewhat by the revelation that the Court exercises this power even when it cannot cohere around a consistent rationale for doing so.

These difficulties aside, it seems clear from these discussions that preferences over the doctrine promulgated in decisions exercising judicial review

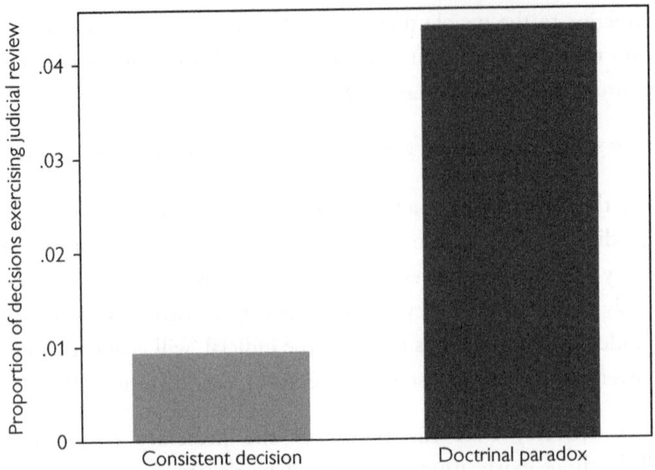

Fig. 3.1. Proportion of Decisions Exercising Judicial Review, by the Doctrinal Paradox

should be, on average, more intense than in other cases, satisfying the doctrinal condition. The *judicial review hypothesis* suggests there should be a positive and significant relationship between exercises of judicial review (over Acts of Congress) and the doctrinal paradox/plurality opinion.

Fourth and finally, as the court of last resort for the American legal system, one of the Supreme Court's primary responsibilities (at least in the eyes of legal scholars) is resolving conflicts that arise among the intermediate circuit courts of appeals (Hellman 1995). When conflicts exist, federal law is interpreted differently in different circuits, meaning that similar disputes result in disparate outcomes depending solely on the geography of the parties. Senators criticized the Roberts Court for failing to resolve enough of these conflicts (Specter 2010), noting that the Court arguably leaves a substantial number of conflicts unresolved for years at a time (George and Guthrie 2009). Lindquist and Klein (2006) and Perry (1991) contend that in conflict cases, the Court behaves in a "jurisprudential mode." As such, when the Court is in such a mode, the justices may be likelier to allow legalistic concerns, such as the consistency of their opinions, to exert more influence. Figure 3.2 shows the percentage of disputes heard to resolve a circuit split, subset by their consistency.[5]

Figure 3.2 shows that of the 7,839 consistent decisions in the data, about 17 percent were decided in order to resolve a circuit conflict. Conversely, only about 5 percent of unreasoned judgments emerged after a hearing to resolve a conflict. The χ^2 value of this comparison is 49.80, $p < 0.001$. Clearly, the

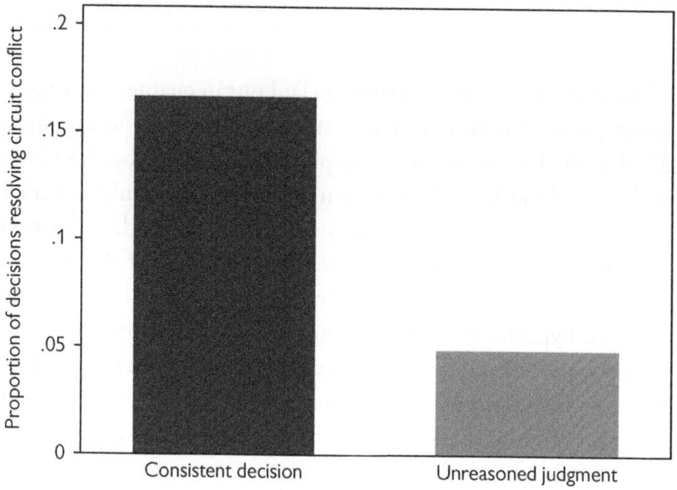

Fig. 3.2. Percentage of Decisions Made to Resolve Circuit Split by Consistency of Decision

Court is unlikely to resolve a circuit split unless it can do so in a consistent manner. Indeed, in the rare instances in which the Court does resolve a circuit split inconsistently, the effect of this inconsistency on the lower courts is substantial (Post and Salop 1992).[6]

Clark and Kastellec (2013) show that the emergence of conflict in the lower federal courts has an ambiguous and nonlinear effect on the probability that the Supreme Court will grant cert. At first, conflict *lowers* the probability of a cert grant, but the conflict eventually encourages the justices to grant cert after sufficient percolation in the lower courts. Clark and Kastellec (2013) present a formal model predicting this dynamic, which posits that percolation allows the justices to learn more about the issue, thus increasing the probability that the Court as a unit resolves the conflict in a manner consistent with its own preferences. Yet George and Guthrie (2009) show that the Court leaves many disputes unresolved, even after years of percolation. As such, other dynamics, such as a desire to avoid inconsistency, might explain the languishing of many unresolved conflicts.

The implication, to be explored more fully in a multivariate setup below, is that allowing the Court the discretion to choose its own agenda carries a significant tradeoff: circuit splits may remain in place indefinitely if the Court cannot resolve these splits with a consistent decision. The *circuit conflict hypothesis* suggests that cases for which the reason for certiorari is the resolution of a circuit conflict should exhibit a negative and significant association with unreasoned judgment.

Data

Here, I follow the measurement strategy laid out in chapter 2 for identifying unreasoned judgments in two manifestations. The more visible manifestation, the doctrinal paradox, arises in plurality opinions by the Court. The less visible manifestation, the opinion per curiam, is only considered an unreasoned judgment if such an opinion is issued alongside at least one separate opinion, following oral argument. The validation of the measurement strategy is discussed in detail in chapter 2.

To test the hypotheses of this chapter, I draw data from several sources. Data on many case characteristics are easily found in Spaeth's database. The analysis below includes binary variables for mandatory cases, civil liberties cases, exercises of judicial review, and the resolution of circuit conflict from this database.[7] Further a variable measuring the count of legal issues the Court faces is also drawn from this source.[8]

To measure case salience, I utilize Epstein's data showing which decisions (through 2009) were mentioned on the front page of the next day's *New York Times*.[9] Finally, to measure disordered coalitions, I constructed a binary variable equal to one for any decision supported by a coalition that deviated from unidimensional ideological alignment. For this variable, I utilized the ideological scores for the justices measured and reported by Martin and Quinn (2002).[10]

Several of the hypotheses above distinguished between plurality opinions and opinions per curiam. As such, I utilize two different statistical models in the analysis to follow. The first set of analyses treats unreasoned judgment as a binary phenomenon: either a decision is unreasoned, in any way, or it is not. I then consider a more nuanced dependent variable that takes on three categorical values: consistent, per curiam, and plurality. Importantly, this latter analysis imposes no ordering on these three opinion types. I do not presume that doctrinal paradoxes are necessarily stronger or more extreme than opinions per curiam. As this chapter's opening vignette of *Bush v. Gore* highlighted, opinions per curiam can themselves manifest quite dramatically.

Results

I relegate the full statistical details of these analyses to appendix B. In brief, there exists statistical support for most of the hypotheses of this chapter. As hypothesized, cases taken to resolve circuit conflicts are negatively and statistically significantly associated with unreasoned judgments. Figure 3.3

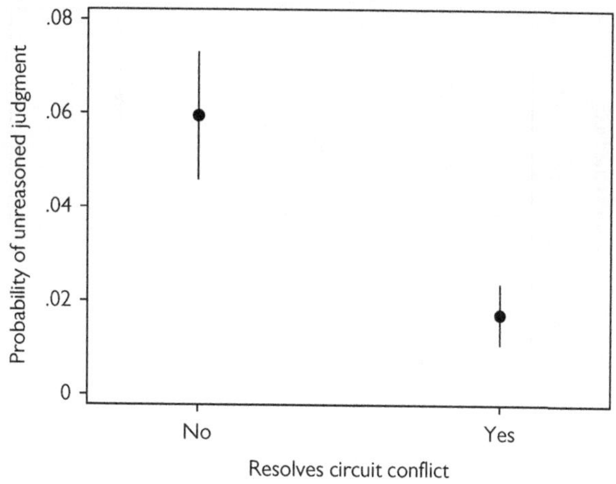

Fig. 3.3. Probability of Unreasoned Judgment by Circuit Conflict, 95 Percent Confidence Intervals

shows that a case heard to resolve a circuit conflict is predicted to have a 1.7 percent chance of resulting in an unreasoned judgment. This probability more than doubles for cases that do not resolve intercircuit conflicts.[11] This finding is strong evidence in favor of the *circuit conflict hypothesis.*

Moving on, disordered (nonsingle-peaked) voting coalitions are positively and statistically significantly associated with unreasoned judgments, as hypothesized. Figure 3.4 shows that a single-peaked outcome voting coalition has about a 6 percent chance of resulting in an unreasoned judgment. This probability essentially doubles to 12 percent when the outcome voting coalition is disordered. This finding is strong evidence in favor of the *disordered coalition hypothesis.*

For two hypotheses regarding unreasoned judgment, there was limited support in the data, and I fail to reject the null hypothesis. A drawback of including both the mandatory jurisdiction and the circuit conflict variables in a single model is that Spaeth's database generally does not code a reason for certiorari for cases arising under the Court's mandatory jurisdiction—that is, the "circuit conflict" variable equals 0 for almost every (all but three) cases arising under the Court's mandatory jurisdiction, meaning collinearity between these variables may bias standard errors upward. Omitting the circuit conflict variable from the estimation reduces the standard error associated with the mandatory jurisdiction variable, and this estimate becomes significant at the $p < 0.10$ level for opinions per curiam, in both binary and categorical analyses. Therefore, on balance there is mixed evidence for

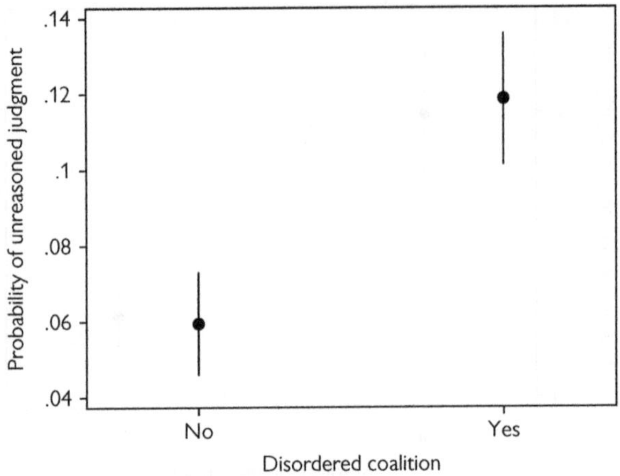

Fig. 3.4. Probability of Unreasoned Judgment by Disordered Coalition, 95 Percent Confidence Intervals

the *mandatory jurisdiction hypothesis.* Conservatively, I fail to reject the null hypothesis.

Moreover, a dispute's count of legal issues is negatively associated with the probability of unreasoned judgment. This finding is the opposite of the hypothesis. Further analysis demonstrates that this effect is driven by opinions per curiam. The count of legal issues is not statistically significantly associated with plurality opinions. This unexpected finding may be the result of the manner in which the Spaeth database measures legal provisions. Provisions are measured by the summary of the case in the Lawyers' Edition for Supreme Court Reports. As opinions per curiam are by nature brief and obscure the full dimensionality of cases, these opinions are particularly likely to undercount legal provisions and issues, a common criticism of the Spaeth database (Shapiro 2009). Moreover, it may be the case that the Spaeth database generally undercounts the amount of issues and provisions at stake in cases. Perhaps a typical case involves more nuance than the Spaeth database allows us to observe. Future work should continue probing along the lines of Shapiro (2009): for all its intellectual value, does the Spaeth database adequately measure the full range of issues and legal provisions in the Court's cases? Whatever the reason, however, the data do not support the *multiple legal provisions hypothesis.* I fail to reject the null hypothesis.

For three hypotheses, I conjectured that various case properties would be associated with plurality opinions (doctrinal paradoxes), but not opinions per curiam. Turning to this categorical analysis, figure 3.5 shows that politically salient cases are positively and statistically significantly associated

Fig. 3.5. Probability of the Doctrinal Paradox by Case Salience, 95 Percent Confidence Intervals

with the emergence of the doctrinal paradox. The probability of a paradox stands at about 2.7 percent for nonsalient cases; this probability nearly doubles to 5.4 percent for decisions that were announced on the front page of the *New York Times* (Epstein, Segal, and Spaeth 2001).

Cases involving civil liberties issues, however coarsely, seem likelier to involve the sorts of weighty doctrinal issues that lead the justices away from issuing opinions per curiam and closer to plurality opinions. As hypothesized, civil liberties cases are positively and statistically significantly associated with the emergence of the doctrinal paradox. Figure 3.6 shows that while civil liberties cases have about a 2.7 percent probability of the paradox, noncivil liberties cases have only about a 0.8 percent probability of resulting in a doctrinal paradox. Thus, going from a noncivil-liberties case to a civil liberties case increases the chances of the paradox by almost 250 percent.

Finally, it was hypothesized that exercises of judicial review over Congress would be positively associated with the doctrinal paradox. Figure 3.7 supports this hypothesis. Exercises of judicial review have about a 7.5 percent probability of being paradoxes. Cases that do not exercise judicial review, however, have only a 2.7 percent probability of being a paradox.[12] Therefore, if a case goes from not exercising judicial review to exercising it, its probability of resulting in the doctrinal paradox rises by almost 200 percent.

In sum, there exists support for many, but not all, of the hypotheses of this chapter. Unreasoned judgments are negatively and statistically significantly associated with cases heard to resolve intercircuit conflicts. Unreasoned

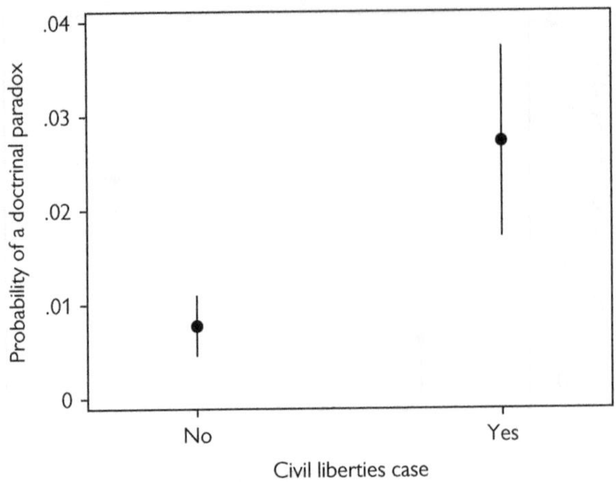

Fig. 3.6. Probability of the Doctrinal Paradox by Civil Liberties Cases, 95 Percent Confidence Intervals

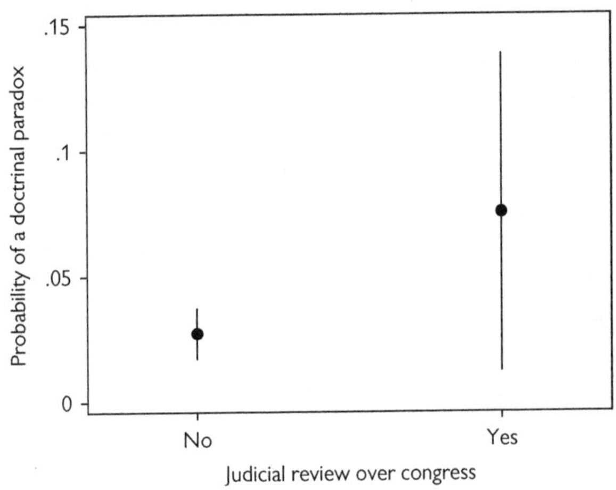

Fig. 3.7. Probability of the Doctrinal Paradox by Judicial Review, 95 Percent Confidence Intervals

judgments are positively and statistically significantly associated with disordered coalitions. The probability of a doctrinal paradoxes is positively and statistically significantly associated with salient cases, civil liberties cases, and exercises of judicial review. I therefore reject the null hypothesis for the the *disordered coalition hypothesis*, the *case salience hypothesis*, the *civil liberties hypothesis*, the *judicial review hypothesis*, and the *circuit conflict hypothesis*. I fail to reject the null *mandatory jurisdiction hypothesis* and the null *multiple legal provisions hypothesis*, for reasons discussed above.

Discussion: Court Curbing and the Doctrinal Paradox

The finding that the doctrinal paradox is more likely when the Court exercises judicial review raises a question: Does Congress take notice when the Court acts against its legislation in an inconsistent manner? Clark (2009; 2011) presents a model of what he terms "Court curbing," in which Congress signals to the Court its displeasure by introducing bills that would punish the Court in some way (usually by limiting its jurisdiction). Clark shows the Court responds to these curbing bills by exercising judicial review less frequently.

The fact that the Court overturns Acts of Congress with doctrinal paradoxes shows that these inconsistencies are more than theoretical curiosities. Rather, unreasoned judgments emerge even when the Court overturns the will of a democratically elected legislature. Ultimately, this result suggests that defenders of judicial review in a democratic society (Rostow 1952) could consider providing renewed justifications for this institution given its particular susceptibility to inconsistency. This result further raises the question as to whether the Court's audiences notice such actions and react accordingly. Using Clark's Court-curbing framework, I explore congressional responses to the Court's unreasoned judgments in a multivariate setup in chapter 6.

Conclusion

This chapter studied the emergence of unreasoned judgment at the case level. Though inconsistencies appear less frequently than consistent decisions, these inconsistencies do not appear randomly. As largely predicted by the theory presented in chapter 1, disputes satisfying a set of conditions are generally more likely to exhibit inconsistency.

Additionally, the Court seems relatively unwilling to resolve a circuit split in an inconsistent manner. Indeed, when the Court hears a case in order to resolve a split, these decisions are significantly less likely to result in either form of inconsistency. Because the justices vote strategically in the certiorari process (Caldeira, Wright, and Zorn 1999; Kleiner and Moldovanu 2017), it seems natural that they would avoid potentially fractious or multidimensional cases, if possible. Thus, the puzzle of unresolved circuit splits (Hellman 1995; George and Guthrie 2009; Specter 2010) may be illuminated by these findings. The justices know the importance of resolving splits for their jurisprudential influence (Clark and Lauderdale 2012), yet perhaps eschew resolving these splits if they could only do so in a manner that would be difficult or impossible for the lower courts to follow consistently (McAleer 2013; Post and Salop 1992). Thus, many splits may remain unresolved for the simple fact that the justices cannot resolve the split in a consistent or satisfactory manner.

Further, disputes for which the justices are likely to be unwilling to compromise on long-run doctrine are more likely to be doctrinal paradoxes. I operationalize this doctrinal condition in three ways. First, decisions reported on the front page of the *New York Times* (Epstein and Segal 2000) are significantly more likely to exhibit the paradox. These decisions are generally more salient than others. This measure is imperfect—most notably, it is biased based on other news events happening at the same time. That said, it offers some advantages over other measures of salient decisions (such as expert surveys or inclusion in law review articles). In particular, the measure is not biased by retroactive or revisionist views of Supreme Court decisions. Since the doctrinal condition requires that the justices themselves perceive the long-run doctrine as more important than the immediate judgment, the lack of revisionist bias in the *New York Times* measure is desirable.

Second, given the imperfection of the *New York Times* measure and the latent nature of the concept of relative preference intensity, additional measures of importance were included to buttress inferences regarding the doctrinal condition. This chapter showed that civil liberties cases have a significant, positive association with the doctrinal paradox. Since the doctrinal condition requires that the justices care more about long-run doctrine than the immediate judgment, civil liberties cases represent a good test of this condition. Civil liberties cases deal with important constitutional issues that the justices typically have strong preferences over (Edelman, Klein, and Lindquist 2008).

Third, when the Court exercises its power of judicial review over Congress, these decisions exhibit the doctrinal paradox significantly more often than other decisions. Even after controlling for salient cases (using the *Times* measure), exercises of judicial review over Acts of Congress are associated with more than triple the probability of exhibiting the paradox, ceteris paribus.

When the Court overturns legislation enacted by elected representatives, it abridges democratic representation. Congress may respond to these inconsistent exercises of judicial review by introducing more Court-curbing bills in subsequent years. This difference is only descriptive, however, and is not statistically significant. I therefore undertake a more comprehensive study of congressional responses in chapter 6.

CHAPTER 4

The Supreme Court's Evolution away from Unreasoned Judgment

Framers of judiciary acts are not required to be seers...it is enough if the designers of new judicial machinery meet the chief needs of their generation.

—Felix Frankfurter & James M. Landis,
The Business of the Supreme Court

Introduction

When asked about the first time the State of Louisiana attempted to execute him, Mr. Willie Francis said, "I felt a burnin' in my head and my left leg and I jumped against the straps. When the straps kept cuttin' me I hoped I was alive, and I asked the electric man to let me breathe" (Miller and Bowman 1982, 8).

Mr. Francis, an African American man, was one of fifteen children. He grew up poor and received little formal education in the segregated South (Miller and Bowman 1982). At the age of sixteen, his life took a dramatic turn for the worse when the police in Port Arthur, Texas, mistook him for another man, one sought for questioning in a drug case. The police realized their mistake and never pursued this case against Mr. Francis. However, while in custody, Mr. Francis wrote a very brief confession to the unsolved murder of a white citizen of his hometown of St. Martinville, Louisiana. Mr. Francis never spoke with an attorney or counselor before making this confession.

Nevertheless, he now returned to St. Martinville to face a murder charge. The primary evidence the State of Louisiana presented against him consisted of his written confession. Mr. Francis pled not guilty at trial. As Miller and Bowman (1982) and King (2008) discuss, Mr. Francis conceivably did not commit this crime. An eyewitness the night of the murder reported seeing a car parked with its lights on right after shots were fired in the victim's house. Mr. Francis lived on about nine dollars a week as a laborer and could not have begun to afford a car of his own in 1945 Louisiana. Moreover, his handwritten confession makes no mention of a car; rather, he confessed to hiding behind the victim's "gorage" in wait (Miller and Bowman 1982, 7).

Mr. Francis's court-appointed attorneys did not present an opening statement or a defense (Miller and Bowman 1982, 7). They called no witnesses and presented no evidence (King 2008). Unsurprisingly, he was convicted and became subject to Louisiana's mandatory death penalty law. His attorneys did not appeal this conviction (Wiecek 2001, 54). At the time, the State of Louisiana executed condemned criminals via the electric chair. The state moved its electric chair around the state, requiring it to be installed anew for each execution.

The installer of this chair for Mr. Francis's execution was not a licensed electrician. Moreover, the executioner reportedly arrived to carry out the sentence drunk (Miller and Bowman 1982, 9). When they strapped Mr. Francis into the chair and flipped the switch, a current ran through his body, very likely causing him extreme pain (King 2008). Yet this current was not sufficient to kill him. The chair shorted out, and officials returned Mr. Francis to a cell to regroup and figure out what to do next.

Describing the scene, Mr. Francis's attorney would later write in a brief to the U.S. Supreme Court (Wood 1947, 1):

> The scene was a disgraceful and inhuman exhibition, that as soon as the switch controlling the current was taken off, the drunken executioner cursed Francis and told him he would be back to finish electrocuting him, and if the electricity did not kill him he would kill him with a rock.

The State of Louisiana scheduled a new date to try to execute Mr. Francis again. Fortunately (though it would be of no good in the end), Mr. Francis had secured the pro bono help of more diligent counsel following this first botched execution (Miller and Bowman 1982, 10, fn. 49).[1] Mr. Francis petitioned the Board of Reprieves and Pardons of the State of Louisiana and then the Supreme Court of Louisiana to have this second execution attempt halted. Both bodies refused unanimously.

Mr. Francis's new legal counsel then filed a for a stay of execution and a petition for a writ of certiorari to the U.S. Supreme Court. Following the death of Chief Justice Stone and given Justice Jackson's absence in Nuremberg prosecuting Nazi war criminals, the Court stood at a bare seven members when this petition came in. There were three votes in favor of granting certiorari, with four opposed. Since four votes are typically required, the clerk of the Supreme Court reported that cert was denied. Mr. Francis's attorney relayed this information to him. Yet, because the Court was short two justices, three votes were considered sufficient to grant cert, and Mr. Francis was informed of this error; the Court would indeed hear his case (Wiecek 2001, 54). The Supreme Court heard arguments in *Louisiana ex rel. Francis v. Resweber* (329 U.S. 459) on November 18, 1946.

The justices grappled with the question of whether a second attempt at an execution was constitutional or not. Certainly the case presented *unusual* circumstances. But were these circumstances cruel, constituting essentially state-sponsored torture? Or were these circumstances an honest technical error: we don't close down the prisons every time a fire breaks out on a cell block, for example.

These unusual circumstances belied the broader legal importance of the case. In particular, the case raised the issue of whether the Fifth and Eighth Amendments to the Constitution ought to be incorporated via the due process clause of the Fourteenth Amendment. That is, could state law violate an individual's rights against double jeopardy and cruel and unusual punishment? If not, and the amendments ought to be incorporated, did subjecting Mr. Francis to a second attempted execution violate either amendment? If the amendments ought not be incorporated, did some other standard of decency prevent such a double execution?

After arguments, the justices came to a preliminary vote of 6-3 in favor of affirming the Louisiana Supreme Court and allowing the state another chance at executing Mr. Francis (Wiecek 2001, 55). Justice Reed's draft opinion avoided addressing the thorny issue of incorporation, allowing only that a second execution would not constitute a due process violation viewed through the lens of national standards of decency (Wiecek 2001, 55). Yet this draft opinion touched off a firestorm: three separate dissents were prepared and circulated by Justices Rutledge, Murphy, and Burton. Justices Frankfurter and Jackson (now returned from Nuremberg) left the majority opinion and signaled they would write separate concurrences. Justice Douglas abandoned the majority altogether, joining Rutledge, Murphy, and Burton in dissent.

Ultimately, these various opinions coalesced: Justice Jackson rejoined the original majority opinion coalition, and the dissenters united behind Justice Burton's draft. The key justice was Frankfurter. Justice Reed's draft majority opinion evolved: it still did not make a dispositive ruling on incorporation but suggested that incorporation likely would be appropriate. Justice Reed's draft opinion nevertheless still found a second execution would not violate either the Fifth or the Eighth Amendment, if they were to be incorporated.

Justice Frankfurter recognized the value in promulgating a coherent majority rationale. He wrote a memo to his brethren stating, in part:

> In order that there be an opinion of the Court, I had hoped to join brother Reed's opinion in addition to expressing my own views...It makes for nothing but confusion in the consideration of constitutional cases under the Due Process clause to cite cases that construed the scope of the double jeopardy provision of the Fifth Amendment. Presumably cases are cited because of their relevance to the problem under discussion.[2]

Justice Frankfurter understood the general importance of avoiding inconsistency in this memo. Yet, in his view, the crucial standard had nothing to do with the Fifth and Eighth Amendments, but whether Mr. Francis's treatment departed from the accepted, prevailing standards of fairness and justice within the State of Louisiana (Wiecek 2001, 59).

Table 4.1 summarizes these positions and highlights the unreasoned judgment in *Francis*. A majority of the Court seems to be in favor, at least theoretically, of incorporating the Eighth Amendment, though the plurality opinion does not go so far as to actually do this.[3] Yet, among those who

TABLE 4.1. Unreasoned Judgment in *Francis*

	Premise (1) Incorporate 8th	Premise (2) Use State standards	Premise (3) Treatment violates	Judgment
Frankfurter	N	Y	N	A
Jackson	Y	N	N	A
Vinson	Y	N	N	A
Reed	Y	N	N	A
Murphy	Y	N	N	A
Rutledge	N	N	Y	R
Black	Y	N	Y	R
Douglas	Y	N	Y	R
Burton	Y	N	Y	R
Court	*Y*	*N*	*N*	*A*

Note: Either premise 1 or 2 and premise 3 must have majority support in the same direction for any result to exhibit consistency.

agreed that incorporation was likely theoretically warranted, there was no majority on the question of whether Mr. Francis's treatment violated the Eighth Amendment. Justice Frankfurter's separate analysis and rejection of Justice Reed's plurality opinion ensured that the Court produced an unreasoned judgment, allowing the State of Louisiana to proceed with Mr. Francis's execution. Of course, because of the unreasoned nature of this judgment, the Court provided no rationale, at the collective level, for why the State of Louisiana was justified in subjecting Mr. Francis to the electric chair a second time.

The story of Willie Francis does not quite end here, however. Justice Frankfurter reported later that this decision weighed on his conscience considerably see (Wiecek 2001, 58–59; Miller and Bowman 1982, 19). Justice Frankfurter, who strongly took the position that the Court should not substitute its private views for those of the elected officials of Louisiana, nevertheless felt that those officials should show mercy to Mr. Francis. "Frankfurter sought to overturn the Supreme Court's *Francis* decision in an extraordinary example of extrajudicial intervention" (Miller and Bowman 1982, 34). Justice Frankfurter wrote to a friend, Monte Lemann, a member of the Louisiana Bar and a fellow Harvard Law graduate, three weeks after the Court issued its ruling (King 2008). He closed this letter by asking the State of Louisiana to grant Mr. Francis clemency (Miller and Bowman 1982, 35). Mr. Lemann then sent a letter to the Board of Reprieves and Pardons of the State of Louisiana, encouraging clemency while vaguely alluding to the correspondence he had with a well-respected attorney. Justice Frankfurter circulated a copy of this letter to the other justices but told only Justice Burton that he had been the instigator of this action. The board denied reprieve to Mr. Francis for a third time, in spite of Mr. Lemann's letter (Wiecek 2001, 64).

How clearly we see that Justice Frankfurter valued the doctrine promulgated (or not promulgated, in the case of incorporation) in *Francis*, as well as his perception of the properly restrained role of a judge, above avoiding what he seems to perceive as an unjust outcome. Indeed, Justice Frankfurter would subsequently vote against petitions for rehearing and habeas corpus on Mr. Francis's behalf, ending the final hopes of preserving Mr. Francis's life through the federal judicial system. "Frankfurter's attempt to gain clemency for Willie Francis can only be recognized for what it was: a pitiful attempt by a jurist to assuage his conscience for allowing a youth to be put to death in the name of abstract principles of federalism" (Miller and Bowman 1982, 39).

Justice Frankfurter participated in an unreasoned judgment that some argue violates normal standards of justice (King 2008; Miller and Bowman 1982). To subject a then eighteen-year-old boy to the electric chair a second time, given the woeful ineffectiveness of his counsel at trial, struck some as particularly barbaric (King 2008). More broadly, we have now seen that unreasoned judgment can emerge in politically salient disputes and in exercises of judicial review. Inconsistent decisions therefore present several significant normative and practical difficulties for the American legal system.

Moreover, it appears that the Supreme Court rarely resolves a conflict between lower courts with an unreasoned judgment, implying that, perhaps, the justices would rather not settle a conflict at all if such resolution would be unreasoned. The justices appear to dislike inconsistency. For example, consider Justice Frankfurter's memo to his brethren in the vignette above. Or refer back to the private dialogue between Justices Blackmun and Scalia in chapter 1. In struggling to craft a coherent majority opinion, both justices (who ended up endorsing contradictory legal doctrines in that case) expressed strong desires to avoid inconsistency if at all possible, just as Justice Frankfurter had expressed decades before. Avoiding conflicts that might have to be resolved without a coherent rationale likely satisfies the justices' desire to be viewed well by the primary consumers of their opinions: the legal community (Baum 2006). Indeed, who did Justice Frankfurter contact to mollify his conscience after casting the decisive vote in *Francis*? A peer, friend, and a member of the legal elite community.[4]

Thus, it seems only sensible that the justices would pursue reforms aimed at reducing the amount of complex and fractious disputes that they would be forced to resolve, potentially with an unreasoned judgment. The Supreme Court in the nineteenth century would decide well over one thousand cases in some terms (Epstein et al. 2012). Even as late as the 1980s, the Court was regularly hearing and resolving between 120 and 150 cases per year. That number has shrunk to between sixty-five and eighty cases per year (Owens and Simon 2012). Did this evolution by the Court have any bearing on its production of unreasoned judgments? If so, what impact has this evolution had on the business of the Supreme Court in the twenty-first century? These issues, viewed in combination with the theoretical threat to just republican governance posed by inconsistency (Pettit 2001), motivate the investigation of the frequency of inconsistency over time. I undertake a dynamic analysis in this chapter to address this question. If inconsistency appears frequently or is on the rise, in spite of the Court's reduced workload, then perhaps drastic reforms to the Court's decision-making procedures, like those suggested by Pettit 2001 and Kornhauser and Sager (2004), might be warranted.[5] If not, then scholars who suggest that theoretical concern over inconsistency is unwarranted or overblown (Rogers 1991; Easterbrook 1982) might be correct.

Beyond answering descriptive questions regarding the raw frequency of unreasoned judgments, this chapter also explores a question of general interest to the study of political institutions. The Court sought and obtained reforms that greatly enhanced the justices' discretion over which conflicts they would hear. Scholars have probed the impacts of agenda control on collective decision making in committees and legislatures for decades (Shepsle and Weingast 1981).

Studying the quality and nature of the Court's output over time allows for the consideration of whether institutional changes affected the aggregate consistency of the Court's output. In this chapter, I explore in detail the effect of the largest change in the Court's control over its agenda since the 1920s. This reform, initiated by congressional action in 1988, allows for the testing of hypotheses regarding the effect of agenda control on unreasoned judgment. While it is well-known that legislative committees can avoid intransitivity and chaos through institutional structure (Levmore 1989; Shepsle and Weingast 1981), this chapter shows that institutional features that collegial courts share with legislative committees also attenuate inconsistent outcomes in these venues.

This chapter also investigates the extent to which these changes impact the overall volume of conflicts resolved by the Court. Given the fundamental results of Arrow (1951) and List and Pettit (2002), it seems clear that societies must choose where in their judiciaries inconsistency is least desirable, since it cannot be eradicated altogether. As the caseload of the circuit courts of appeals rises, so to do cert petitions to the Supreme Court. Further, the Court faces increasingly intense criticism for failing to resolve long-simmering splits between the circuits. Yet the Court resolves fewer and fewer cases every year. Even as inconsistency falls at the Supreme Court level, disputes that could result in unreasoned judgments are increasingly left to the devices of the circuit courts. Thus, outcomes for litigants in these disputes may therefore depend arbitrarily on the geographic region in which their suit is filed. Moreover, the Court issues fewer total politically salient decisions on a year-over-year basis today, while the rate of such judgments remains flat. This dynamic implies that the Court did not utilize their newfound agenda control to resolve controversial disputes that they previously lacked the capacity to handle.

I continue with a descriptive presentation of unreasoned judgment over time. I then develop hypotheses regarding agenda control and unreasoned judgment in aggregate. I then test these hypotheses and conclude with a discussion regarding the implications of the findings.

Unreasoned Judgment over Time

In this chapter, I examine two manifestations of unreasoned judgment in the aggregate over many decades at the Supreme Court. I continue to follow the measurement strategy outlined in chapter 2. The first, more visible, manifestation is the discursive dilemma or doctrinal paradox, wherein the Supreme Court produces written opinions such that no rationale for the judgment of the Court carries the support of a majority of justices. The second manifestation occurs when the reasoning of the justices for their conclusion is opaque—that is, opinions per curiam. These are brief, unsigned opinions announcing a judgment; in these instances, it is usually impossible to ascertain whether the legal rationale for the Court's judgment carries a majority or not, hence it is a less visible variant of inconsistency.

Because reforms at the Supreme Court reduced its aggregate workload over the course of the twentieth century, the best way to understand the promulgation of inconsistency at the Court is by considering the rate of unreasoned judgments compared to the Court's overall workload. Figure 4.1 shows this rate between 1946 and 2010. The rate of unreasoned judgments fluctuates considerably over the latter half of the twentieth century. This rate appears to fall in the mid-to-late 1980s, stabilizing at a lower level by 2010. Is this secular decline a coincidence? Or is it a function of changes vigorously sought by the justices during this period?

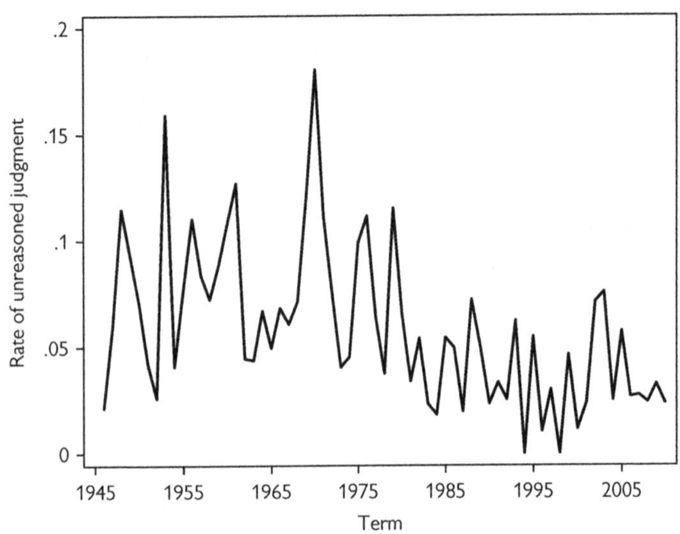

Fig. 4.1. Rate of Unreasoned Judgments, 1946–2010

Figure 4.1 demonstrates that the rate of unreasoned judgment rises as high as about 18 percent of the Court's output in a given year.[6] This amount would constitute a sizable minority of the Court's output. Indeed the rate might be worrying if the consequences of unreasoned judgment prove to be both substantial and societal in nature. Moreover, given that chapter 3 showed that unreasoned judgments arise with greater frequency in salient and contentious decisions, this rate might prove even more troubling to those who view the very existence of any collective inconsistency as unacceptable.

Agenda Control and Unreasoned Judgment

What might explain the dynamics shown in figure 4.1? Theoretical work on intransitivity in legislative committees motivates hypotheses about how the Court's formal and informal institutions curb or encourage inconsistency in the aggregate (Shepsle and Weingast 1981; Tullock 1981; Levmore 1989). Moreover, the justices' own internal deliberations shed light on how the justices might pass on potentially fractious cases if possible. A complex mess of a case might be avoided unless the broader legal and societal implications of the dispute are so pressing that resolution cannot wait for further percolation (Clark and Kastellec 2013).

Shepsle and Weingast (1981) describe a structure-induced equilibrium, where institutional features of legislatures serve to prevent chaotic results such as cycling and intransitivity. Legislatures can avoid these unstable results through structure and processes. In practice, legislatures do evolve away from chaos (Levmore 1989) in large part through these measures. Institutional features that the Court has in common with legislatures should exhibit similar effects on inconsistency.

One of these institutional features is agenda control. Generally speaking, legislatures avoid chaos through *restrictions on the domain of exchange* (Shepsle and Weingast 1981). That is, some proposals or amendments are restricted from being brought to the floor for a pure majority vote, even if these amendments might defeat an allowable alternative. Further, other proposals or amendments are prioritized; for instance, the final vote is the status quo position against some alternative, prioritizing the status quo position over others.

In legislatures, this requirement that winning proposals must succeed in a vote against the status quo attenuates chaos (Shepsle and Weingast 1981, 514). In legislatures, there is always a status quo reversion point. The legislature is in the business of creating new policies that amend or replace existing policies. The existing state of the world, the status quo, is never off of the agenda in a legislature. The ability to revert to the status quo and to prioritize the status quo in the voting order facilitates a structure-induced equilibrium in legislatures, preventing chaos.

At the Supreme Court, however, there is variance in the Court's discretion to revert to a status quo point when making decisions. Much of the Court's docket is discretionary. That is, the Court reviews petitions for certiorari and only hears arguments and issues opinions in the small subset of cases it chooses to decide. However, a varying portion of the docket over the years is composed of mandatory jurisdiction cases, cases in which the Court is obliged to issue a ruling of some sort.

The discretionary nature of much of Court's docket allows the justices to decide *not* to hear many cases, allowing whatever decision the lower court made to stay in place. By not hearing a case and issuing opinions, the Court allows the legal status quo to remain in place when it exercises its discretion in docketing cases. If a case appears to be especially complex, multidimensional, or fractious, the justices might prefer to leave the status quo in place rather than potentially issuing an inconsistent opinion.

To be sure, the very notion of structure-induced equilibrium generates controversy in the academic literature. Perhaps most strongly, Diermeier and Krehbiel (2003) contend than any collective decision-making body that is fundamentally majoritarian can simply alter structures that are displeasing whenever they want. Diermeier and Krehbiel looked prescient in 2017 as Senate Republicans voted by simple majority to eliminate the filibuster on Supreme Court nominees in order to confirm Justice Neil Gorsuch by a less than filibuster-proof margin (Archer and Liptak 2017). Indeed, if a group of actors is free to change their rules whenever they see fit by majority vote, why do we care all that much about rules and structure at all?

The answer, in this case, is two-fold. First, Congress, not the Court, sets the Court's jurisdiction. So, while the Court can indeed change many of its rules by majority vote, its discretion over the agenda is not under the direct control of the justices. That is, even if the justices wanted to go back to a largely mandatory docket, they could not do so via a majority vote among themselves. Since the germane element of the Court's structure under analysis here cannot be altered by a majority vote of the justices, Diermeier and Krehbiel's (2003) criticism does not apply directly.

Second, it would underscore the general argument of this chapter if a majority or more of the justices sought out the institutional change of enhanced agenda control themselves. That is, the justices seem to desire the ability to avoid potentially fractious disputes if possible. If they lobbied Congress directly, indicating strong support for a structural change, this activity would indicate clearly the direction in which the justices desired the Court to evolve. So, while Diermeier and Krehbiel's (2003) criticism of structure-induced equilibrium bites at many studies focused on the effect of institutional characteristics on collective decision making, it seems less relevant here.

When the Court is obliged to decide a case, defaulting to the status quo is no longer an option. Moreover, the Court does not enjoy the ability to alter its mandatory caseload by a majority vote of the justices. While cases arising under the discretionary portion of the Court's docket can successfully be avoided by denying certiorari and reverting to the status quo, cases arising under the Court's mandatory jurisdiction must be decided in some fashion. The structure of this discretion, then, arguably plays a role in dictating the equilibrium of cases resolved and unreasoned judgments produced by the Court.

Unreasoned judgments garner criticism from legal audiences (McAleer 2013). Indeed, given that the legal audience may exert the most influence on the justices' behavior (Baum 2006), avoiding disputes that might be potentially unreasoned seems a natural behavior for the justices to engage in. Both psychological and rational choice theories point toward the same prediction: cases arising under the Court's mandatory jurisdiction should be more prone to exhibit judgment–rationale inconsistency than cases arising under the Court's discretionary jurisdiction. Indeed, bivariate analysis shows that a case arising under mandatory jurisdiction is about 1.3x as likely to result in an unreasoned judgment, relative to cases arising under discretionary jurisdiction.

Further, there is a positive and statistically significant correlation between the Court's mandatory caseload and its production of unreasoned judgments. Specifically, the correlation between the Court's mandatory caseload and the incidence of unreasoned judgments is 0.71.[7] The correlation between the rate of unreasoned judgments and the Court's mandatory caseload is 0.47. Both correlations are statistically significant at conventional levels. These dynamics indicate that the mandatory caseload at the Court likely represents a key driver of the aggregate production of unreasoned judgments.

Any reforms at the Court that eliminated portions of this mandatory caseload thus eliminated disputes that are more likely to result in inconsistency. It is hypothesized that increased agenda control will be associated with fewer incidences of inconsistency. Congress eliminated most of the remaining mandatory caseload in 1988.[8]

The justices lobbied hard for this change. They submitted a letter to the House Judiciary Committee, signed by all nine active justices, stating in part: "Unfortunately there is no correlation between the difficulty of the legal issues presented in a case and the importance of the issue to the general public. For this reason, the Court must often call for full briefing and oral argument in difficult issues which are of little significance."[9] The justices lobbied for increased agenda control out of a desire to avoid complex and difficult cases if such difficult issues could be avoided for lack of general relevance to the public. Members of Congress acquiesced to this lobbying in passing the bill, later signed by President Reagan.

This episode mimics a similar incident in the 1920s. Chief Justice Taft lobbied Congress for legislation that eventually became known as the Judges' Bill (Frankfurter and Landis 1928). This bill created the certiorari process and gave the Court partial discretion to set its own docket. It is fair to view the 1988 Case Selections Act as a furthering of the goals of the Judges' Bill. The lobbying activity of the justices throughout the twentieth century aimed at reducing the Court's mandatory caseload and increasing discretion. That is, at multiple moments in Supreme Court history, the justices pushed hard away from decisiveness in favor of discretion. The justices became freer and freer over time to avoid disputes that may have resulted in unreasoned judgments; the complaints about the complexity of the mandatory caseload speak to this point. The promise implied by the justices at both of these junctures in history is that the Court would continue to maintain the uniformity of federal law by continuing to resolve important conflicts between lower courts as they arose (Starr 2006). Whether the Court is living up to that promise is a question for debate; many scholars and politicians appear to believe otherwise (Specter 2010; Hellman 1995; George and Guthrie 2009).

Of course, the 1988 legislation also opened the door for the justices to simply hear fewer cases. Prior work shows that the 1988 reform did indeed result in a lessened workload for the Court (Owens and Simon 2012). Figure 4.2 below shows the same: the average number of cases decided annually at the Court falls dramatically after 1988. From 1946–1988, the Court decided approximately 145 orally argued cases per year. From 1989 to 2010, the Court disposed of only roughly 94 cases in this manner per year. This trend seems unlikely to reverse itself if the justices continue to be left to their own devices regarding agenda setting. For example, in the 2015 term, the Court decided 69 cases with argument.[10]

The difference in workload before and after 1988 at the Court is statistically significant at conventional levels.[11] As such, and consistent with

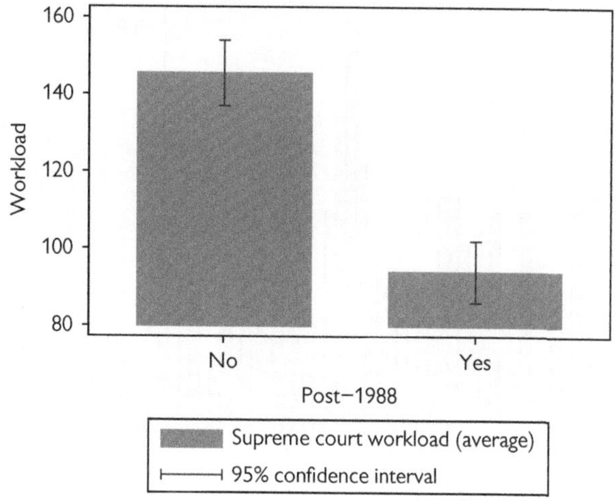

Fig. 4.2. Workload of the Supreme Court, Before and After 1988

prior work (Owens and Simon 2012), it is clear that the 1988 legislation substantially depressed the volume of business at the Supreme Court.

Figure 4.2 suggests that perhaps a decline in the absolute number of unreasoned judgments after 1988 may well be the result of a reduced amount of opportunity for such judgments. Yet the theory presented above suggests that the rate of unreasoned judgments should fall as well following increases in the Court's control over its agenda. That is, declines in unreasoned judgment should result from the justices deciding not to decide more potentially fractious cases. Under this argument, the volume of total work at the Court is not expected to have much of an effect on the production of unreasoned judgments. Thus, it is hypothesized that *after 1988, both the rate and the incidence of unreasoned judgment at the Court fell.*

Descriptive Analysis

Figure 4.3 shows that the incidence of unreasoned judgments in on a downward trajectory.[12] After the 1988 legislation, the highest number of unreasoned judgments in a single term was seven (in 1989). Further, in four terms after 1988 (1994, 1996, 1998, and 2000), the Court produced either zero or only one unreasoned judgment. For comparative purposes, the minimum number of unreasoned judgments in a term before 1988 was three. The term with the most unreasoned judgments, twenty-six, occurred prior to 1988 in 1970. Prior to the 1988 reform, the Court issued more

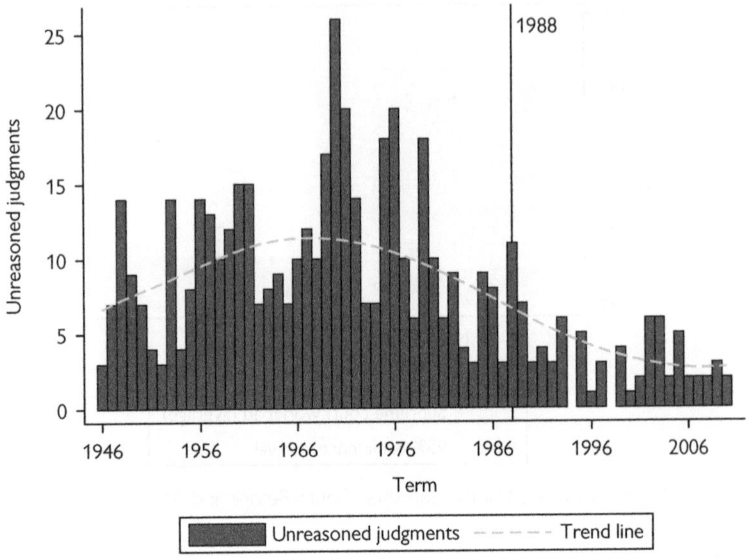

Fig. 4.3. The Trajectory of Unreasoned Judgments, 1946–2010

than seven (the highest number after 1988) unreasoned judgments in no less than twenty-eight separate terms. Bivariate analysis shows that the incidence of unreasoned judgments before and after 1988 is statistically significant at conventional levels.[13]

The aggregate production of unreasoned judgments does appear to have been impacted by the 1988 legislation, at least in this simple descriptive analysis. The Court produced about ten unreasoned judgments a year, on average, before 1988. After 1988, this average drops to about three, a 70 percent decline, and a drop of well over the standard deviation.

Of course, this decline in the incidence of unreasoned judgments does not tell the whole story: perhaps the Court simply issued fewer unreasoned judgments because their overall workload declined. Figure 4.4 shows that the rate of unreasoned judgments relative to the Court's overall workload is on the decline as well. As before, the difference in the rate of unreasoned judgments before and after 1988 is statistically significant at conventional levels.[14]

Substantively, the average rate of unreasoned judgments before 1988 was about 0.07. Seven percent of the Court's output could be expected to be unreasoned before the agenda control reforms. This rate drops to about 0.03 after 1988. The rate is more than cut in half following 1988. Again, this decline is well over a full standard deviation decrease.

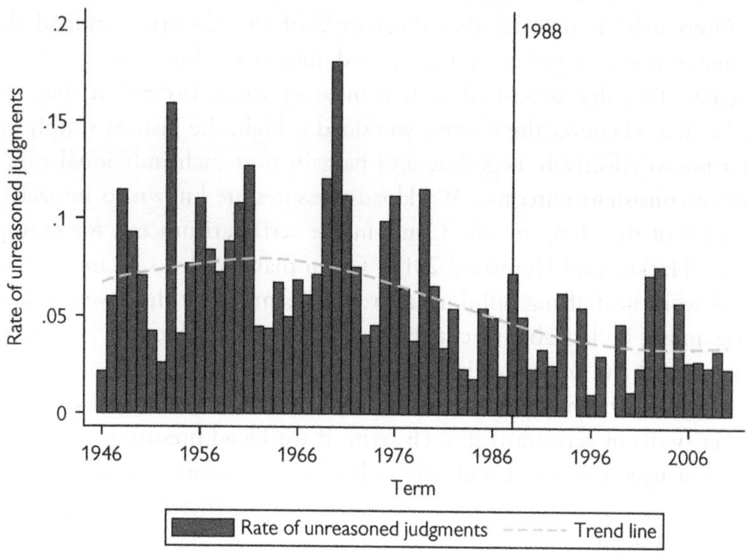

Fig. 4.4. The Trajectory of the Rate of Unreasoned Judgments, 1946–2010

Control Variables

Of course, these associations are descriptive in nature and should certainly not be viewed as causal relationships. To help ensure that any inferences about the relationship between the 1988 legislation and unreasoned judgments are not spurious, I also consider two possible alternate explanations for the variance in unreasoned judgments over time.

First, it is possible that the Court may exhibit more inconsistency between its rationales and judgments when the preferences of the justices are more divergent and agreement on any proposition is more difficult. That is, as the justices diverge from each other ideologically, forming a majority consensus must become more difficult (Maltzman, Spriggs, and Wahlbeck 2000). This difficulty would be present whether or not the justices were required to hear certain cases. Thus, I control for the standard deviation of the justices' Martin–Quinn scores (Martin and Quinn 2002) in each term; if preference divergence generated more inconsistency, then the coefficient on this variable should be positive. Using the standard deviation allows for a simple summary index of how spread out the justices' preferences are from each other. This control is preferable to a scale that depends only on the values of extremists on the Court, such as the absolute distance between the most liberal and conservative justice in a given term.

Alternately, it may be that the nature of the Court's workload does influence the emergence of unreasoned judgment, but not due to any inherent difficulty associated with mandatory cases. Instead, it may simply be that whenever the Court's workload is high, the justices simply lack the time to effectively negotiate and bargain over each individual case to reach a consistent outcome. Workload pressures are known to impact the behavior of the clerks on the Court in the certiorari process, for example (Blake, Hacker, and Hopwood 2015). Given that the clerks do much of the initial work in drafting opinions as well, it seems likely that overburdened clerks might be less able to cut the Gordian knots of doctrine involved in controversial and complex disputes.

I include the number of cases accepted via the Court's discretionary docket (writs of certiorari) in each term. If workload pressures, rather than the challenges associated with the lack of agenda control, were associated with increased unreasoned judgments, then the coefficient on this variable should be positive.

Analysis

These data are dynamic in nature. That is, each variable in the analysis constitutes a time series—a series of repeated observations on the same variable at regular intervals in time. Extra precautions must be taken to guard against false inferences (Box-Steffensmeier et al. 2014).

I relegate the full technical details of the multivariate time series analysis to appendix B. In brief, it is necessary to ensure that the data analyzed have been appropriately tested and preprocessed in order to avoid the spurious regression problem (Yule 1926). We must purge the effect of a random drift upward (or downward) from every time series we analyze. Otherwise, it is easy to mistake sets of unrelated secular trends for meaningful relationships.

After pretesting and processing each individual series, I then included the control variables listed above in a multivariate time series statistical model. Because the Court's discretionary workload is including in the calculation of the rate of unreasoned judgment it would be inappropriate to also include workload as an independent variable in that analysis. The full results are presented in appendix B. In summary, there exists a negative and statistically significant association between the 1988 reforms and both the incidence and rate of unreasoned judgments.[15]

Interestingly, ideological divergence between the justices is not statistically significantly associated with either the rate or the incidence of

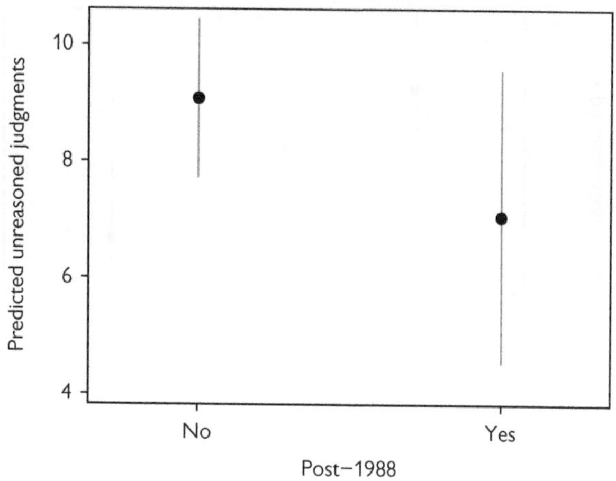

Fig. 4.5. Effect of 1988 Legislation on the Incidence of Unreasoned Judgments

unreasoned judgments. Nor is the Court's discretionary workload statistically significantly associated with the incidence of unreasoned judgments.

To put these findings in context, figure 4.5 shows that after controlling for the dynamic properties of the series, as well as the other independent variables, the 1988 legislation is associated with a decrease of approximately two unreasoned judgments per year. This decrease is equivalent to roughly a third of a standard deviation.[16]

Results are similar for the rate of unreasoned judgment. Figure 4.6 highlights these effects. The 1988 legislation is predicted to have lowered the rate of unreasoned judgment by about 2.5 percent, nearly two-thirds of a standard deviation. As such, the evidence is decidedly against the null hypothesis of this chapter. The substantive impact of the 1988 agenda control legislation is profound: an average of seven fewer total instances of unreasoned judgment emerge in the Court's output per term following this legislation. Further, after 1988, the rate of unreasoned judgment falls by two-thirds of a standard deviation. The Court's discretionary caseload is also lower on average after 1988. However, the correlation between discretionary workload and unreasoned judgment was never both positive and significant, neither before nor after 1988.[17] As such, the results indicate that the agenda control reforms of 1988 played a role in the reduction of unreasoned judgments at the Court, as opposed to a general secular decline in all decisions the Court issues.

As I detail in appendix B, I subject this finding to a supplementary analysis for robustness. While the year 1988 is statistically significantly associated with changes in the incidence and rate of unreasoned judgment, this

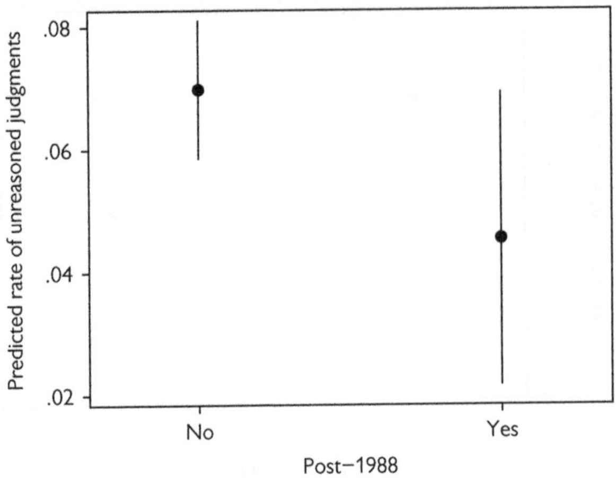

Fig. 4.6. Effect of 1988 Legislation on the Rate of Unreasoned Judgments

association could also be a spurious byproduct of a trend that began earlier for other reasons. Caporale and Grier (2005) advised analyzing a time series for the location of unknown structural breaks as a guard against false inferences based on this potential confound. As detailed in appendix B, both the rate and incidence time series appear to have undergone a structural break around 1988. This finding provides even greater confidence that this year was a turning point in the generation of unreasoned judgments by the Court.

The data suggest that there may be a positive and significant relationship between unreasoned judgment and the Court's mandatory caseload. After the elimination of much of this caseload by congressional action in 1988, the amount of inconsistency in the Court's output fell dramatically. Multivariate analysis that accounts for the dynamic properties of the data and several competing explanations support this conclusion. Regarding the control variables, there is no evidence in the data that variance of preferences among the justices in a given term has any impact on the emergence of unreasoned judgment. The coefficients on this variable fail to attain significance in any specification. There is also no support for the alternate argument that simple workload pressures explain the relationship between mandatory caseload and inconsistency; the coefficients on the Court's discretionary caseload is negative, though not statistically significant. This dynamic, if anything, suggests that a higher discretionary workload is associated with *fewer* unreasoned judgments.

Discussion

The relationship between the Court's mandatory caseload and the emergence of unreasoned judgment has important practical implications. Had Congress not intervened to eliminate a substantial portion of the mandatory docket, these results suggest that inconsistency would have persisted at the pre-1988 rate. Importantly, the amount of petitions to the Court continues to rise, as shown in figure 4.7. While some cases that would have been part of the Court's mandatory docket before 1988 surely are now filed as petitions for certiorari (Stern, Gressman, and Shapiro 1988), the Court today has discretion to avoid resolving these cases.

If the Court's mandatory caseload remained as large today as it was before 1988, then perhaps the criticisms of Pettit (2001) would require serious consideration, as inconsistencies presented themselves at a nontrivial rate before 1988. Of course, such a debate would require a better understanding of the consequences of unreasoned judgments as well. That subject is the focus of the latter half of this book.

As it stands here, these decisions, marked by their fractured and difficult to interpret reasoning, resolved many disputes over time. While the volume and rate of unreasoned judgments appears lower today, they were hardly eradicated.

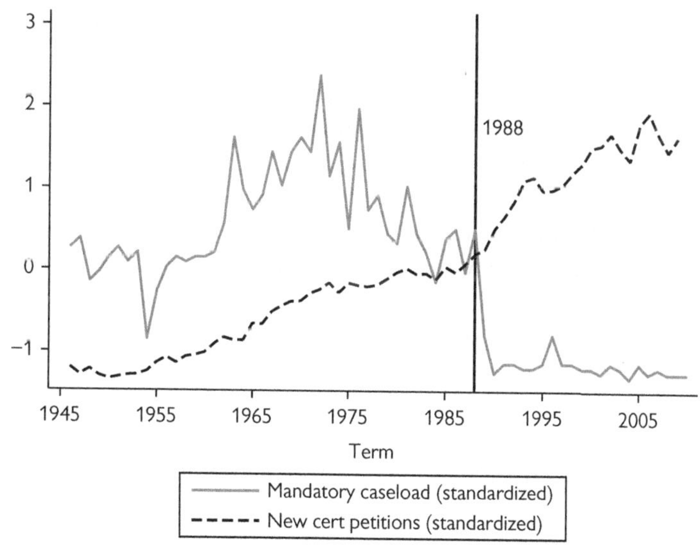

Fig. 4.7. Mandatory Caseload and Petitions 1946–2010

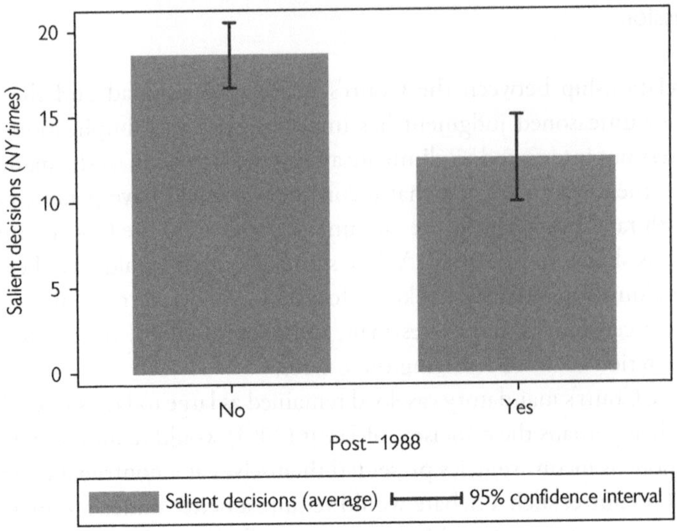

Fig. 4.8. Salient Decisions by the Court, Before and After 1988

That said, no judgment aggregation system guarantees consistency (Arrow 1951; Easterbrook 1982; List and Pettit 2002). And it does appear that the introduction of greater agenda control at the Court in 1988 substantially reduced the emergence of inconsistencies. As such, given that perfect consistency (the wholesale elimination of unreasoned judgments) is an unattainable goal for the Supreme Court (Easterbrook 1982), the dramatic reforms suggested by Pettit (2001) for all collective decision-making bodies are arguably unneeded at the Supreme Court, so long as the Court retains the level of agenda control it currently enjoys.

This chapter demonstrated that the Supreme Court evolved away from decisiveness and toward consistency. The Court resolves today many fewer cases than it did in the recent past. Moreover, its rate of unreasoned judgment is also substantially lower. While this dynamic might help the justices satisfy personal goals in terms of producing good and praiseworthy doctrine in the eyes of their professional peers (Baum 2006), it is not at all clear that this development should be viewed positively at a societal level.

As Starr (2006) pointed out, the justices promised Congress to continue behaving decisively to ensure conformity of the law across the country. Moreover, as articulated earlier in chapter 1, one of the key purposes of the Court, according to Hamilton and others, is the resolution of important constitutional questions. How is the modern Court doing on that score? Figure 4.8 shows that the Supreme Court today is issuing fewer salient decisions than it did before 1988. This difference is statistically significant at conventional levels.[18] Here, as earlier, salience is measured as a binary variable that equals one if a decision is announced on the front page of the following day's *New York Times* (Epstein and Segal 2000). As such, figure 4.8 shows that the reduced business of the Court means that it is also potentially dealing with fewer politically salient or controversial disputes. It is not the case that the Court used its newfound agenda control to eliminate busy work from the docket. Rather, it appears that cases of interest and importance to the country go ignored more often today than they may have before the agenda control reform of 1988.

The rate of salient decisions, measured by the *New York Times* variable, is unchanged after 1988. Thus, the Court engages with salient and nonsalient issues in similar proportions today. Yet the Court's reduced business means that on balance it is weighing in less often on issues of importance to society writ large.

Conclusion

Increases in agenda control reduced unreasoned judgments in the United States Supreme Court. Whether that inconsistency is manifested transparently as a doctrinal paradox/plurality opinion or opaquely as a per curiam opinion, the amount of inconsistency in the Court's output appears to be tied to the amount of mandatory cases they are required to hear. Congressional action in 1988, which removed most of the Court's remaining mandatory caseload, reduced the amount of inconsistency in the Court's output.

Before 1988, inconsistency at the Court was more common, appearing in hundreds of decisions from 1946–1988. Given that prior to 1925, the Court had very little control over its agenda, this research suggests that this problem was even worse in earlier eras, though a lack of reliable data precludes testing this hypothesis.[19]

After 1988, however, unreasoned judgments appear less frequently. If societies prioritize consistency over decisiveness (a very debatable point), then the lesson here is that before courts and other bodies consider drastic reforms (such as changing decision rules, per Pettit (2001) and Kornhauser and Sager (2004)), collective decision-making bodies should first seek to create an institutional structure that significantly reduces the probability of inconsistent outcomes. As seen in legislative committees (Shepsle and Weingast 1981), agenda control is one of these institutional features. The ability to "decide not to decide" as it were, allows collective decision-making bodies to keep high-dimensional, complex, or fractious problems off the table, avoiding an inconsistent outcome. Of course, to maintain a stable equilibrium, it may be necessary for other institutions to set the parameters of a collective choice body's agenda control. Otherwise, the members could undo this stability by changing the rules regarding agenda setting by majority vote whenever it suited them (Diermeier and Krehbiel 2003). This issue does not perturb the analysis above, however; Congress, not the Court, sets the limits of the Supreme Court's control over its agenda.

These results suggest a possible answer to a troubling question: why does the Supreme Court leave so many circuit splits unresolved (Hellman 1995)? To be sure, at times the circuits split over issues that appear to be of little national-level consequence (Hellman 1995). Perhaps the justices recognize that some circuit splits, while problematic from a legal point of view, represent complex, multidimensional cases of little national importance. If nothing else, the justices might wisely avoid taking such cases until the key questions are sufficiently refined and clarified (Clark and Kastellec 2013).

Thus, in order to avoid creating an inconsistency, the justices might avoid such disputes altogether when given the discretion to do so. Of course, the upshot of this behavior is that arbitrariness remains in the legal system. When a circuit split exists, citizens can expect different outcomes in similar disputes depending solely on their geography, a different but still undesirable form of arbitrariness.

Moreover, agenda control does not "solve" the overriding problem of inconsistency. That is, a dispute that generates inconsistent outcomes at the Supreme Court does so because the dispute involves complex, multidimensional issues that fracture the justices away from coherent unidimensional voting alignments (see chapter 3). When the justices exercise agenda control and decide not to adjudicate such disputes, these inconsistencies do not evaporate.

Rather, these complex and fractious disputes remain settled by the decision of a lower court, usually a federal circuit court of appeals. Figure 4.9 demonstrates that the caseload of these appellate courts has swollen considerably over the last six decades. Concurrently, the Supreme Court hears fewer and fewer cases through its discretionary jurisdiction. Arguably, it is more appropriate for society to wrangle with difficult problems openly and transparently, even if only incomplete progress can be made (Sunstein 2007).

Given these countervailing trends, scholars and politicians criticize the modern Court for failing to adjudicate more cases (George and Guthrie 2009; Specter 2010; Starr 2006). Critics argue that the Court routinely fails to settle conflicts between the various circuits. This failure introduces

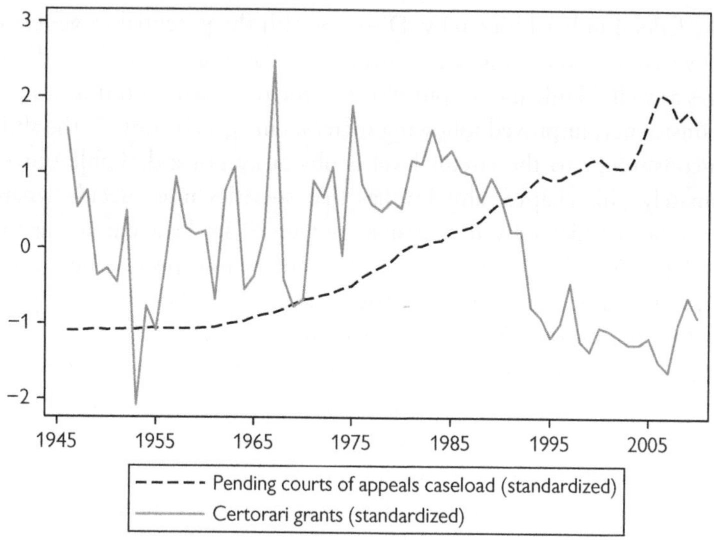

Fig. 4.9. Courts of Appeals Caseload and Certiorari Grants 1946–2010

arbitrariness and volatility in the American legal system. Unresolved circuit conflicts may cause similar litigants to obtain different outcomes, depending on which part of the country they happen to bring their case. Further, these unresolved conflicts encourage strategic forum shopping by litigants (George and Guthrie 2009), an inefficient and arbitrary manipulation of the legal system. Indeed, evidence shows that the geographic nature of most of the circuit courts of appeals' jurisdiction encourages considerable forum shopping: well-to-do litigants selectively file their lawsuits in the circuit most favorable to their interests (Atkinson, Marco, and Turner 2009). Unresolved circuit conflicts may exacerbate the inequality of legal outcomes in the United States, as not all litigants possess the wherewithal or resources to shop for the most favorable jurisdiction.

An unresolved circuit conflict is perhaps arguably analogous to inconsistency—it implies the arbitrary exercise of judicial authority over citizens (Pettit 2001). Additionally, circuit judges themselves may produce contradictory or fractious reasoning in their own opinions (McAleer 2013). A worthy area for future study would be the frequency of inconsistency in circuit court opinions.

The rule of law in the United States requires that citizens receive predictable and nonarbitrary treatment when they seek relief in the judicial system (Pettit 2001; Scalia 1989). Yet it seems likely that inconsistent and arbitrary outcomes may now increasingly populate the intermediate level of the federal judicial hierarchy. Disputes with the potential to generate an inconsistency at the Supreme Court level likely fracture and divide other judges as well. While the output of the Supreme Court, in terms of its logical consistency, improved following increases in agenda control, the shifting of inconsistency to the circuit level is obviously not a desirable outcome. Ultimately, this chapter also implies that societies must decide where in their judiciary hierarchy inconsistent outcomes are least damaging to the rule of law. As I discuss later, it is not reasonable to expect a single court of last resort to simultaneously prioritize decisiveness and consistency: perhaps these functions should be split between different bodies.

Agenda control reduces the probability that the Supreme Court will produce an inconsistent decision, but the mechanism by which this result is achieved seems to be that the Court may simply avoid cases that are potentially problematic. What then happens to these cases that are avoided, particularly if they involve unresolved questions of federal law? The implication of this chapter is that the benefit of agenda control comes at the cost of providing rulings on potentially important but fractious cases. By picking and choosing its cases with almost total discretion, there is no assurance other than the word of the justices that the current Court adequately fulfills its obligation to resolve important conflicts of federal law (Starr 2006). So while the Court itself avoids inconsistency through agenda control, there is no reason to think that this particular institutional arrangement is optimal for the American legal system. Indeed, this arrangement assures that complex but important questions go unresolved. Future work should explore the tradeoffs implied in this choice. Moreover, it is crucial to understand the consequences of unreasoned judgment, so these institutional design choices can be understood in their proper context. I now turn to this question: how do unreasoned judgments impact three key audiences: other judges, Congress, and the public?

CHAPTER 5

The Deference Shown to Unreasoned Precedents

If they are to truly guide the lower courts, and help individuals and legislators to understand the demands of the law, appellate courts must work to prevent serious splintering of opinions.

—David P. Leonard, "The Correctness Function of Appellate Decision-Making: Judicial Obligation in an Era of Fragmentation"

It might seem obvious that any American citizen enjoys the same constitutional rights, regardless of where in the country they live. Obvious, but wrong. The Constitution provides certain protections for citizens residing in the *states* of the country. For instance, Article III of the Constitution permits citizens in a given state to file lawsuits in federal court for grievances caused by citizens in different states. Citizens enjoy federal jurisdiction and relief based on the *diversity* of their citizenship, not the presence of a substantial federal question. Article III §2 of the Constitution reads in part: "The judicial Power shall extend to all Cases...between Citizens of different *States* [emphasis added]." This clause might seem straightforward in interpretation.

Yet what if a citizen lives not in a state but in the District of Columbia? Should the word "States" in Article III §2 be taken to mean "States or the District of Columbia?" Or should the word "States" be taken to imply that as the District of Columbia is not a state, its residents should not be able to sue citizens of the states in federal courts based solely on the diversity of their citizenship? Did the framers of the Constitution intend to exclude citizens residing in the capital city from the protections and liberties enjoyed by residents of the states? The varying shades of meaning in ordinary words and the difficulties associated with ascertaining the intention of the drafters of legal documents regularly bedevil judges tasked with interpreting these documents (Curtis 1949).[1]

The Supreme Court addressed the diversity jurisdiction rights of citizens of the District of Columbia early in its tenure. In *Hepburn & Dundas v. Ellzey* (6 U.S. 265, 2 Cranch 445 [1805]), Chief Justice John Marshall's opinion ruled that "States" in Article III §2 refers to citizens residing in states exclusively and not citizens residing in the District of Columbia.

The Court took up this question again more than a century later. Congress passed a law in 1940 granting citizens of the District of Columbia the right to pursue lawsuits against citizens residing in states for civil actions not involving federal questions.[2] This statute appeared to stand in direct violation of the Supreme Court's reading of Article III in *Hepburn.* It therefore was likely inevitable that the Court would hear a case involving this statute before long.

A canonical example of unreasoned judgment is 1949's *National Mutual Insurance Co. v. Tidewater Transfer Co.*, 337 U.S. 582 (Leonard 1984; Nash 2003; Post and Salop 1992; Stearns 2000). *Tidewater* naturally centered on whether "citizens" (here a corporation) of the District of Columbia could file lawsuits in federal court against a Virginia business based upon the diversity of their citizenship.

The justices debated two legal premises in the case. First, does the Constitution permit citizens residing in the District of Columbia, which is not a state, to file lawsuits in federal court against citizens of Virginia? That is, ought *Hepburn* be overruled either directly or indirectly? Second, if not, can Congress give the federal courts the authority to hear lawsuits from citizens of the District of Columbia against citizens of Virginia? That is, does Congressional power as defined in Article I of the Constitution permit it to supersede via statute the dictates of Article III? A majority of justices would logically have to support at least one of these premises for the Court to find in favor of diversity jurisdiction and therefore in favor of the D.C. corporation (Leonard 1984; Stearns 2000).

Only a minority of justices supported either premise. Yet a majority found in favor of diversity and thus for the D.C. corporation. Had the justices taken a majority vote on the first premise and then on the second, binding themselves to issue a judgment based upon their votes over the premises, they would have found against diversity. Table 5.1 illustrates the paradox of *Tidewater.* Two justices support the first premise; three the second, combining for a five to four majority in favor of diversity. A majority held that Article III of the Constitution does not permit D.C. citizens to file lawsuits in federal

TABLE 5.1. Unreasoned Judgment in *Tidewater*

	Premise (1) D.C. Article III	Premise (2) Congress	Judgment
Douglas	N	N	A
Frankfurter	N	N	A
Vinson	N	N	A
Reed	N	N	A
Murphy	Y	N	R
Rutledge	Y	N	R
Black	N	Y	R
Jackson	N	Y	R
Burton	N	Y	R
Court	*N*	*N*	*R*

Note: Either premise 1 or 2 must have majority support for a reversal to be reasoned.

court against citizens of Virginia. A majority also held that Article I does *not* extend to Congress the authority to empower the federal courts to hear such lawsuits. Yet a majority ruled that D.C. citizens may file lawsuits in federal court against citizens of the states.

Justice Jackson commented, in his handwritten notes on the case, that the position of at least some justices at the preliminary conference was "affirmance is logical." Yet he authored an opinion reversing the lower court.[3] The plurality opinion, authored by Justice Jackson, does not explicitly overrule *Hepburn*. He would allow diversity jurisdiction because Congress can alter certain dictates of Article III via statute under its Article I powers. Justices Rutledge and Murphy explicitly rejected this argument; they instead would directly overrule *Hepburn* and change the interpretation of Article III (Leonard 1984, 312).

Because neither premise for this judgment carried a majority, *Tidewater* proved quite difficult for lower judges to interpret and apply (Leonard 1984; Post and Salop 1992). Could a judge cite *Tidewater* to claim that Article III's invocation of "States" now included the District of Columbia and, by extension, perhaps territories of the United States? Such a position was rejected by a majority of the justices. Could a judge cite *Tidewater* to support a ruling that found Congress's Article I authority allowed it to alter the meaning of Article III by statute? Again, such reasoning garnered only a small minority of the justices' support. "After *Tidewater*...the lower courts, future litigants, and Congress only knew that Congress had the power to confer jurisdiction upon federal courts to hear non-federal question actions between citizens of the District of Columbia and those of a state. No guidance was provided as to the source of this power or its limits" (Leonard 1984, 313).

As luck would have it, federal judges would be presented with an opportunity to apply *Tidewater* just eight days after the judgment was announced (Post and Salop 1992, 767). At the time, Hawaii was not a state but a territory of the United States. A citizen residing in Hawaii attempted to bring a diversity action in federal court. The Ninth Circuit Court of Appeals considered whether the same statute challenged and upheld in *Tidewater* also applied to citizens residing in territories, as opposed to states. Leonard (1984, 313) describes the Ninth Circuit's difficulty:

> The court held that under *Tidewater*, Congress did have the power to confer such jurisdiction on the federal courts...the court admitted...that Article I does not expressly provide for Congressional power over the territories as it does for power over the District of Columbia. Nevertheless, quoting from both of the Supreme Court opinions in *Tidewater* which asserted the constitutionality of the jurisdictional statute, the Circuit Court determined that jurisdiction could be conferred in the case before it.

As other scholars summarized this outcome: "The appeals court's discomfort in trying to wrest workable precedent from *Tidewater* is apparent to any reader" (Post and Salop 1992, 767). More generally, as Leonard (1984, 314) asks, what happens when the Supreme Court promulgates a rule or standard in an incoherent and unreasoned fashion?

Unreasoned judgments could therefore represent a threat to the operation of the rule of law in the United States. Or they could represent a frustrating but inevitable byproduct of the Court's business, necessitated by a need to make some progress on difficult societal issues. As the Supreme Court evolves away from decisiveness and toward consistency in its output (see chapter 4), the relative virtue or vice of this evolution depends in part on how unreasoned judgments impact the Court's various audiences.

Therefore, what effect does unreasoned judgment have in a common law system like the United States? Is the Court wasting its time, at best, with unreasoned judgments and at worst harming the rule of law in the United States with such opinions? Or do precedents supported by unreasoned judgments receive equal or greater deference and attention when compared with consistent precedents? Moreover, is the federal judicial hierarchy capable of recognizing and criticizing inconsistent precedents as they arise?

As is often the case in the social sciences, a methodological question is implied by this theoretical inquiry. Answering this question requires a careful definition and application of exactly what is meant by the term "precedent." That is, an important measurement question is implied in seeking to determine the precedential value of unreasoned judgments.[4] Because of these concerns, in this chapter I propose a new method for measuring precedent. I show that unreasoned judgments are less influential by this measure in the lower federal courts. That is, federal judges cite and defer to precedents supported by unreasoned judgments less frequently than precedents supported by consistent opinions. However, lower federal judges do not criticize unreasoned judgments any more frequently than consistent opinions.

More broadly, any understanding of the Court's role in American society should arguably include an understanding of which precedents exert the most legal influence and why (Clark and Lauderdale 2012). Yet the broader impact of any precedent promulgated by a constitutional court on a judicial hierarchy should arguably focus more on the reactions of the lower judges in that hierarchy (Hitt 2016). If a Supreme Court justice shows deference to a precedent that that justice herself previously authored, such a behavior should not be characterized as influence per se.

Approaches to measuring precedent that rely on citations in Supreme Court opinions seem likely to capture such self-referential behavior (Clark and Lauderdale 2012; Fowler et al. 2007; Fowler and Jeon 2008; Patty, Penn, and Schnakenberg 2013). These scholars aim to measure the general relevance and importance of Court precedents, and they do so quite well. However, we cannot simply apply their various useful metrics to the problem at hand. It is irrelevant to this research whether the justices themselves cite their own precedents approvingly or whether the Supreme Court's own citation behavior changes when handling unreasoned judgments. Rather, the fundamental question is to what extent other judges utilize or ignore precedents arising from unreasoned judgments.

To resolve this issue, I propose a new methodology for measuring the broader legal influence of precedent. Analysts must make two methodological choices when measuring legal precedent. First, in any hierarchical legal system, analysts must decide at which level or levels of that system they wish to measure the significance of individual precedents. In the United States, judges at the district, circuit, and Supreme Court levels face different operative incentives and constraints (Baum 1994).

For instance, federal district judges face a nontrivial probability of review by a randomly assigned appellate panel. They have a professional incentive to avoid reversals (Choi, Gulati, and Posner 2012; Epstein and Knight 2013). Compared with other federal judges, ideology exerts the least influence on district judge behavior (Pinello 1999), and their workload and professional incentives make nonideological goals more operative (Baum 1994; Epstein and Knight 2013).

Due to these constraints, perhaps district judges are more likely than others to allow legalistic concerns to predominate when crafting opinions. Similarly, in other contexts, it could be expected that the lower rungs of any judicial hierarchy would be least able to innovate ideologically, due to resource and opportunity constraints (Choi, Gulati, and Posner 2012; Epstein and Knight 2013; Pinello 1999; Wold and Caldeira 1980).

Conversely, Supreme Court justices at times behave in a "jurisprudential mode," allowing legalistic concerns to dominate. This "mode" arguably explains the justices' behavior when they resolve intercircuit conflicts at the certiorari and merit stages (Lindquist and Klein 2006; Perry 1991). At other times, however, the justices appear to behave in a manner quite unconstrained by stare decisis (Lax and Rader 2010; Segal and Spaeth 1993, 1996). Further, at times the justices arguably have the obligation to criticize or overturn bad precedents (Schauer 1987) and to grapple with and clarify fractious, challenging, or ambiguous areas of doctrine (Sunstein 2007). Thus, citations to precedent may suggest different underlying processes at different levels of a judicial hierarchy. Focusing on the lower levels of the hierarchy reduces these ambiguities.

The second choice analysts face is whether to consider the language of the citing opinions directly. Some citations to precedent are incidental, others are negative, and some are deferential. Fowler et al. (2007); Fowler and Jeon (2008), and Patty, Penn, and Schnakenberg (2013) focus on a citation's networked position and analyze all types of citations—positive, negative, and neutral—together. Alternatively, Hansford and Spriggs (2006) consider the nature of citations when measuring precedent at the Supreme Court level exclusively. Considering only deferential treatments may better capture jurisprudential treatments than would considering all citation types together. Ultimately, a reasonable method for measuring the broader jurisprudential significance of Supreme Court precedent involves aggregating how often a precedent is *followed* (according to *Shepard's Citations*) across the lower two levels of the federal judicial hierarchy.[5] However, when analysts set out to measure which precedents are relevant to a given court in a more broad sense (Fowler et al.; Fowler and Jeon 2008; Clark and Lauderdale 2012), considering all citation types appears to be the better option. Therefore, I present an analysis of original data on the treatment of every Court precedent from 1946–2010 in the lower two levels of the federal judicial hierarchy to determine how unreasoned judgments fare according to this new metric.[6]

Case study evidence shows that lower courts struggle to follow unreasoned judgments because it is unclear which line of reasoning ought to apply (Leonard 1984; Post and Salop 1992). Recently, several judges complained that following doctrinal paradoxes is near impossible (McAleer 2013). Yet we lack evidence as to whether precedents supported by unreasoned judgments receive less deference as a general matter. Given this case study evidence, unreasoned judgments also represent an excellent vehicle for testing the face validity of any method for measuring the legal influence of precedent. A metric that captures legal influence should therefore rate precedents arising from paradoxes lower.

I show below that doctrinal paradoxes receive *fewer* positive treatments or citations in district and circuit court opinions. In this instance, then, the second analytic choice mentioned above (pooling all citations or only considering positive treatments) does not influence the results; however, Hitt (2016) presents some differences. I demonstrate the robustness of this approach by analyzing how Court precedents that resolve circuit conflicts are followed and cited across levels of the judicial hierarchy. Conflict case precedents are cited and followed more in the lower courts relative to other precedents. These conflict cases, which are more numerous than unreasoned judgments, show that when the Court promulgates precedents in its "jurisprudential mode" (Perry 1991) it appears to exert more legal influence on the system as a whole. I next discuss the theoretical concept of precedent. I then present the empirical test and discuss the implications of these findings.

What Is Precedent?

Precedent is the focus of many theories and empirical analyses (Black and Spriggs 2013; Bueno De Mesquita and Stephenson 2002; Clark and Lauderdale 2012; Fowler et al. 2007; Fowler and Jeon 2008; Hansford and Spriggs 2006; Lax 2007; Lax and Landa 2009; Lax and Cameron 2007; Patty, Penn, and Schnakenberg 2013; Landes and Posner 1976; Spriggs and Hansford 2001*b*). The education and socialization of judges inculcates a norm of citing authorities in written opinions. These citations clothe opinions in an air of principle and formalism, beneficial to judicial legitimacy (Friedman 2005). Attorneys and judges undoubtedly can identify which well-known cases ought to be cited when dealing with different branches of the law.

Legal scholars define precedent pithily as "something done in the past that is appealed to as a reason for doing the same thing again" (Landes and Posner 1976, 250). Lawyers and judges are taught to reason by analogy: find a precedent case with a similar fact pattern, determine and define the appropriate legal rule or standard from the precedent case, and then apply the rule or standard to the current case (Levi 1948). This short definition does leave aside the complexity inherent in the fact that at times it is desirable for the Supreme Court to alter or overturn a precedent entirely (Schauer 1987; Maltz 1987).

Thus, if a precedent is ambiguous, fractious, and promulgates multiple conflicting rules or standards, then lawyers and judges should struggle to apply the precepts of legal reasoning when considering that precedent. Therefore, unreasoned judgments represent a class of precedents for which the standard model of legalistic deference to precedent breaks down.

Types of Citations across a Judicial Hierarchy

When a judge cites a precedent, this citation may be deferential in nature. Even at the Supreme Court, the justices at times arguably enter a "jurisprudential mode." Justices enter this mode when their preferences over a case's potential outcome are not strong and legalistic considerations (such as stare decisis) are allowed to dominate their decision-making process (Perry 1991; Lindquist and Klein 2006). A deferential, or "following," citation appears more jurisprudential in nature, consistent with the definition of precedent in legal scholarship (Landes and Posner 1976; Maltz 1987; Schauer 1987). Conversely, at times judges cite precedent critically or neutrally.

Why might a judge feel compelled to cite a precedent without deferring to it? The quality of a judicial opinion relates to its future probability of being overruled (Clark and Carrubba 2012). Citations to precedent are the main rhetorical device judges can use when crafting an opinion. As such, a future iteration of the Supreme Court would likely view a precedent that cited no authorities unfavorably. Additionally, judges have multiple goals to satisfy in making their decisions and writing opinions, not all of which are policy oriented (Baum 1994, 2006; Epstein and Knight 2013). Judges desire to be respected and taken seriously by their peers and the legal academy. Judges can help satisfy this goal by writing high-quality opinions laden with citations to precedent.

If a precedent is frequently cited in a passing, neutral, or critical fashion, but not a deferential or jurisprudential fashion, can it be said that such a precedent exerts much legal influence? Such a precedent, which would enjoy high citation counts (due to its general relevance), is not guiding legal doctrine. The links between it and future decisions might be the result of shared ideology (homophily), or its general noteworthiness, or the fact that it is so multifaceted and malleable that it can be massaged to justify almost any decision. Thus, the fact that a precedent is well known enough to be well cited by judges who have a negligible probability of audit is insufficient evidence to classify a precedent as jurisprudentially influential across an entire legal system. A measurement of the broader jurisprudential influence of precedent should consider both the content and the location of citations across all levels of a judicial hierarchy.

To be sure, even judges at the lowest levels of a judicial hierarchy undoubtedly invoke precedents for extralegal/nonbinding reasons at times. It would be incorrect to assume that even federal district judges do not have ideological preferences over some of their caseload. Yet district judges are provided with fewer opportunities for ideological innovation. Moreover, they face incentives and constraints that encourage the primacy of legalistic considerations in many cases. Indeed, Pinello's (1999) meta-analysis showed that ideology exerts a much weaker influence on the behavior of district judges compared with higher federal judges. Two factors explain why district judges should be much more likely to issue jurisprudential treatments of precedent than any other federal judges.

First, district judges face audits by randomly assigned three-judge panels whose ideology is at times difficult to forecast. As district judges desire to avoid reversals their incentives to constrain their behavior are stronger than those of appellate judges (Choi, Gulati, and Posner 2012; Randazzo 2008). For instance, Randazzo (2008) shows that a district judge's ideology is less predictive of her behavior when that judge faces a higher probability of review by an ideologically hostile panel. This finding indicates that district judges moderate their behavior to avoid reversals and that the anticipation of review influences district judge behavior.

Second, the business of district judges tends to make nonideological goals related to their working environment more operative. These judges have high caseloads, do not have discretion to select only cases that allow them to innovate ideologically, and in short face a working environment that favors expedient case processing rather than ideologically charged judicial policymaking. In the words of one district judge:

> "the federal district courts' primary roles in civil cases have become...office tasks...not umpiring trials. In criminal cases, the judge's work...has become law elaboration and fact finding at sentencing, supervising federal offenders after prison, and safeguarding the integrity of a criminal process that sends defendants to prison without a trial." (Hornsby 2007, 468)

If managerial concerns and expediency are the foci of these judges, why would they favor precedents with nebulous, multidimensional, or complex holdings (such as doctrinal paradoxes) that would require considerable effort to interpret and justify and might increase the probability that their opinion would be overturned? Instead, applying straightforward rules and standards in a routine fashion to minimize the risk of reversal and maximize efficiency seems a much more plausible account of district judge citation behavior. Therefore, while ideology certainly matters in the federal district courts, the institutional constraints, professional incentives, and working environment of these judges combine to imply jurisprudential treatments of precedent should be most likely in these courts, as compared with the rest of the judicial hierarchy.

Sitting between the extremes of the Supreme Court and the district courts are the intermediate federal circuit courts of appeals. The citation behavior of these judges appears to be in part a function of ideology (Choi and Gulati 2008). Further, the probability of audit by either en banc review or the Supreme Court is quite low, allowing for more flexibility (Bowie and Songer 2009). Appellate courts may also need to grapple with clarifying issues of law in ways trial courts may not; as such, it may be the case that ambiguous or fractious precedents are cited more frequently in the circuits than in the district courts but less perhaps than at the Supreme Court. Therefore, *unreasoned judgments should receive fewer citations and positive treatments in the opinions of lower federal judges relative to consistent opinions.*[7]

Measuring Precedent

Empirically, how might these different types of citations be analyzed? One avenue lies in the application of network methods. Whenever a case X cites a precedent Y, a "tie" or "edge" is formed between them. These ties combine to form a network amenable to study. The simplest network-based metric of precedential influence is degree centrality. The degree centrality of a given node (opinion) in a network is simply the number of ties it has to other nodes. For the purposes of measuring the significance of a given Court decision, the precedent's indegree centrality (how many cases cite the precedent rather than the other way around) is the quantity of interest. But there are more sophisticated network-based methods for measuring precedent.

A common method for adding precision to degree centrality involves weighting the centrality of a case according to properties of other cases that cite it.[8] For instance, Fowler et al. suggest Kleinberg's (1999) hub and authority scores. Kleinberg's method, a variant of the more common eigenvector centrality (Bonacich 2007), is well described in Fowler and Jeon (2008, 17): "The authority score of a case depends on the number of times it is cited and the quality of cases that cite it." In essence, a case's authority score is its indegree centrality weighted by the quality of the cases by which it is cited. "Quality" here means that the citing case also cites a number of other precedents with high authority scores. The authority score method shares much in common with another method—eigenvector centrality.[9] These methods seem promising for measuring the general relevance of precedents, especially at the Supreme Court level. Indeed, as Fowler and Jeon (2008) shows, Supreme Court cases deemed "important" by experts are highly ranked by these network approaches: these methods generally accomplish their intended purpose. Yet these methods theoretically do not seem to capture the notion of jurisprudential influence as well.

Precedents are cited in a variety of positive and negative ways, a fact not captured by these measures as applied in prior work. And, of course, measuring influence via citations in subsequent opinions of the same court runs the risk of ascribing influence to self-citations. Further, since Supreme Court justices handle only a tiny fraction of the judicial workload of the United States and work in an institutional environment that differs considerably from that of lower federal courts, a different approach to measuring precedent is called for—one that both measures the behavior of judges at the lower levels of the judicial hierarchy while taking the context of citations into account.

For this analysis, I measure jurisprudential influence of precedents by a count of citations that are "follows," aggregated across the lower two levels of a judicial hierarchy. In the United States, "follows" are defined according to *Shepard's Citations*. "*Shepard's Citations* is a citation index that, among other things, provides a list of all U.S. court opinions that refer to any U.S. state or federal court case decided since the beginning of the U.S. legal system" (Spriggs and Hansford 2000, 328–329). *Shepard's* also indicates how a particular court opinion is legally interpreted by the opinions that cite it. *Shepard's* citation reports classify many different ways in which a precedent can be cited.[10] These classifications (other than distinctions among the more ambiguous neutral classifications) are quite reliable when hand-validated by scholars (Spriggs and Hansford 2000). Of particular interest is the classification "followed," which *Shepard's* uses to indicate "that a citing case's majority opinion 'expressly' relied on a cited case as precedent. According to the manual, "followed" is only to be applied if the citing opinion contains language that goes beyond a 'mere going-along' with the cited case" (Spriggs and Hansford 2000, 330). Thus, the number of follows a precedent receives in the lower courts is a good indication of its broader legal influence.

Of course, the levels of the American judicial hierarchy process caseloads of different sizes. As such, simply summing the number of times a precedent is followed, at any level of the hierarchy, would disproportionately favor precedents followed in the federal district courts. In the appendix, I consider an alternative method that first standardizes treatments at each lower level of the hierarchy, yielding a z-score for that precedent at each level, then summing the two z-scores. This approach equally weights precedents' relative influence at each lower level of the judicial hierarchy. The results reported below are robust to this alternative (see appendix B).

A possible tradeoff arising from using aggregated follows instead of Supreme Court citations is that this metric may measure legal influence without capturing broad, general relevance. Indeed, some precedents set down rules or standards that are frequently followed and applied but are not of especial interest or prominence to scholars and journalists. Further, the Supreme Court may consider precedents like these to be settled law, so they may not be frequently cited at that level regardless of their broader influence. Since the Supreme Court hears a small number of cases (Owens and Simon 2012; Starr 2006) and since the Court does not perceive its role to include the correction of erroneous judgments in the lower courts (Shapiro 2006), the fact that a precedent is not often cited at the Court does not imply that that precedent enjoys little legal influence.

To illustrate this tradeoff, consider that of all precedents issued between 1946 and 2010, the one most-followed in district court opinions is 1993's *Farmer v. Brennan* (511 U.S. 525). *Farmer* dealt with a transgender woman housed in a male prison. She sued the prison after being beaten and raped in her cell. The Supreme Court ruled that prison officials' deliberate indifference to a substantial risk of serious harm to the inmate violated the Eighth Amendment. The Court further established a two-part test for lower courts to apply when determining when prison officials may be held liable due to negligence in cases of prisoner-on-prisoner violence.

This precedent has been followed close to ten thousand times in district court opinions. Yet it has only been cited in three U.S. Supreme Court opinions. The mean amount of citations at the Supreme Court for precedents generated between 1946 and 2010 is about 10.7, with a range of 0 to 266.[11] Yet it can hardly be said that *Farmer* has little significance; while other precedents may enjoy more noteworthiness, *Farmer* exerts a sizable influence on the American legal system.

To illustrate precisely what is captured by the approach I suggest, table 5.2 shows the top ten precedents between 1946–2010, as measured by their aggregated count of positive treatments at the lower two levels of the judicial

TABLE 5.2. Top Ten Precedents by Supreme Court Citations and Aggregated Follows

Rank	Supreme Court citations	Aggregated follows
1)	*Gregg v. Georgia*	*Farmer v. Brennan*
2)	*Vignera v. New York*	*Williams v. Taylor*
3)	*Gideon v. Wainwright*	*Heck v. Humphrey*
4)	*Abernathy v. Sullivan*	*Miller-El v. Cockrell*
5)	*NAACP v. Button*	*Monell v. Dept. of Social Services*
6)	*Roth v. United States*	*Saucier v. Katz*
7)	*Gebhart v. Belton*	*Celotex v. Catrett*
8)	*Mapp v. Ohio*	*Anderson v. Liberty Lobby Inc.*
9)	*NAACP v. Alabama ex rel. Patterson*	*West v. Atkins*
10)	*Baker v. Carr*	*Slack v. McDaniel*

hierarchy. For contrast, table 5.2 also shows the top ten precedents according to their citations in subsequent Supreme Court decisions; a commonly utilized alternative (Clark and Lauderdale 2012; Fowler et al.; Fowler and Jeon 2008; Patty, Penn, and Schnakenberg 2013).

Table 5.2 further demonstrates the tradeoffs inherent in the methodological choices analysts must make when measuring precedent. Many precedents in the top ten according to Supreme Court citations are broadly well-known constitutional decisions. Conversely, precedents in the top ten according to aggregated positive treatments tend to be those that set down clear rules, tests, or instructions for lower court judges (e.g., *Farmer v. Brennan*). Several of the top ten (e.g., *Miller-el v. Cockrell*) deal with habeas corpus relief for imprisoned individuals. These precedents, which may not be as well known as high profile constitutional decisions, nonetheless provide substantial guidance and structure to future judges, who accordingly follow these precedents at extremely high rates.

Criticizing Unreasoned Judgments

Of course, judges do more than neutrally cite or show positive deference to precedents. At times, judges criticize precedents in their opinions. Criticism of precedent should be a normal and untroubling element of any common law system. As precedents age and society changes, many decisions will fade in their applicability and appropriateness (Black and Spriggs 2013). And as judges wrestle with the difficult social and legal problems, it is natural that some sets of opinions will arguably fall short in their reasoning and interpretability.

Sunstein (2007) contends that the only way to make progress in a society with diverse preferences is through partial agreements, which Sunstein calls "incomplete theorization." Essentially, it is unreasonable to expect that a group of judges can resolve in a single collective opinion not only the immediate judgment but also the underlying foundational questions of legal doctrine, social welfare, and moral values as well. Partial agreements, based on intermediate rules or standards, are to Sunstein the best path forward. The very incompleteness of argumentation in any set of opinions addressing a foundational disagreement in society means that the development of law likely depends on judges at times calling for the refinement of doctrine through criticism.

A precedent's legal value diminishes when a judge treats it negatively in an opinion (Hansford and Spriggs 2006). Undoubtedly many law clerks utilize *Shepard's* citation service to research case law in drafting opinions for judges. When *Shepard's* reports that a precedent received prior negative treatment, the service offers a clear, color-coded warning signal in electronic search results. The legal vitality of a precedent cannot be strengthened by such a development. Perhaps most fundamentally, precedents that are previously treated negatively are more likely to be overruled wholesale in the future (Spriggs and Hansford 2001*a*). Negative treatment flags the precedent as potentially problematic for future law clerks, judges, and attorneys. Given this valuable function of criticism, it is worth knowing whether unreasoned judgments attract a greater degree of negative attention from federal judges.

Indeed, perhaps the most prominent approach for measuring the vitality of Supreme Court precedent discounts a precedent for every negative treatment it receives in subsequent Court opinions (Hansford and Spriggs 2006). The sooner such negative treatment occurs, the sooner the overall vitality of the precedent diminishes. Further, the sooner a case is marked with the warning label of negative treatment, the sooner the Supreme Court may seriously consider altering or overturning it. Thus the speed of criticism matters a great deal. A precedent that enjoys high vitality for decades impacts countless future disputes. The impact of a precedent that is quickly marginalized is naturally less.

The likelihood that future judges will not follow a precedent faithfully is theoretically increasing in the precedent's ambiguity (Staton and Vanberg 2008). Indeed, ambiguity and inconsistency appear to lower the probability of a precedent's positive treatment. By implication, then, ambiguity potentially raises a precedent's probability of negative treatment. Corley and Wedeking (2014), for example, find that Supreme Court opinions featuring greater linguistic certainty were more likely to be positively interpreted by future lower court opinions.[12]

If future judges value certainty and clarity in positively applying precedent, then unreasoned judgments should be both more likely to be criticized than similar but consistent precedents. Plurality opinions in general receive fewer positive treatments in the lower courts (Corley 2009); I expand this inquiry to include all unreasoned judgments. Unreasoned judgments, which offer conflicting or opaque rationales, may cause other judges to complain that in this circumstance it is impossible to discern what the narrowest grounds might be (McAleer 2013). Indeed, case study evidence shows that lower court judges do struggle in practice to apply doctrinal paradoxes to future disputes (Leonard 1984; Post and Salop 1992).

If a judge recognizes that an unreasoned judgment is the most recent controlling precedent on a given subject, yet that precedent offers only unreconcilable rationales or standards, it is only natural that frustration and criticism should ensue. As such, I expect that *precedents supported by unreasoned judgments should receive more negative treatments in future federal court opinions than precedents supported by similar but consistent opinions.*

Interestingly, the most criticized opinion in the data is 1957's *Conley v. Gibson* (355 U.S. 41). This precedent was overturned in 2007 in *Bell Atlantic Corp. v. Twombly* (550 U.S. 544).[13] A doctrinal paradox discussed in detail by Stearns (2000), *Pennsylvania v. Union Gas Co.* (491 U.S. 1 [1989]), also lands in the top ten for negative treatments.

The broader definition of unreasoned judgment encompasses a spectrum of related phenomena. In this chapter and throughout, I focus on readily measurable manifestations of inconsistency: the doctrinal paradox (plurality opinion) and certain opinions per curiam. Yet the law's complexity and nuance suggest that many nonparadoxical decisions will nonetheless present their own challenges in interpretation. Indeed, unreasoned judgment may be best thought of as a spectrum: Some decisions openly reject competing, orthogonal rationales (e.g., doctrinal paradoxes). Still others may be facially consistent, meaning that separate opinions do not directly reject competing rationales.

Yet the very presence of additional commentary increases the complexity of interpretation. And, "as any law student knows, virtually any judicial decision can be analogized to or distinguished from any other fact pattern" (Maltz 1987, 371). The complexity of judicial opinions suggests that even facially consistent decisions will in fact offer sufficient raw material for potential criticism. As such, it might be unreasonable to expect that consistent decisions receive no criticism.

Data

For the analysis to follow, I utilize both data from Fowler and Jeon (2008), graciously made publicly available by Fowler, and original data on the treatment in the federal courts of every Supreme Court precedent promulgated between 1946–2010, collected by the author from LexisNexis. The Fowler data contain valuable information about the properties of individual precedents, for example, which cases are considered legally important by independent experts.

These original lower court citation data incorporate all published decisions with selective coverage of unpublished decisions, along with all unpublished decisions from 2005–2010, due to data availability from LexisNexis. These data were collected using the LexisNexis "Get and Print" function to collect the raw *Shepard's* reports for about twenty to twenty-five precedents at a time. These raw reports were then parsed using the R programming language (R Core Team 2014) to extract the count of follows, citations, and negative treatments at each level of the judicial hierarchy.

Interestingly, while the network-based metrics in Fowler and Jeon's (2008) data (degree centrality, authority scores, and eigenvector centrality) all differ theoretically, they correlate at high levels. A principal components factor analysis shows that these metrics load onto a single factor with an eigenvalue well above one, with no other factor approaching one. The results indicate that these diverse statistics all capture the same underlying phenomenon (Kaiser 1960). As such, for parsimony and simplicity, I avoid utilizing the more complex network statistics, and I conduct the analysis going forward on only indegree centrality (i.e., raw counts of citations, follows, and criticisms in the lower courts).

To consider deferential citations, overall citations, and negative treatments in lower courts, I collected citation data from *Shepard's Citations* via LexisNexis for all cases for which the relevant covariates from Fowler and Jeon's (2008) data and Spaeth's database were also available. I utilized *Shepard's* citation service, available via LexisNexis, to create three distinct dependent variables for analysis.

Shepard's is a service the classifies citations to precedent in judicial opinions according to a variety of separate categorizations. Several of these categorizations are clearly negative in nature: for example, criticized, overruled, limited, revoked. These negative categories are quite reliable when validated by human coders (Spriggs and Hansford 2000). Moreover, the positive category, "followed," also shows strong reliability when validated by human coders (Spriggs and Hansford 2000). Distinguishing between the neutral categories of *Shepard's* proves more difficult, but fortunately making such distinctions is not necessary to the analysis here.

It is expected that unreasoned judgments will receive fewer positive and neutral treatments and more negative treatments than others. As discussed throughout this book, unreasoned judgments are opinions of the Court for which the justices provide no reasons for the judgment that are collectively supported by a majority of the justices. Chapter 2 details my measurement strategy for identifying unreasoned judgments. I propose that any method for measuring the jurisprudential influence of precedent should score unreasoned judgments lower than other similar precedents.

In brief, I consider two classes of opinions to be unreasoned judgments: first, plurality opinions, in which the rationale applied in the opinion of the Court to resolve a dispute is not itself supported by a majority of the justices. Second, certain opinions per curiam, in which the justices do not a provide a formal rationale to which a majority of the justices affix their names. I only consider opinions per curiam issued after oral argument and accompanied by at least one separate opinion as unreasoned judgments. Chapter 2 indicates that this strategy better captures controversial cases, as opposed to legal housekeeping.

The analysis I propose is simple: analyzing every precedent for which all citation data at both of the two lower levels of the judicial hierarchy could be collected, what is the relationship between unreasoned judgment and its subsequent treatment by federal judges?

An Alternative Test of Construct Validity: Conflict Cases

While using unreasoned judgments as a face validity test makes theoretical sense, there are other options. Perry (1991) noted that one of the key legalistic concerns of Supreme Court justices (when they were in "jurisprudential mode") was the existence of a intercircuit conflict. Lindquist and Klein (2006) go on to show that the Court's decisions on the merits in conflict cases also appear to be more influenced by legalistic concerns.

As such, precedents stemming from conflict cases would seem to be natural candidates for jurisprudential citations. Therefore, if a metric for measuring precedent captures legal influence, its relationship to conflict cases should be the *opposite* of its relationship to unreasoned judgments. That is, the coefficient on conflict resolving precedents should be positive and significant, if a given metric is capturing legal influence.

Control Variables

In studying circuit courts of appeals' responses to a sample of plurality opinions, Corley (2009) suggests several covariates worthy of inclusion. Corley suggests that a precedent's "legal importance," by which she means that the precedent either declared a statute unconstitutional or overturned a previously existing precedent, should be related to that precedent's treatment in the lower courts. In the analysis below, I include separate dummy variables equal to one for precedents that declare statutes unconstitutional or alter precedent, respectively.

Corley, Steigerwalt, and Ward (2013, 160), show that unanimously decided cases at the Supreme Court in the modern era differ from nonunanimous cases in many important respects—particularly cases in which there is a high degree of legal certainty as to the strongest legal answer as well as nonsalient cases involving economic or government power issues. I include a dummy variable equal to one for nonunanimous cases in the analysis below.

Owens and Simon (2012) explore the Supreme Court's docket and find that a significant reason for the decline in the number of cases heard at the Court in recent years is in large part a function of the elimination of most of the Court's remaining mandatory jurisdiction. A case heard under mandatory jurisdiction is one in which the Court has no option but to decide. The remainder of the Court's workload (and virtually all of the cases it has heard since 1989) arrives via a discretionary process. As mandatory and discretionary cases may vary in important substantive ways—that is, mandatory cases are less likely to deal with issues of broad national significance—I include a binary variable for mandatory cases in the analysis below.

Black and Spriggs 2013 show that Supreme Court precedents depreciate over time. That is, as precedents age, they receive fewer and fewer citations on average. I include a variable equal to the age of the precedent, in years, as of 2015, to account for this dynamic.

Fowler and Jeon (2008) use data from the Legal Information Institute, highlighting "important" cases at the Supreme Court, as determined by experts. This variable is equal to one if the panel of experts at the Legal Information Institute labeled a precedent as "important."

Finally, Fowler and Jeon (2008) presented a counterintuitive finding: precedents that are later overturned are found to be more authoritative than other precedents. As reversed precedents by definition no longer influence the American legal system, I include a dummy variable in the analysis below for overturned precedents to investigate whether this finding holds when measuring precedent via other methods.

Results

Here, I present an analysis of the associations between unreasoned judgments and the count of positive, negative, and total treatments each precedent in the data received in the lower levels of the judicial hierarchy. As such, I utilize a statistical method appropriate to the multivariate analysis of count data. I relegate the full details of this analysis to appendix B.

Figures 5.1 and 5.2 present the predicted counts of positive treatments and total citations for unreasoned vs. consistent judgments, respectively. Unreasoned judgments are negatively and statistically significantly associated with both positive treatments and citations in the lower federal courts. This result is robust to measuring citation behavior at only the district or circuit court level and to analyzing plurality and per curiam opinions separately.

Figure 5.1 demonstrates the magnitude of this effect. An unreasoned judgment should, as predicted by the statistical model, receive about eleven positive treatments in the subsequent opinions of lower federal judges.[14] In contrast, consistent decisions should receive about thirty-four positive treatments, according to the model. Thus, holding all else constant, a consistent decision ought to receive over 200 percent more positive treatments when compared to an unreasoned judgment. This result indicates that unreasoned judgments receive considerably less deference from other federal judges.

Figure 5.2 shows a similar pattern: unreasoned judgments are predicted to receive about twenty-nine citations. Holding all else constant, judgments

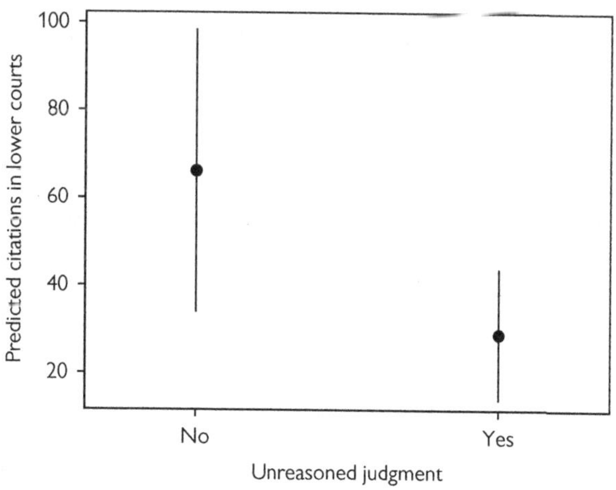

Fig. 5.1. Predicted Count of Positive Treatments, Unreasoned Judgments vs. Consistent, 95 Percent Confidence Intervals

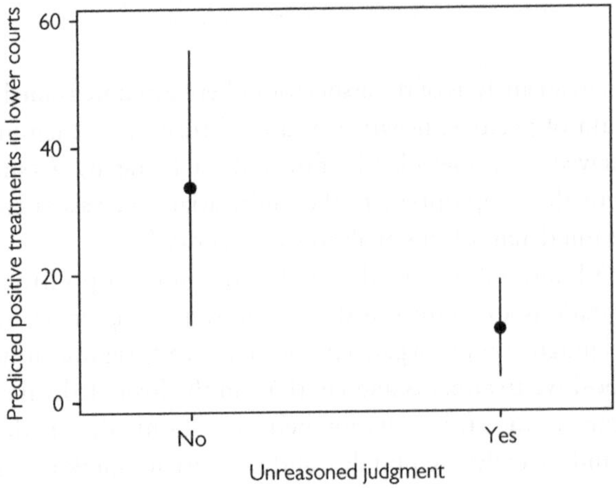

Fig. 5.2. Predicted Count of Total Citations, Unreasoned Judgments vs. Consistent, 95 Percent Confidence Intervals

supported by consistent opinions should receive about sixty-six citations, a 127 percent increase. In sum, there is evidence that federal judges interact with unreasoned judgments less frequently and show these opinions less deference. I therefore reject the null associated with these hypotheses.

However, unreasoned judgments are not statistically significantly associated with negative treatments. These judgments are not singled out for criticism uniquely by lower federal judges. Of course, these judges may feel reluctant to criticize the precedents of the Supreme Court. After all, these judges can be overruled by the Court, and at least some of them might have eyes on promotion to higher judicial office (Black and Owens 2016; Budziak 2013). Moreover, it could easily be the case that judges simply ignore precedents that are too complex to understand and apply, as opposed to levying outright criticism. Nevertheless, I fail to reject the null hypothesis regarding negative treatments and unreasoned judgment. Other federal judges do not appear to single out unreasoned judgments for special censure.

Moving on, precedents that resolve circuit conflict cases are positively and statistically significantly associated with follows and citations at the district and circuit court levels. An opinion that does not resolve a circuit conflict should receive about thirty-three positive treatments, while an opinion that does resolve a conflict should receive roughly forty-five positive treatments, an increase of approximately 36 percent. Further, precedents that resolve circuit conflicts are predicted to receive about eighty-three total citations, compared to roughly sixty-six citations for precedents that do not resolve conflicts—a difference of about 25 percent.

This supplementary result shows that jurisprudential influence can indeed be measured (at least in part) if analysts consider deferential citations, incorporate lower levels of the judicial hierarchy, or, ideally, both. However, conflict cases are also positively and statistically significantly associated with negative treatments as well. To be sure, the count of negative treatments is substantially smaller than either the count of positive treatments or citations. Even with this statistically significant result, conflict cases are still predicted to receive less than one negative treatment, holding all else equal.

This analysis also buttresses and extends Fowler and Jeon's (2008) finding. Fowler and Jeon (2008) showed that "important" cases, in the views of independent experts, are statistically significantly associated with greater counts of citations in Supreme Court opinions. Here, I find that these same "important" cases are positively and statistically significantly associated with positive treatments and citations in lower federal courts as well. Important cases are predicted to receive sixty more positive treatments and approximately 118 more citations in the lower two levels of the federal judiciary, relative to unimportant cases. Intriguingly, these same important cases are positively and statistically significantly associated with negative treatments as well. This result indicates that the "important" designation likely enjoys a nuanced and conditional relationship with the legal influence of precedents. Unlike the statistically significant association between conflict cases and negative treatments, this effect is substantively meaningful as well. An "important" case is predicted to receive roughly 1.8 negative treatments, compared with roughly 0.63 negative treatments for unimportant cases, a difference of 185 percent.

Interestingly, exercises of judicial review are not statistically significantly associated with follows or citations in either the circuit or district courts. Once a statute is declared unconstitutional, it seems likely that less litigation regarding that statute will arise in the lower courts, perhaps explaining this nonsignificant association.

Precedents that alter or overturn prior precedents are themselves significantly more followed and cited at all levels of the judicial hierarchy. Precedents stemming from nonunanimous decisions have a positive and statistically significant association with citations in subsequent lower court opinions, but not with positive treatments. Cases that are brought to the Court under its mandatory jurisdiction are followed, cited, and criticized significantly less in the lower courts. Perhaps because the Court tends to hear cases that have a broad impact on the American legal system under its discretionary jurisdiction (Shapiro 2006), precedents arising from mandatory cases are less likely to generate much additional litigation, all else equal.

The significant association between reversed precedents and citations at the Supreme Court, reported by Fowler and Jeon (2008), is buttressed and expanded in this analysis as well. Precedents that are later reversed are positively and statistically significantly associated with follows, citations, and negative treatments in the lower levels of the judicial hierarchy. A precedent that is later reversed should receive approximately fifteen negative treatments in the lower courts. In contrast, a precedent that was not subsequently reversed should receive less than one negative treatment, all else equal: a decrease of nearly 2,300 percent. This dynamic shows that the Supreme Court may heed the advice of lower judges who criticize its previous work. Therefore, if unreasoned judgments garnered substantial criticism, then perhaps they would be overturned more rapidly. The data, however, show the lower federal judges do not criticize unreasoned judgments any more frequently than other precedents.

Taken together, the findings indicate that an acceptable method for measuring the jurisprudential influence of precedent could be an aggregation of deferential or neutral citations across all levels of the judicial hierarchy. Considering negative treatments as well does not appear to be as useful, given its null relationship with unreasoned judgment. More importantly, unreasoned judgments receive fewer citations and positive treatments in the subsequent opinions of other federal judges.

Conclusion

Inconsistency seems both impossible to avoid (List and Pettit 2002) and, arguably, preferable to the alternative of not resolving fundamental conflicts of federal law (Sunstein 2007). Federal judges appear somewhat able to discern unreasoned judgments from other similar decisions: they invoke and defer to them less often. Yet the limits of this doctrinal correction are clear: federal judges do not seek out and mark unreasoned judgments with criticism. If they did, the evidence shows that the Supreme Court might listen to this criticism and potentially revisit these judgments. Moreover, given the U.S. Supreme Court's minuscule docket, every unreasoned judgment represents a waste of resources that could perhaps have been spent on the promulgation of a more useful precedent, at least in terms of utility to the federal judicial hierarchy.

This chapter grappled with a methodological question as well: measuring the legal influence of precedent using judicial citation data requires considering both the content and context of judicial opinions. Addressing these measurement concerns allowed for the investigation of the treatment of unreasoned judgment as precedent in the United States federal judicial hierarchy. Scholars must make two choices when attempting to measure the influence or significance of legal precedents using subsequent citations in judicial opinions. First, from which level of a judicial hierarchy subsequent citations are to be measured. Second, whether to use all citations, be they positive, negative, or neutral, or to consider only those that express deference (i.e., explicitly "follow") the precedent (Hansford and Spriggs 2006).

The import of these choices is by no means limited to the United States. Measuring precedent in any country that utilizes a hierarchical, common law judicial system seems likely to be susceptible to similar tradeoffs. Scholars should explicitly decide which theoretical construct, general relevance, or jurisprudential influence they aim to measure. Analysts must then consider which type of citations (only deferential or everything) and which level(s) of the hierarchy to analyze based on their theoretical target. The jurisprudential significance of precedent appears to be adequately captured via measuring deferential or neutral citations only, aggregated across the lower two levels of the American judicial hierarchy.

This argument is intentionally convergent; case study evidence (Leonard 1984; Post and Salop 1992) and commentary from judges (McAleer 2013) suggests that doctrinal paradoxes *cannot* be routinely followed. This chapter shows that these paradoxes are indeed seldom followed or cited across the judicial hierarchy. This finding demonstrates simultaneously that paradoxes do little to shape the law (at least in a positive direction), and that, relatedly, that aggregating deferential citations may adequately measure the jurisprudential influence of precedent.

The results further suggest that courts of last resort exert broader legal influence most frequently when promulgating rules or standards that apply across a wide range of disputes. These process-oriented precedents may attract less attention than polarizing civil liberties disputes. However, judges across the American judicial hierarchy defer to these precedents at higher rates. Future scholars could consider analyzing how these highly influential process-oriented precedents impact litigants of various identities. Are the processes they stipulate neutral? Further, measuring precedent by aggregating deferential citations across a hierarchy will likely identify the important process-oriented precedents in other contexts. A comparative study of these precedents would be a worthy aim for future work.

These results imply that the generation of inconsistent precedents arguably harms the legal system at large. The Supreme Court adjudicates very few disputes each year. Some of the Court's limited resources are wasted promulgating precedents that are difficult to apply in theory and are seldom followed in practice. As such, each unreasoned judgment likely squanders an opportunity for the Court to provide consistent direction to the lower courts in a different area of law.

Interestingly, the justices themselves may actually utilize doctrinal paradoxes with some frequency: a plurality opinion averages about twice as many citations at the Supreme Court level compared to other precedents. As Judge Easterbrook said, "The availability of inconsistent precedents allows the justices to "prove" anything they like, without fear of contradiction" (Easterbrook 1982, 831). From this perspective, precedents supported by unreasoned judgments may offer a useful tool. The multiple and conflicting rationales of these precedents give opinion authors considerable flexibility in crafting opinions justifying different outcomes.

Alternatively, it may be that the high citation counts of unreasoned judgments in Supreme Court opinions reflect the justices attempting to correct the inconsistencies of the past. Whatever the pathway, the broader pattern is clear: promulgating unreasoned judgments is, at a bare minimum, a waste of the Court's time and resources not easily corrected by the lower rungs of the judicial hierarchy. I turn next to exploring whether a similarly undesirable response to unreasoned judgment emerges from other audiences for the Court's opinions: Congress and the public.

CHAPTER 6

Does Congress Curb an Inconsistent Court?

The Supreme Court today, therefore, will have to bear with its customary dignity the slings and arrows of occasionally outraged members of the legislative branch.

—Shelden D. Elliott, "Court-Curbing Proposals in Congress"

Clarice Covert told her psychiatrist that she was "just going to explode" (*We Want Them Accountable* 1955). Twenty-four hours later, she would crawl into bed next to her husband, immediately after murdering him with an ax (Raustiala 2007). Mrs. Covert confessed the murder to the same psychiatrist the next day (Raustiala 2007). This psychiatrist, like the slain Master Sergeant Edward Covert, served at an English base of the United States Air Force. Mrs. Covert, however, was a civilian.

At the time, the United States Uniform Code of Military Justice stipulated that all persons accompanying the armed forces outside the continental limits of the country were subject to the Code (Huston 1956). Britain waived the opportunity to try Mrs. Covert in their civil courts, per an executive agreement between Britain and the United States (*We Want Them Accountable* 1955). The Air Force then subjected Mrs. Covert to a court-martial. Crucially, court-martial proceedings violate a civilian's right to a trial by a jury of their peers, as guaranteed under the Sixth Amendment to the Constitution (Raustiala 2007).

Mrs. Covert was convicted and sentenced to life imprisonment. She appealed her conviction, arguing that this court-martial proceeding violated her constitutional rights. The Eisenhower Administration, however, contended that "the Constitution does not go overseas" (Raustiala 2007). That is, Mrs. Covert had no reasonable expectation of constitutional protections, given that she was not currently in the United States at the time of her crime. Mrs. Covert's conviction was overturned in federal district court for violating the Sixth Amendment (*We Want Them Accountable* 1955). The government ultimately appealed the verdict to the Supreme Court.

In *Reid v. Covert*, 354 U.S. 1 [1956], the Court considered a broad and fundamental question: whether American citizens abroad retained the protections afforded to them by the Bill of Rights.[1] The Court initially ruled that these trials were legal, reversing the district court. In a remarkable and unusual turn of events, the justices expressed reservations and called for an additional round of arguments in the case. While losing litigants routinely petition for a rehearing at the Court, these rehearings are seldom granted, and the results rarely change.

Yet in *Reid*, in a historical first, the Court reversed itself on rehearing, invalidating the offending section of the Uniform Code of Military Justice. As no rationale for this reversal carried a majority (indeed, three separate opinions upheld the judgment), *Reid* is a doctrinal paradox. This unreasoned judgment was created in part by Justice John Marshall Harlan II. In his solo concurrence in the judgment, he expressed uneasiness with the notion that the Constitution applied in full overseas (Moorhead 1960). Alone among the justices participating in this case, Justice Harlan switched his vote on the merits after reargument. His view was that the "circumstances" and "necessities" implied a constitutional requirement for a jury trial, but this requirement, in his view, likely should not extend to lesser offenses (Moorhead 1960, 20). Justice Harlan's desire to secure what he viewed as the correct outcome in the case itself balanced with a seeming desire to limit the doctrinal impact of the opinion, resulting in an unreasoned judgment by the Court.

Congress enacted by statute the 1950 Uniform Code of Military Justice that had subjected Mrs. Covert to a court-martial. Therefore, if the justices affirmed the district court ruling, they would be exercising judicial review over this Act of Congress, rendering the germane provisions unconstitutionally void. The justices themselves showed awareness of the difficulties they created when they thusly exercised judicial review inconsistently.

Justice Clark, in his dissent, summarized these difficulties:

> The Court today releases two women from prosecution though the evidence shows that they brutally killed their husbands, both American soldiers, while stationed with them in quarters furnished by our armed forces on its military installations in foreign lands. In turning these women free, it declares

> unconstitutional an important section of an Act of Congress governing our armed forces...it is unable to muster a majority. Instead, there are handed down three opinions. But, worst of all, it gives no authoritative guidance as to what, if anything, the Executive or the Congress may do to remedy the distressing situation in which they now find themselves. (*Reid v. Covert*, 354 U.S. at 78, Justice Clark dissenting)

Did member of Congress take notice when the Court overturned portions of this statute? Certainly, the three branches of government at times come into conflict. While Congress can pass statutes aimed at overriding judicial decisions they dislike (Christiansen and Eskridge Jr. 2014), the constitutional nature of the Court's decision removed this possibility. Therefore, if members of Congress wished to express their displeasure, they would need to attack the Court via other means (Chafetz 2017).

Elected officials seem to delight in heaping derision upon judges who make controversial or unpopular rulings. President Barack Obama inveighed about corporations spending freely in American elections as a result of *Citizens United v. FEC* (552 U.S. 1278 [2010]) during the 2010 State of the Union address (Liptak 2010). President Donald Trump mocked a district judge (James Robart) who ruled against the first iteration of the 2017 travel ban (Nash 2017), calling him a "so-called judge." Generally, members of the other branches of government attack the judiciary with some frequency and relish (Chafetz 2017).

Of course, the judiciary lacks the mandate of popular election. The Supreme Court, famously in "Federalist No. 78," is the "least dangerous branch," lacking the power of purse or sword. Therefore, the judiciary remains ever vulnerable to attack by the other two branches of government (Hamilton, Madison, and Jay 2008). Criticism of the judiciary, even criticism that lacks any formal sanction or punishment, harms the Supreme Court in a variety of ways.

For example, these attacks could potentially politicize perceptions of the Supreme Court, making ordinary people think the Court is a partisan, insincere institution. When people perceive the Court in this way, perceptions of the Court's legitimacy decline (Baird and Gangl 2006; Woodson 2015; Zilis 2015).

Moreover, as Clark (2009; 2011) showed, at times attacks on the judiciary transcend mere words into potential legislative action against the Supreme Court. Members of Congress can and do introduce bills to punish or "curb" the Supreme Court by, for example, limiting its jurisdiction (Elliott 1958). While these proposals rarely advance far in the legislative process, they nevertheless indicate to the justices and the nation that the other branches of government are displeased with the Court.

Unreasoned judgments issued by the Court can resolve important questions or conflicts in the American legal system. Yet these judgments might carry substantial costs to the Court as well. Arousing the ire of the other branches of the federal government would constitute such a cost.

The Court depends on the other branches to enact and enforce its rulings. Further, the Court lacks any mechanism to ensure that the other branches obey its dictates. Therefore, if Congress responded to unreasoned judgments in a hostile manner, then efforts by the Court to minimize the frequency of these outcomes would be well justified. If, however, the wrath of Congress were unrelated to the consistency of the Court's reasoning, then perhaps the Court's evolution away from decisiveness and toward coherent doctrine should be viewed in a less generous light.

So, does Congress take notice when the Court acts against its legislation in an unreasoned manner? Members of Congress certainly take umbrage at individual judgments they dislike. Yet legislators do not have to interpret and follow legal doctrine with the same care and fidelity as federal judges. Indeed, members of Congress may care more about the judgments the Court renders than the Court's reasoning. Of course, poor or incoherent reasoning could be mentioned as a deficiency in the Court's actions in a particular case. But the reasoning seems likely to be a secondary concern for actors who do not have to directly apply the Court's rationale in a legal sense. It is unsettled terrain, then, as to whether Congress responds negatively (or at all) to the quality of the Court's collective reasoning.

How Congress Curbs the Court

Clark (2009; 2011) presented several analyses of Court-curbing by Congress.[2] In Clark's theory, Congress signals to the Court its displeasure by introducing a curbing bill. He showed that the Court responds to these curbing bills by exercising judicial review less frequently. The mechanism for this effect, in this theory, is that the legislative branch is better connected to the public mood. Ultimately, the Court's legitimacy rests on the views of the mass public. Indeed, political conflict between the three branches may be rooted in each branch's desire to maintain and increase its public standing and legitimacy (Chafetz 2017).

Therefore, when the Court receives the signal of a curbing bill, the justices may infer that they have contradicted the public mood with their most

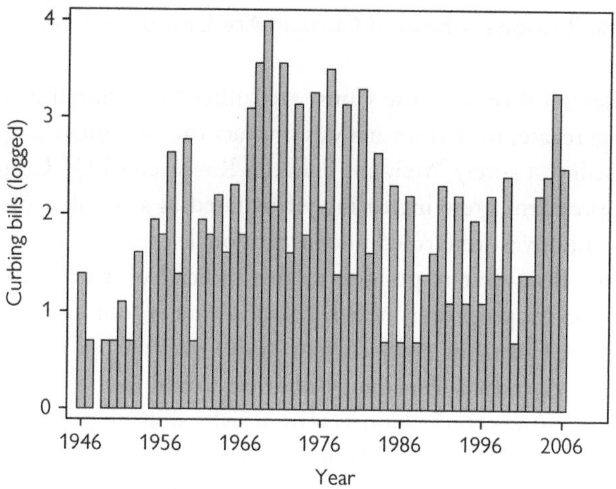

Fig. 6.1. Court Curbing Bills 1946–2010

recent rulings. Thus chastened, the justices avoid overruling congressional legislation in the following term. Figure 6.1 shows the volume of curbing legislation during the general period of this study, 1946–2010.

Clark's data, generously made publicly available, show that many curbing bills do not in fact discuss a specific decision by name.[3] The bills often discuss broader policy areas, but constructing a one-to-one mapping between specific decisions and specific bills would be an exercise in guesswork much of the time. His approach, which I adopt and invert here, is instead focused at the aggregate, term-by-term level.

The curbing bills in Clark's data vary considerably in their effectiveness in navigating the legislative process. Some attract dozens of cosponsors, while others attract none at all. Most are referred to a committee and never see further action, the most minimal level of legislative activity (Volden and Wiseman 2014).

Therefore, these bills should not be viewed as credible threats to the institutional structure of the Supreme Court. Rather, they are an elevation of rhetoric beyond public statements to the level of institutionalized criticism. It is doubtful that the justices believe most of these bills are likely to be enacted. But their existence shows the justices that a more "dangerous" branch of government is monitoring their work with displeasure.

Clark's inquiry focuses on how the Court responds to being curbed, in the spirit of strategic models of judicial behavior (Epstein and Knight 1998; Murphy 1964). Here, the question is reversed: does Congress respond differently when the Court issues many unreasoned judgments?

Institutional Responses Beyond Curbing Are Limited and Unsuccessful

More existential threats to the Court are sufficiently limited historically to make an aggregate, over-time analysis impractical. The most severe of these episodes is almost surely President Franklin Roosevelt's 1937 Court-packing plan. The president grew increasingly frustrated as a number of New Deal legislative initiatives were ruled unconstitutional.

President Roosevelt responded to this judicial obstruction of his economic agenda by proposing new legislation that would allow him to add a justice to the Court for every current justice over the age of seventy years, six months. In practice, President Roosevelt would have then been able to add up to six justices to the Court, substantially shifting the ideological balance in his favor. Caldeira (1987) demonstrated that public support for the Court buoyed it against this attack, particularly following several pro-New Deal rulings by the Court and subsequent media coverage thereof. The plan ultimately died, and the Court's membership remained at nine justices.

The Court-packing incident showed that elite reactions to the Court's behavior can rise above criticism to serious proposals. Moreover, accounts of this incident focus on the *outcomes* the Court reached, not its reasoning. Whatever doctrine the Court used to invalidate New Deal legislation likely would not have satisfied President Roosevelt. Further, it seems quite unlikely that the coherence of the Court's reasoning dominated media coverage of this episode.

While the Court-packing episode remains historically unique, it does provide support for the argument that elected officials focus more on outcomes as opposed to rationales when evaluating the Court. Further, it highlights the ability of the Court to provoke substantial reactions with its rulings, demonstrating that it is possible for the Court to attract existential threats from other branches by dint of its behavior.

Can the Court Inspire Curbing with Unreasoned Judicial Review?

So, if the Court can inspire heavy criticism from other institutions with its rulings, what sorts of rulings might be likeliest to enrage members of Congress? As Clark (2009) and others emphasize, the Court treads most obviously on the congressional domain when it rules Acts of Congress unconstitutional.

When the unelected branch of government exercises its authority over an elected branch of government, this action by definition violates the

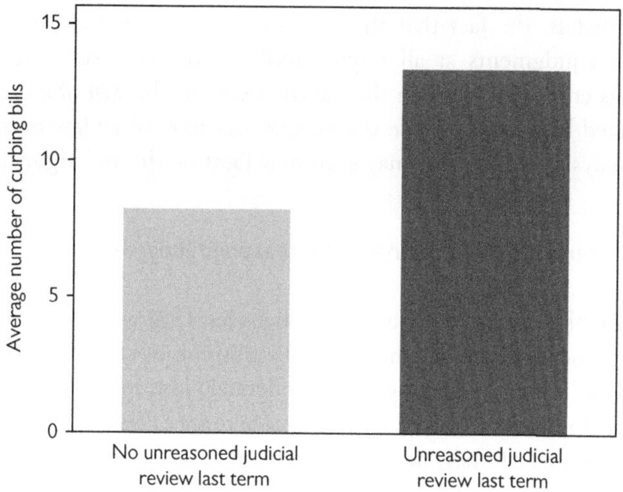

Fig. 6.2. Court Curbing Bills and Unreasoned Exercises of Judicial Review

concept of majority rule (Waldron 2006). In such a fraught environment, presumably the Court's reasons for overruling the legislative branch would be of paramount importance. As such, we might expect that when the Court exercises judicial review via an unreasoned judgment, it invites the wrath of Congress, expressed perhaps via the introduction of Court-curbing legislation.

Figure 6.2 shows the average number of curbing bills introduced in Congress the year following an unreasoned exercise of judicial review. Figure 6.2 indeed shows that more curbing bills are introduced the year after an unreasoned exercise of judicial review. About thirteen curbing bills are introduced in such years, compared with only around eight in other years.

While suggestive, this difference is not statistically significant at conventional levels.[4] Therefore, we cannot be sure whether this difference in average bills is the result of random chance or not.

Why can't we be sure? It may be that Congress simply isn't responding to this behavior. It may also be the case that we simply do not have enough data to make a precise inference. In the data analyzed here, there are only nine years in which Congress could evaluate an unreasoned exercise of judicial review by the Court in the previous term. This small number of years makes statistical analysis challenging. Therefore, we can also turn to analyzing not just these limited incidents of judicial review via unreasoned judgment but the response of Congress to the overall frequency of unreasoned judgments generally.

Nonetheless, the fact that the Court overturns Acts of Congress with unreasoned judgments at all might trouble some observers. Unreasoned judgments emerge even when the Court overturns the will of a democratically elected legislature. While the debate over judicial review is tangential to this analysis, these results may shed new light on this old argument.

Can the Court Inspire Curbing via Unreasoned Judgment?

Turning to the systematic relationship between Court-curbing and unreasoned judgment, figure 6.3 shows the distribution of curbing bills in years immediately following terms of low, moderately low, moderately high, and high rates of unreasoned judgment.[5] Rates here are calculated as before, with the total number of orally argued and decided cases at the Court in a given term serving as a denominator, while the sum total of unreasoned judgments (plurality decisions and certain opinions per curiam) serve as the numerator. Using rates recognizes the fact that the Court's workload fluctuated substantially during the period under study.[6]

Figure 6.3 shows that there is a contemporaneous increase in the amount of curbing bills in terms with higher rates of unreasoned judgments in the previous term. Interestingly, the frequency of curbing appears greatest in years following terms with only moderately high rates of unreasoned judgment. Following such a term, about thirteen curbing bills are introduced

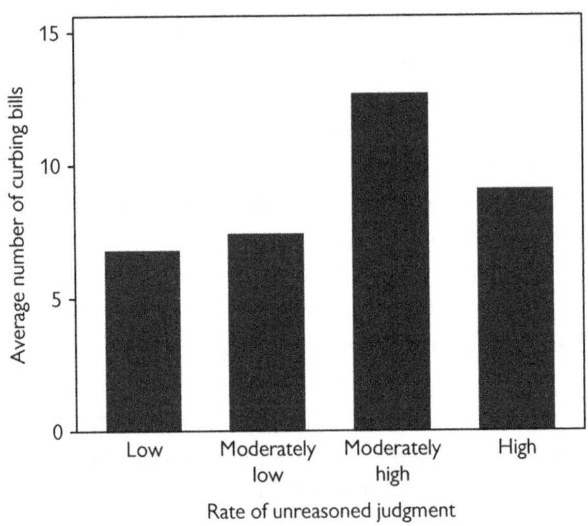

Fig. 6.3. Court Curbing Bills by Previous Term's Rate of Unreasoned Judgment

on average. Comparatively, only approximately nine curbing bills are introduced on average following a term with the highest rates of unreasoned judgment. In contrast, roughly seven curbing bills are introduced on average following terms with very low and moderately low rates of unreasoned judgments. However, as before, this rate of increase is not statistically significant: we cannot tell whether these differences are systematic or are more likely the product of noise.[7]

Taken together, the bivariate analyses fail to provide evidence that Congress responds to unreasoned judgments by the Court by increasing the volume of curbing legislation introduced. There are some increases, both following the exercise of judicial review with an unreasoned judgment, as well as after terms with higher than normal rates of unreasoned judgments. Yet these differences are not so large or clear-cut to give confidence that a meaningful difference exists.

Multivariate Analysis

To interrogate these relationships more systematically, we can control for a variety of other potential causes of Court-curbing in a multivariate statistical analysis. For the analysis to follow, I continue to utilize replication data made publicly available by Tom S. Clark for the dependent variable: Court-curbing. The control variables include a measure of ideological divergence between the Court and the public mood. This measure of divergence tracks the absolute distance between the liberalism of the public and the liberalism of the Court's rulings. This approach to measuring ideological divergence via the public mood was first presented by Durr, Martin, and Wolbrecht (2000). Additionally, following Clark, I control for partisan opposition in Congress with a dummy variable that equals one whenever the House and the Senate are controlled by the opposite party of a majority of the justices' appointing president. Perhaps most importantly, I further control for the total count of laws invalidated by the Court in the contemporaneous and preceding terms of the Court to ensure that any potential effect of unreasoned judgments is not an artifact of judicial review in and of itself.

The key variables of interest in the following analysis are a dummy variable set equal to one if the Court exercised judicial review with an unreasoned judgment in the preceding term and the contemporaneous and lagged rates of unreasoned judgments by the Court. If Congress responds to unreasoned judgments with greater curbing, there should be positive and statistically significant relationships between these variables and the frequency of curbing legislation.

The full technical details of this analysis are relegated to appendix B. For our purposes here, know that we must deal with the fact that the data we seek to analyze are dynamic in nature. That is, we are interested in the behavior of a series of data points over time. It is quite likely that these data points are correlated: the value of the series in one year is related to the value of the series in the previous year (Box-Steffensmeier et al. 2014). The past is helpful in predicting the present, so to speak. In the statistical models summarized below, I account for the dynamic nature of the data in a number of ways; see appendix B for full details. Because the time series of Court-curbing bills contains several years with extremely high levels of curbing, I analyze the natural log of curbing bills in these analysis to ameliorate the undue influence of outliers.

After controlling for the dynamic properties of the data and the other variables, the marginal effect of judicial review supported by an unreasoned judgment on subsequent curbing bills is vanishingly small. This effect is not statistically significant at traditional levels. Moving on, there is a virtually flat relationship between prior rates of unreasoned judgment and Court-curbing activity. In short, Congress does not appear to respond to unreasoned judgment with an uptick in its criticism of the Court.

Conclusion

The generation of unreasoned judgments carries practical and normative consequences in the eyes of some scholars (Pettit 2001). One such practical consequence could have been a fiery reaction from the other elite branches of the national government. If the "least dangerous branch" attracted intense opposition from Congress as a consequence of the issuance of unreasoned judgments, then the Court would do extremely well to do what it could to limit such outcomes. If instead Congress behaves no differently when its members observe unreasoned judgments utilized to justify an exercise of judicial review, or the overall rate of unreasoned judgments, then the Court can be decisive without fear of congressional backlash if an unreasoned judgment is the result.

This latter scenario is precisely what the data indicate. The frequency of legislation introduced to punish the Court is not impacted by the Court's issuance of unreasoned judgments. Therefore, the Court does not invite legitimacy-damaging action from the legislative branch with such judgments.

Congress's failure to punish the Court for exercises of inconsistent legal reasoning gives the Court the latitude, in a separation-of-powers sense, to resolve conflicts without an existential compulsion to also produce a fully reasoned and coherent opinion or set of opinions. Viewed in this way, the Court's evolution away from decisiveness and toward consistency is less promising: the Court may have traded away progress and certainty in American law while failing to gain any new insulation from congressional attack.

However, the fact that Congress fails to curb the Court when the Court overturns Congress with an unreasoned judgment underscores the limitations inherent in a separation-of-powers system that relies on elective representation in one or more branches of government. Criticism of the Court seems much more likely to be rooted in ideological dissatisfaction with the conclusions the Court might reach, not the logical or legal quality of the Court's doctrine. Indeed, given that the courts are likelier to interpret more complex legislation, it may be that members recognize that when the Court issues an unreasoned judgment in exercising judicial review, this judgment will by necessity of the statute's complexity itself be quite nuanced and complicated (Maltzman et al. 2014).

Therefore, criticism of the Court from the elective branches must be viewed with considerable skepticism. Moreover, this potential ideological bias in criticism of the Court means that citizens cannot rely on their elected officials to monitor the quality of the Court's reasoning and doctrinal output. Therefore, the Court is potentially free to issue sets of opinions with minimal logical coherence, knowing that the other branches will not mind so long as the ideological direction of the judgments themselves are satisfactory.

This possibility raises a final question for empirical analysis: if the other branches may not monitor the Court's reasoning effectively, do ordinary people mind when the Court issues unreasoned judgments? Or is a bad outcome equally undesirable, no matter how the Court justifies it? I explore this question in the next chapter.

CHAPTER 7

Unreasoned Judgment and Public Support for the U.S. Supreme Court

Does the content of the Court's rulings—the rationales that Justices provide to explain their votes—influence the Court's institutional well-being?

—Dion Farganis, "Do Reasons Matter? The Impact of Opinion Content on Supreme Court Legitimacy"

How long does it take to break a man's will? In 1947, an African American man from Indiana, Mr. Robert A. Watts, was arrested on an assault charge. Later in the day, officers found the corpse of a white woman near the scene of the previous assault. Preliminary evidence indicated that perhaps the earlier assault also involved a shotgun slaying. Mr. Watts rapidly became the sole subject of the police's interest in solving this brutal crime.

Mr. Watts remained in police custody, without being formally arraigned, for six days. That is, during this period, he was never informed of the any charges against him, nor was he allowed to respond with a plea of guilty or not guilty. He did not speak to a friend, attorney, or any other counselor during that time.

During his stay in custody, Mr. Watts would be removed from his cell in the early evening and questioned by police about the murder until 2 or 3 in the morning—with no attorney present (Paulsen 1954). For long stretches during this time, he was placed in solitary confinement (Paulsen 1954, 420).

The solitary confinement cell lacked both a bed and a toilet. Officers also denied Mr. Watts adequate food. They took Mr. Watts out of his cell at times during the day, driving him around town for hours while asking him probing questions about the murder.

At some point during this intensive questioning, Mr. Watts led a deputy to a secluded area and revealed a shotgun: the murder weapon. Mr. Watts's confession was used as evidence to convict him of murder, and the Indiana Supreme Court affirmed his conviction.

The U.S. Supreme Court granted certiorari and heard the case on April 25, 1949. In the Court's judgment in *Watts v. Indiana* (338 U.S. 449 [1949]), the justices wrestled with a challenging question: how do we *know* when someone has been coerced, threatened, or tortured to the point where their confession is involuntary and therefore inadmissible as evidence against them? By a vote of 6-3, the Court agreed that Mr. Watts had been subjected to treatment that violated the due process clause of the Fourteenth Amendment, and his confession was therefore inadmissible.

From a doctrinal perspective, however, this six justice majority splintered into four distinct camps on the question of how future courts should consider the question of involuntary confessions. Writing for a three justice plurality, Justice Frankfurter advocated an essentially holistic approach. As Paulsen (1954, 422) recounts, under Frankfurter's approach:

> Illegal arrest, illegal detention, the length of the questioning periods, the manner of the inquiry, the denial of a chance to see friends and counsel, the general treatment of the accused, as well as his age and experience would all be matters which these three Justices would consider in deciding whether an accused's constitutional right to remain silent had been undermined and hence whether the use of a confession should be forbidden in state court.

Conversely, Justice Douglas advocated a much simpler, bright-line rule: *any* confessions taken between arrest and arraignment were presumably coercive or potentially coercive. Therefore, to err on the side of ensuring that coerced confessions were never used against a defendant, no confessions taken during this period at all would be allowable.

Justice Black, in a brief concurrence in the result, appears to promote a different bright-line rule, one he articulated in the majority opinion of an earlier decision, *Ashcraft v. Tennessee* (322 U.S. 143 [1944]). In *Ashcraft*, Justice Black's opinion stated that interrogation techniques that would not be admissible in a courtroom trial could not be used to elicit confessions. In *Ashcraft*, the accused was subjected to a thirty-six-hour interrogation. Justice Black pointed out that a witness would never be subject to thirty-six hours of cross-examination. Justice Black's special concurrence is brief, but it refers to what Justice Black presumably considers to be the controlling precedent of *Ashcraft*. Since the questioning of Mr. Watts similarly would never have been allowed in a courtroom, Justice Black would also overturn the conviction.

Finally, Justice Jackson took a considerably more deferential view to the judgments of local police, judges, and juries. Justice Jackson concedes that Mr. Watts's treatment amounted to "threats, promises, or inducements, which torture the mind but put no scar on the body" (*Watts v. Indiana*, 338 U.S. at 60, Justice Jackson, concurring). Yet Justice Jackson emphasized that the reason he was able to come to this conclusion is that the State of Indiana conceded as much at trial. That is, federal judges should not substitute their judgment above that of local officials about what constitutes coercive treatment. In this (for the time at least) unusual case, the prosecutor for the State of Indiana generally agreed with Mr. Watts's characterization of how he was treated. This admission by the local authority was the deciding factor for Justice Jackson. Indeed, in Justice Jackson's draft opinion, he takes care to both add and emphasize the word "solely" in this sentence in his final concurring opinion: "If the opinion of Mr. Justice Frankfurter in the Watts case were based *solely* on the State's admissions as to the treatment of Watts, I should not disagree" (*Watts v. Indiana*, 338 U.S. at 60, Justice Jackson, concurring).[1]

Table 7.1 summarizes these four distinct rationales. The first premise, upon which there was majority agreement, was whether Mr. Watts's treatment constituted coercion. The second premise is upon what grounds should courts determine whether coercive treatment occurred. The three dissenters' views on the premises are left intentionally blank. They simply stated that they would affirm the Indiana Supreme Court and Mr. Watts's conviction, without engaging in this debate. Therefore, we cannot determine their revealed preferences on these doctrinal questions. Given their dissent, one could conjecture that their views might be closest to those of Justice Jackson, but we cannot be certain.

TABLE 7.1. Unreasoned Judgment in *Watts*

	Premise (1) Coercive?	Premise (2) Standard	Judgment
Frankfurter	Y	Holistic	R
Murphy	Y	Holistic	R
Rutledge	Y	Holistic	R
Douglas	Y	Never Admissible	R
Black	Y	Courtroom Rules Apply	R
Jackson	Y	Defer to Local Judgment	R
Vinson			A
Reed			A
Burton			A
Court	*Y*	No Standard Has Majority Support	*R*

Note: Premise 1 and some standard in premise 2 must have majority support for a reversal to exhibit consistency.

Because a majority of justices could not agree on a proper standard for determining that a confession is coercive, *Watts* is an unreasoned judgment. Rogers (1991) correctly notes that Justice Douglas's concurrence in *Watts* is expansive: he likely doesn't mind the holistic approach but preferred his own more extreme rule. Even so, that would only make four votes, a minority, for the holistic standard. Perhaps Justice Black agreed with the plurality as well, but his short concurrence is explicitly in the judgment only and makes reference to an entirely separate doctrine.

In 2017, protests and counter-protests raged over police conduct and misconduct toward racial and ethnic minorities (Gallagher et al. 2016). While the #BlackLivesMatter and #BlueLivesMatter/#AllLivesMatter movements surely would differ vigorously in their approval of the Court's judgment in *Watts*, one wonders whether the fractured quality of the Court's reasoning would intensify this disapproval among people who identify with the pro-police #BlueLivesMatter movement? Or is the simple fact that the outcome gave less deference to local police all that matters?

Put another way: do the reasons matter to ordinary people when they consider a judicial decision they disagree with? Or might the reasoning be only a secondary concern to the mass public? Is the Court's reasoning simply something to praise when it supports a favorable ruling and criticized if it supports an unfavorable ruling, independent of the opinion's logical quality and clarity?

Judges usually show precedents supported by unreasoned judgments less deference than other precedents. Chapter 5 showed that these opinions are followed and cited considerably less in the lower levels of the American judicial hierarchy. These results perhaps lend weight to the argument that the U.S. Supreme Court should reform its procedures to promulgate as few inconsistent outcomes as possible (Pettit 2001). Yet critics of paradoxical outcomes do not just invoke the practical difficulties posed by these decisions to judges (Post and Salop 1992). The heart of the criticism lies instead with the notion that inconsistent outcomes represent an illegitimate exercise of governmental authority over its citizens (Pettit 2001).

Pettit's (2001) criticism of the discursive dilemma (doctrinal paradox) in multimember courts rested on the idea that when a court cannot provide reasons for its judgment at the collective level, then its exercise of state authority was arbitrary and therefore illegitimate. Because it is the court itself, and not the justices who comprise it, that ultimately exercises the authority of the state, Pettit contends that the court as a collective must promulgate logically consistent reasoning for its judgments in order to behave in a legitimate fashion.

Yet other works define the legitimacy of courts differently. Research in political science defines the legitimacy of the U.S. Supreme Court and other judicial bodies via Easton's concept of diffuse support: "a reservoir of favorable attitudes or good will that helps members to accept or tolerate outputs to which they are opposed" (Easton 1965, 273).[2]

Diffuse support differs fundamentally from approval or disapproval of individual decisions by courts (Gibson, Caldeira, and Spence 2003*a*). The antecedents for this support may be exposure to the legalistic symbols of the Court (Gibson and Caldeira 2009*a*) as well as commitments to abstract democratic values (Gibson and Nelson 2015). Conversely, whether individuals agree with and accept a given decision embodies instead the notion of specific support (Gibson, Caldeira, and Spence 2003*a*).

For both kinds of support (diffuse and specific), legitimate decision-making behavior as conceptualized by Pettit (2001) does not appear to be a necessary condition. Individuals can theoretically possess a reservoir of favorable attitudes toward the Court whether or not the Court lives up to Pettit's (2001) standard of "legitimate" decision making. And while it is possible that individuals extend more specific support to logically consistent decision, it is perhaps more reasonable to assume that specific support for a decision is largely a function of ideological preferences as opposed to preferences over the logical structure of the judgment (Bartels and Johnston 2013).

Even leaving preferences aside, perhaps logically consistent decisions are extended more specific support, but perhaps not. Salamone (2014) shows that acceptance of some decisions actually *increases* with the presence of dissensus, suggesting that consensus in and of itself is not a necessary condition for specific support.[3]

Baird and Gangl (2006) and Gibson and Caldeira (2011) present similar evidence: perceptions of sincere, principled disagreement at the Court do not lower individuals' evaluation of the Court and its outputs. And as Gibson and Caldeira (2009*a*) show, exposure to the Court and its symbols increases loyalty to the institution. Reading the Court's opinions, laden as they are in legal jargon, may if anything increase diffuse support, even if the rationales provided are not logically consistent. In sum, the literature suggests that the public will not necessarily follow Pettit's (2001) lead in viewing unreasoned judgments as illegitimate.

This tension motivates inquiry into three questions. First, do unreasoned judgments, illegitimate by Pettit's definition, decrease diffuse support for the Court? Second, given that evidence shows a single decision may not have a significant impact on diffuse support (Gibson, Caldeira, and Spence; Gibson and Nelson 2015), does inconsistency at least reduce individuals' specific support (agreement with and acceptance of) for a decision? Third, do unreasoned judgments undermine more abstract commitments to democracy, such as trust in government? Addressing this third question in particular is useful in evaluating the broader consequences of unreasoned judgment not only for the Court but for American governance more generally.

I address these questions in this chapter via a survey experiment conducted on a nationally representative sample of American adults. Generally, I find that unreasoned judgment does not significantly affect diffuse or specific support, nor does it impact trust in government. Further, supplementary analysis lends support for Gibson and Caldeira's (2009*a*) positivity theory: those with greater knowledge of the Court extend it more diffuse support. Interestingly, this dynamic is not impacted by the experimental condition; it arises whether subjects are exposed to an unreasoned judgment or a consistent control opinion. Finally, the impact of unreasoned judgments do not appear to be a function of individual differences in political knowledge and sophistication; the effects appear similarly flat across levels of knowledge with one exception: exposure to an unreasoned judgment may reduce trust in government, but only among low-knowledge individuals who pay little attention to politics to begin with.

Decision Attributes and Institutional Support

The effect of any individual decision on diffuse support is minimal in the aggregate (Gibson, Caldeira, and Spence). National high courts do vary in the amount of diffuse support they enjoy (Gibson, Caldeira, and Baird). As such, the relatively large and stable reservoir of diffuse support the U.S. Supreme Court enjoys may be susceptible to declines if the Court promulgated a steady stream of very unpopular decisions. Of course, decisions salient enough to attract widespread public reaction likely involve issues upon which public opinion is polarized. As such, the impact of salient decisions largely washes out in the aggregate, even if individual-level diffuse support can actually be moved by specific decisions (Christenson and Glick 2015; Nelson and Smith 2014). More plausibly, diffuse support could suffer declines if the public's perception that the Court behaves in a politicized/insincere fashion were to increase (Gibson and Nelson 2017).

Conflicting evidence exists on whether individual-level diffuse support can be moved by ideologically disagreeable decisions. Bartels and Johnston (2013) present evidence that a single ideologically disagreeable decision can reduce individual-level diffuse support, while Gibson and Nelson (2015) rebut this claim. Gibson and Nelson (2015) argue that the moderating effects of commitments to abstract democratic values and alternative measurements of perceived Supreme Court ideology largely explain the associations reported by Bartels and Johnston (2013). This debate appears to be ongoing as of this writing. As such, this question remains arguably open.

Given the unsettled state of the literature regarding decisions and diffuse support, it is even less clear what we should expect in terms of a relationship between unreasoned judgment and diffuse support. Three divergent dynamics seem plausible or at least possible.

First, logically consistent messages have been shown to be more persuasive than inconsistent messages (McGuire 1960). This psychological dynamic underpins the normative disquiet expressed by some over the lack of a coherent rationale in doctrinal paradoxes (Pettit 2001). That is, if the Court attempts to justify itself with an unpersuasive rationale, subjects might revisit whether it is appropriate to continue allowing it such expansive authority. Therefore, *exposure to an unreasoned judgment will reduce diffuse support relative to exposure to a consistent decision.*

Second, because even evidence to date regarding diffuse support and ideological agreement is only mixed at best, perhaps the logical properties of Court reasoning are irrelevant to subjects' evaluation of the Court as an institution. Indeed, theories of motivated reasoning (Taber and Lodge 2006) would suggest that *whatever* reason the Court gives, it will be rather uncritically accepted by those who agree with the decision and criticized by those who disagree. The reasoning may simply stand as a second-order device used rhetorically by individuals whose position on the judgment is a function of the ideological direction of the outcome only. As such *exposure to an unreasoned judgment will have no effect on diffuse support relative to exposure to a consistent decision.*

Third and finally, exposure to a doctrinal paradox/plurality opinion requires individuals to read and evaluate the Court's opinions. In so doing, individuals will consume legalistic language and arguments as a function of this exposure. Given the legitimacy-enhancing effects of exposure to legal symbols (Gibson and Caldeira 2009*a*), reading the opinions supporting such a judgment might actually increase diffuse support rather than reduce it.

Of course, exposure to the reasoning of any Supreme Court decision might have a similar effect on diffuse support. But perhaps the convoluted reasoning of doctrinal paradoxes require more attention and energy to process than the reasoning supporting a consistent decision. This heightened focus may then amplify the priming effect of exposure to legal symbols. If this dynamic holds, then *exposure to a doctrinal paradox will increase diffuse support relative to exposure to a consistent decision.* Opinions per curiam, however, are quite brief and do not require the same depth of processing to comprehend. Therefore, *exposure to a doctrinal paradox will increase diffuse support relative to an opinion per curiam.* This argument also implies that *exposure to an opinion per curiam will reduce diffuse support relative to a consistent decision with opinions.*

More broadly, given that more abstract commitments to democratic values appear to underpin diffuse support for institutions (Gibson, Lodge, and Woodson), it is possible that causality goes in both directions. Perhaps undesirable output from institutions weakens more abstract commitments and trust in government.

Indeed, Keele (2007) demonstrates that trust in government in the aggregate appears to respond to government performance (as well as declines in social capital). Further, evidence shows that lack of trust constitutes a key element in conspiracy theory beliefs regarding the government (Miller, Saunders, and Farhart 2016). This dynamic suggests that government performance may be tied to beliefs that the government is looking out for ordinary people.

If exposure to unreasoned judgment reduces trust in government, such a result would indicate societal consequences arising from such judgments. On balance, then, the Court's evolution away from producing such judgments would stand as a positive development for American governance. If not, however, then this evolution might be viewed more pessimistically, given that the primary cost of this evolution is an increase in the amount of unresolved conflicts in American law and policy.

Why might an unreasoned judgment reduce trust in government? If the quality of the Court's reasoning constitutes at least an element of how it is viewed, then its general performance could be implicated by the promulgation of such opinions. Given the immense authority and independence enjoyed by the justices, perhaps perceiving the Court's performance as poor, arbitrary, or inconsistent would then lead individuals to conclude that the government does not represent them. Such a conclusion would likely lead to a decline in an individual's trust that the government is looking out for them. As such, *exposure to an unreasoned judgment should reduce self-reported trust in government.*

Less controversially, specific support for a judgment of the Court seems to be in part a function of perceptions of procedural fairness (Salamone 2014), adherence to legalistic norms (Zink, Spriggs, and Scott 2009), and ideological support for the ruling (Bartels and Johnston 2013). Specific support entails both agreement with a particular judgment, as well as acceptance of that judgment (the belief that the decision should stand unchallenged).

The literature is divided on whether unanimous decisions increase specific support—see Zink, Spriggs, and Scott (2009) for evidence to that effect, and Salamone (2014) for evidence to the contrary. Generally, acceptance of the Court's decisions relies on the perceptions of a sincere, legalistic, principled process (Baird and Gangl 2006; Gibson and Caldeira 2011; Gibson and Nelson 2017).

Woodson (2015) advances this literature by showing that among individuals who do perceive such a principled decision-making process, loyalty to the Court intensifies acceptance of decisions. When individuals perceive instead a politicized decision-making process, agreement with the policy implications of the decision instead drives acceptance.

While Woodson's (2015) work represents a theoretical development in this literature, that analysis arguably does not resolve the possibility of reverse causality between loyalty and the perceptions of a principled process. Admittedly, since loyalty cannot be randomly assigned, this issue will be difficult for future researchers to address. It does suggest, however, that scholars should not necessarily ascribe too much credit or blame to the two modes of evaluation theory above and beyond positivity theory (Gibson and Caldeira 2009*a*) until this issue can be satisfactorily addressed.

Whether unreasoned judgments are perceived as less sincere and/or more politicized than consistent decisions is an open question left to future research. The literature generally shows that decision attributes can affect specific support, although these effects are conditional on the ideological congruence between individuals and the ruling, as well as the salience of the issue (Salamone 2014). As of yet, it is unknown whether the defining feature of unreasoned judgments, the lack of a coherent majority rationale for the judgment, can have similar effects on specific support.

This literature suggests that ideological preferences drive specific support for Supreme Court decisions, and I do not doubt that a similar dynamic could be obtained in this study. I do not seek to test here the conditions under which acceptance of ideologically incongruent decisions can be increased (see Zink, Spriggs, and Scott (2009); Salamone (2014); and Woodson (2015) for a review).

Finally, positivity theory (Gibson and Caldeira 2009*a*) suggests that, in essence, to know the Court is to love it. Indeed, legal elites typically extend the Court a much greater degree of diffuse support (Bartels, Johnston, and Mark 2015). And legal training seems to condition and lessen the psychological biases when processing specifically legal information

(Belton, Thomson, and Dhami 2014). It may be the case that more sophisticated respondents will recognize the complexity of the problems the Court faces. Perhaps more knowledgeable subjects will subscribe to Easterbrook's (1982) argument that logical inconsistency is probably unavoidable sometimes, so inconsistency should not constitute grounds for criticizing the Court. *Subjects with greater political knowledge exposed to unreasoned judgments will exhibit greater levels of agreement with and acceptance of these decisions relative to subjects with lower knowledge.* Further, *subjects with greater knowledge exposed to unreasoned judgments will exhibit greater levels of diffuse support for the Court relative to subjects with lower knowledge.* Finally, *subjects with greater knowledge exposed to unreasoned judgments will express greater trust in government relative to subjects exposed to unreasoned judgments with lower knowledge.*

A standard scale for assessing political knowledge is utilized by the American National Election Studies and many other scholars (Carpini and Keeter 1996). It asks general knowledge questions about government (e.g., how long is the term for a U.S. Senator) to gauge respondents' knowledge and awareness of political issues. While scholars routinely include some version of this scale on many surveys and experiments in American political behavior, recently Lupia (2015) levied an important critique. In particular, Lupia recommended that knowledge scales be customized to the particular research question at hand rather than relying on a single battery of five to fifteen questions for all studies.

To that end, the effect of knowledge on diffuse and specific support following exposure to an unreasoned judgment may in fact be conditional not on general political knowledge but knowledge of the Supreme Court specifically. As such, *subjects with greater knowledge of the Court exposed to unreasoned judgments will exhibit greater levels of agreement with and acceptance of these decisions relative to subjects with lower knowledge.* Further, *subjects with greater knowledge of the Court exposed to unreasoned judgments will exhibit greater levels of diffuse support for the Court relative to subjects with lower knowledge.* Finally, *subjects with greater knowledge exposed to unreasoned judgments will express greater trust in government relative to subjects exposed to unreasoned judgments with lower knowledge.*

Finally, measuring knowledge of the Court implicates the predictions of Gibson and Caldeira's (2009*a*) positivity theory, which suggests that knowledge of the Court is associated with greater diffuse support for the Court. As such, independent of the treatment conditions, *subjects with greater Supreme Court knowledge should express greater levels of diffuse support relative to subject with lower knowledge.*

Experimental Design

The experiment needed to test these conjectures requires holding constant as many decision properties as possible, but for the presence of unreasoned judgment. A design in which subjects read stylized and manipulated versions of actual disputes at the Court fits this requirement.

Zink, Spriggs, and Scott (2009), Farganis (2012), Salamone (2014), and Woodson (2015) all utilized similar designs. Those scholars variously probed the effects of coalition size, unanimity, and the type of reasoning employed by the Court to justify its decision. As these matters are shown to influence specific support for Court decisions, all of these factors are held constant in the design employed.

Following a battery of demographic questions, subjects were randomly exposed to a stylized Supreme Court decision. For the two treatment conditions, subjects were also exposed to bolded text indicating that a nonpartisan analyst strongly criticized the Court's lack of a collective reason. Subjects responded to two manipulation checks, ensuring that they understood the nature of the subject matter as well as the nature of the nonpartisan analyst's criticism. Only subjects who correctly responded to these checks are included in the analysis below.

Subjects were then asked items relating to four outcomes. These outcome variables are: agreement with the decision and acceptance of the decision (specific support), a standard six-item battery measuring diffuse support (Gibson and Nelson 2015), and a four-item battery measuring trust in government (Poznyak et al. 2014). Diffuse support and trust in government are measured as the factor score from the aggregation of these respective sets of items.[4]

The hypothetical case utilized was a stylized version of *McDonald v. Chicago* (561 U.S. 742 [2010]) dealing with the rights of cities and states to implement bans on handgun ownership. Chapter 1 details the background of this case and its status as an unreasoned judgment. In particular, the actual decision constituted a doctrinal paradox (Cohen and Stearns 2010).

The three experimental conditions were: a doctrinal paradox/plurality opinion, an opinion per curiam, and a consistent (control) opinion. In each condition, the case facts and discussion were held identical, as was the winning coalition size (a 5-4 vote). The only variation was the type of opinion generated. Appendix C presents the experimental materials in full.

Subjects were asked to rate the importance of various political issues to them on a one to seven scale. The mean salience of gun control to respondents was about 5.3 on this seven-point scale. Relative to other policy issues, gun control rated more salient than the environment, equally salient to taxation, and less salient than health care. The study was fielded in June 2017. The ongoing debate at that time regarding the American Health Care Act, and its (failed) attempt to repeal the Affordable Care Act, in Congress may have placed health care top of mind for subjects. Regardless, gun control appears to have been an issue of moderately high salience to the experimental subjects.

Additionally, ideological congruence should naturally increase decision agreement (Bartels and Johnston 2013; Gibson, Caldeira, and Spence 2005; Gibson, Lodge, and Woodson 2014). If subjects expressed greater specific or diffuse support after being exposed to an agreeable decision, it would be difficult to attribute this effect to the quality of the Court's reasoning as opposed to its judgment. As such, the experiment exposed subjects only to an ideologically incongruent decision. To establish incongruence, subjects were given some background information on the hypothetical case and asked directly what they thought the Court should do.

Woodson (2015) points out there are several ways of eliciting preferences in studies of this type. Gibson, Caldeira, and Spence (2005) also utilize the direct method seen here, but indirect strategies based on abstract ideological questions exist in the literature as well.

Woodson (2015, 198) discusses the tradeoffs between these choices: the direct approach used here guarantees subjects in the incongruent condition receive a disagreeable decision. The cost of this approach is that this approach potentially raises the accessibility of issue-specific attitudes, making it more likely that issue opinions drive specific support. Of course, this cost is constant across the treatment and control conditions in the design utilized here. As such, differences between treated and control subjects could not be reasonably attributed to the accessibility of issue opinions. Further, the salience of this issue is so high that it seems unlikely that subjects would not be able to easily access their issue-specific ideological prior opinions with or without such priming.

The adult sample was recruited via Qualtrics Panels between June 2 and June 8, 2017. Subjects took the survey online; Qualtrics sampling aimed for demographics that were nationally representative. A sample of 451 American adults was thus obtained. Table 7.2 shows the demographic breakdown of the sample.

As table 7.2 shows, the typical respondent to the survey was a fifty-year-old, white male Republican with an income between $30,000 and $50,000 and some college education. The sample is particularly well-balanced on sex. The sample included 226 males and 225 females.

While 451 subjects is a reasonably large sample for an experimental study with three conditions, it was anticipated that more subjects than usual would fail manipulation checks. The experimental manipulation is somewhat complicated and cognitively demanding, requiring subjects to keep track of information regarding the hypothetical case facts, the positions of the various justices, the consistency of the Court's reasoning, and the criticism of an unnamed analyst. Indeed, only 59 percent of subjects answered all the manipulation check questions correctly.

Subjects who answered these questions correctly tended to be older and more educated than those who did not.[5] However, subjects who answered these questions correctly were no more likely to be wealthier, female, or white than those who did not. Thus, while the manipulation checks damaged the representativeness of the sample in several ways, they do provide greater confidence that the data collected reflect the responses of individuals who fully understood the material.

Results

Figures 7.1 through 7.4 present the treatment effects for the various hypotheses concerning the unconditional effect of exposure to an unreasoned judgment. The bars in these figures show the mean value of the given dependent variable across treatment conditions. The vertical lines represent a 95 percent confidence interval. If these intervals overlap across treatment conditions, this overlap implies that there does not exist a statistically significant difference between these conditions for the given dependent variable.

Figures 7.1 through 7.4 show that there are no statistically significant differences between the treated and control groups. That is, the confidence intervals for the estimated effects of the treatment conditions overlap with

TABLE 7.2. Demographic Characteristics of Experimental Sample

Variable	Mean/Proportion	Range
Age	50	18–85
White	78%	
Female	50%	0–1
Education	3.3	1–6 (No HS Grad – Graduate Degree)
Income	3.3	1–5 (< 10k – > 70k)
Party ID (inc. Leaners)	35% D, 45% R	
N	451	

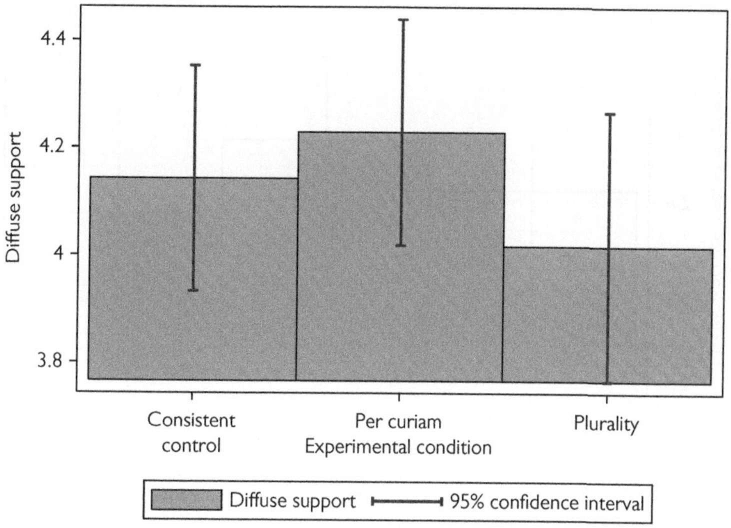

Fig. 7.1. Effect of Unreasoned Judgment on Diffuse Support

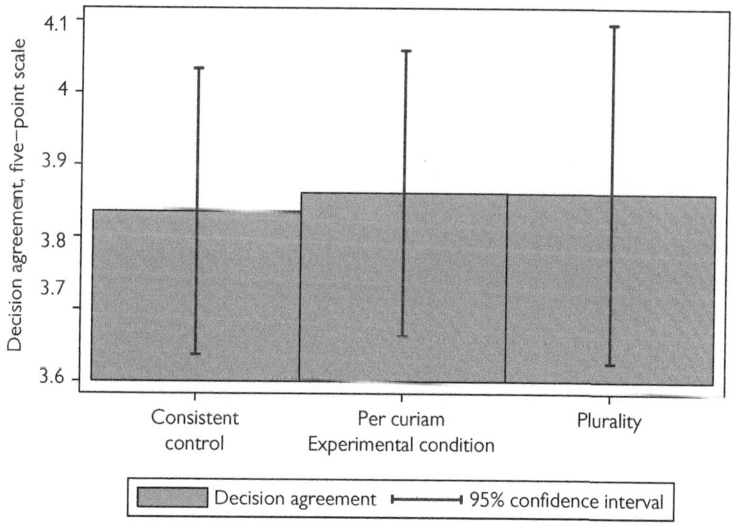

Fig. 7.2. Effect of Unreasoned Judgment on Decision Agreement

the confidence intervals of the control condition for all four dependent variables.[6]

Exposure to a doctrinal paradox or an opinion per curiam does not appear to cause lessened agreement with decisions, acceptance of decisions, diffuse

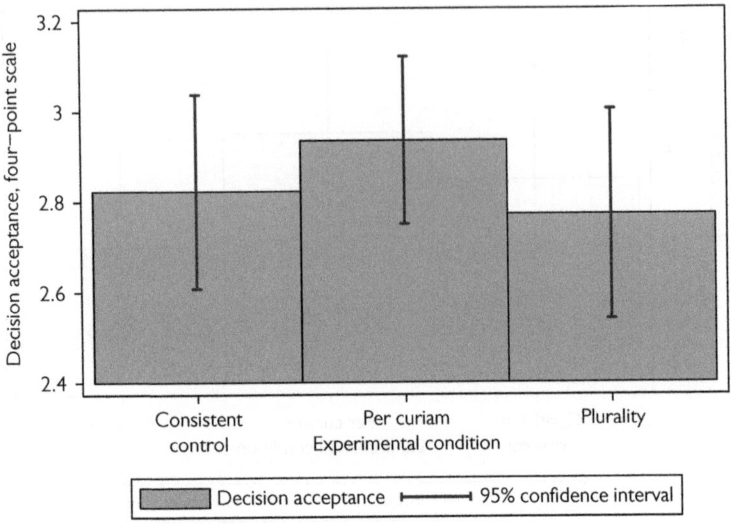

Fig. 7.3. Effect of Unreasoned Judgment on Decision Acceptance

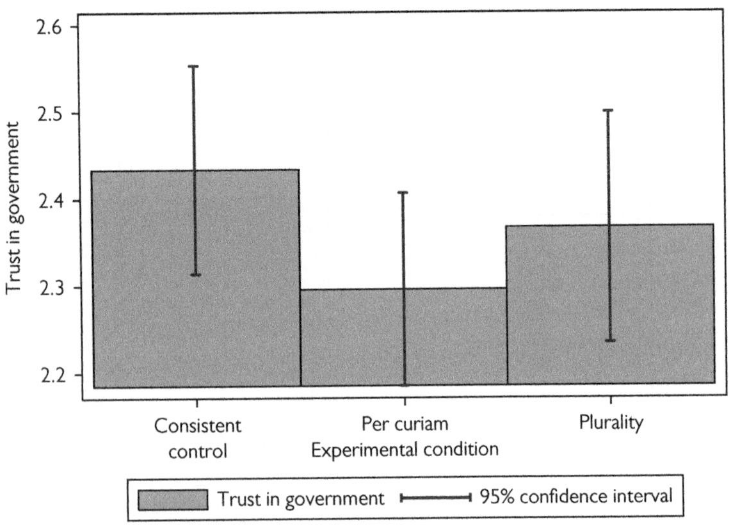

Fig. 7.4. Effect of Unreasoned Judgment on Trust in Government

support, or trust in government. For all hypotheses that were not conditional on an individual difference in knowledge, I fail to reject the null. In particular, there is no evidence that unreasoned judgment affects diffuse support, which was one of three competing conjectures raised above.

There is little evidence to suggest that there exist statistically significant treatment effects in the above figures. The nearest any of these associations comes to approaching statistical significance is the relationship between the per curiam treatment and trust in government. Relative to control, there is a negative association between this condition and trust in government. This association is statistically significant at the $p<0.10$ level. We cannot conclude definitively based on this relationship alone that per curiam opinions negatively affect trust in government. However, absence of evidence should not be construed as evidence of absence: future work should probe whether unreasoned judgments in the form of opinions per curiam impact abstract commitments to the government more generally. Indeed, further analysis, shown in the next section, indicates that this marginally significant unconditional effect is being driven almost entirely by subjects with lower knowledge.

In sum, there does not exist robust statistically significant evidence that the doctrinal paradox (plurality decision) or opinions per curiam cause decreases in specific or diffuse support or trust in government (unconditionally) relative to a similarly ideologically incongruent but consistent decision with the same coalition size in the same issue area.

However, while there are no unconditional treatment effects, it remains possible that these effects depend on respondents' levels of political sophistication. More knowledgeable subjects could well be better positioned to critically evaluate the complicated web of opinions in an unreasoned judgment. Certain higher-knowledge individuals exhibit heightened susceptibility to cynical, even conspiratorial, thinking about politics (Miller, Saunders, and Farhart 2016).

Conversely, because evidence shows that knowledge of the Court is associated with greater loyalty to the Court (Gibson and Caldeira 2009*a*), it may be that only lower-knowledge subjects respond negatively to unreasoned judgments. It is possible that anterior commitments to law and justice among higher-knowledge subjects buttress their impression of the Court against the impact of a single unreasoned judgment. Moreover, when faced with a barrage of complex information coupled with an undesirable outcome, individuals with lower cognitive ability may default to a heuristic or cynical response (Mérola and Hitt 2016).

The Moderating Effects of Knowledge

To test these conjectures regarding the conditional effect of sophistication on exposure to an unreasoned judgment, I first constructed two knowledge scales. The first scale measured subjects' general knowledge of politics, while the second scale was specific to research question at hand (Lupia 2015). This second scale dealt only with questions on the United States Supreme Court.

These scales were administered to subjects before they read the experimental treatment message. This order of administration matters: we need to be sure that subjects' responses to these knowledge questions could not have been impacted by the treatment itself. The exact wording of the knowledge scales can be found in appendix C.

For analysis, it is necessary to transform these multi-question scales into single composite variables. Several reasonable methods exist for the construction of such scales. Researchers must take caution to ensure that their results are not sensitive to data-processing choices like these (Gelman and Loken 2014).

As such, I constructed these composite knowledge variables according to two different commonly utilized methodologies. First, and most simply, I created dummy variables equal to one for subjects who correctly answered the median number of scale items or more, and zero otherwise. These types of simple median splits are commonly utilized in behavioral research (Mérola and Hitt 2016).

As an alternative, however, I created continuous composite variables using factor analysis.[7] I do not present the results of analyses using this composite variable here. See appendix B for details. The results reported below are robust to the usage of either the binary or continuous composite knowledge variable.

Beginning with political knowledge: for three of the four dependent variables, no treatment was statistically significantly associated with a change in the outcome for either higher or lower knowledge subjects.[8] That is, the general null finding presented above is not a function of higher and lower knowledge subjects cancelling each other out.[9]

However, for one outcome, trust in government, political knowledge did statistically significantly moderate the treatment effect. In particular, as figure 7.5 shows, lower political knowledge subjects exposed to an opinion per curiam reported a lower level of trust in government relative to the control.[10] Substantively, the treatment caused a bit more than half a standard deviation decrease in trust in government relative to the control.

Plurality decisions, conversely, did not cause any statistically significant changes in trust in government relative to control among lower knowledge subjects.

This effect may be due to frustration arising out of a lack of knowledge regarding how the Court operates. The per curiam opinion's total lack of

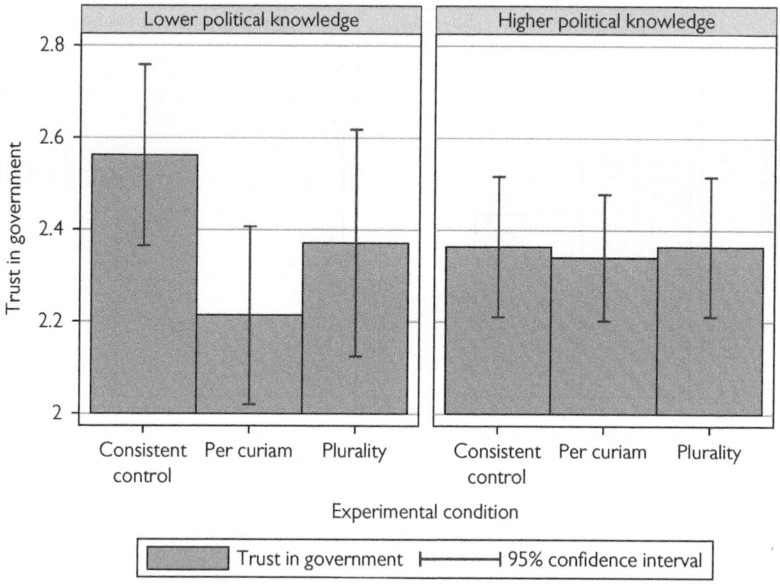

Fig. 7.5. Effect of Unreasoned Judgment on Trust in Government, by General Political Knowledge

reasoning might strike some subjects as particularly egregious, if they were not familiar with the workings of the government generally.

Of course, as Lupia (2015) points out, a generalized political knowledge scale may not be well suited to every study in political behavior. I consider an alternative metric of knowledge: that of the Supreme Court as an institution specifically. Subjects responded to a three-item battery on factual information about the Court (items listed in appendix C). As above, I analyze the simple median split composite variable here. A majority of the subjects who passed the manipulation check also answered all three questions correctly. As such, this dummy variable takes on a value of one if a respondent answered all three items correctly, and zero otherwise.

As with political knowledge, the moderating effect of Supreme Court knowledge is not uniform across the four dependent variables. Indeed, as before, there were no statistically significant treatment effects for either higher or lower knowledge subjects in three of the four conditions.[11]

However, Supreme Court knowledge does exert a statistically significant moderating effect on trust in government. As figure 7.6 shows, subjects with lower knowledge report a statistically significantly lower level of trust in government when exposed to a plurality decision relative to the consistent

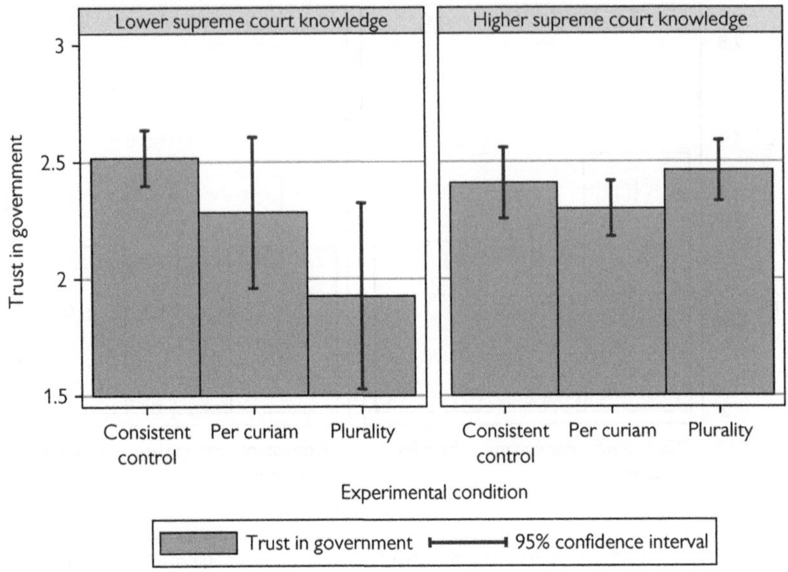

Fig. 7.6. Effect of Unreasoned Judgment on Trust in Government, by Court Knowledge

control. Conversely, there are no statistically significant treatment effects among higher knowledge subjects.

This dynamic suggests that perhaps lower knowledge subjects to view the government with more suspicion when exposed to the messiness and inconsistency of governmental behavior. However, interestingly, the condition under which a statistically significant moderating effect of knowledge emerges is conditional upon whether a general political knowledge scale is used or a subject-matter-specific scale. This sensitivity underscores the importance of Lupia's (2015) argument: the choice of a scale to measure a latent concept may well influence the inferences drawn. We might prefer to measure latent variables such as sophistication with scales that are specific to topic of the research at hand.

Taken together, figures 7.5 and 7.6 indicate that among less sophisticated individuals, exposure to unreasoned judgments may undermine trust in government. However, the differential patterns of significant moderating effects make it difficult to ascertain the mechanism for this effect. Providing an incoherent rationale weakens trust among those with lower knowledge of the Supreme Court itself, while providing no rationale at all weakens trust among those with lower knowledge of politics generally. This mixed result suggests that neither form of unreasoned judgment is necessarily more damaging than the other in the eyes of the less sophisticated members of the

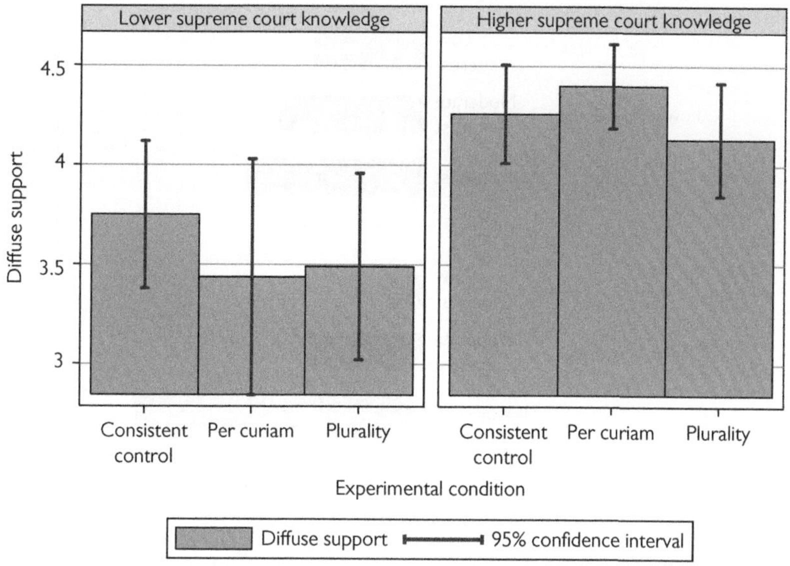

Fig. 7.7. Effect of Unreasoned Judgment on Diffuse Support, by Court Knowledge

mass public. However, it does provide some evidence that the Court may reinforce cynical attitudes about government among some citizens when it fails to provide coherent rationales for its judgments.

While Supreme Court knowledge only moderated treatment effects related to trust in government, Gibson and Caldeira's (2009*a*) positivity theory would predict that Supreme Court knowledge exerts an independent effect on diffuse support for the Court. As predicted, figure 7.7 provides new evidence in favor of positivity theory. Across all experimental conditions, subjects with high Supreme Court knowledge professed greater institutional loyalty to the Court when compared to lower knowledge subjects.

Substantively, higher knowledge subjects reported about two-thirds of a standard deviation more diffuse support than lower knowledge subjects, a sizeable difference. This finding demonstrates, yet again, that to know the Court is to love it. Moreover, this result shows that to know the Court is to love it, *even in the face of an undesirable and unreasoned judgment.*

Discussion and Conclusion

Importantly, it does not appear that the Court damages the acceptance of its decisions or its institutional loyalty when it issues an unreasoned judgment. It does appear that the Court can damage trust in the government

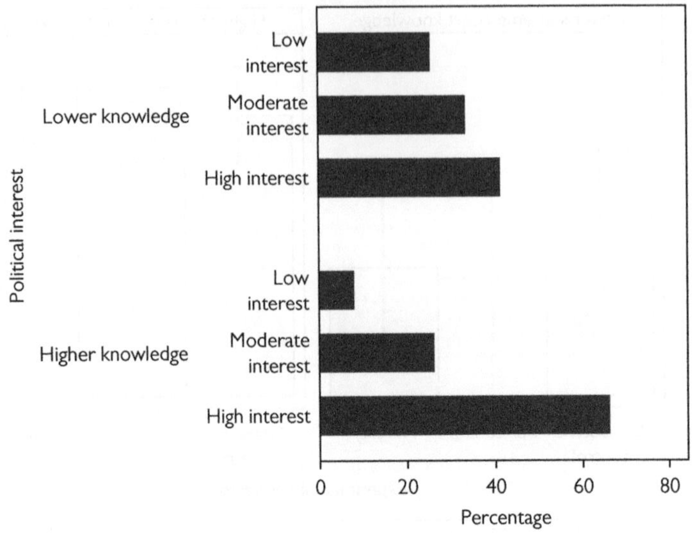

Fig. 7.8. Political Interest by Supreme Court Knowledge

with these judgments, but only among individuals with lower knowledge of politics or the Court. Among subjects with lower political knowledge, opinions per curiam cause lowered trust in government relative to control. Among subjects with lower Supreme Court knowledge, plurality decisions/doctrinal paradoxes cause lowered trust in government relative to control. This mixed result emphasizes the importance of selecting the appropriate knowledge scale for the research project at hand (Lupia 2015). Further, this mixed result precludes a definitive statement about which form of unreasoned judgment is most damaging, leaving resolution of this question to future inquiry.

Should the Court worry about this dynamic and therefore prize consistency over decisiveness in its institutional setup? Perhaps not. Figure 7.8 shows the percentage of lower and higher Supreme Court knowledge respondents who self-reported low, moderate, and high levels of interest in politics. This item was asked before subjects were exposed to the experimental treatments. Among subjects who successfully answered the manipulation check questions, about a one-fourth of lower knowledge subjects reported minimal interest in politics. Only about 8 percent of higher knowledge subjects reported such lackluster interest. Similarly, figure 7.8 shows that while only about 40 percent of lower knowledge subjects reported high interest in politics, over 60 percent of higher knowledge subjects reported high interest. These differences are statistically significant conventional levels.[12]

Figure 7.8 demonstrates that while the Court might harm trust in government among lower knowledge individuals with unreasoned judgments, these individuals are much less likely to pay attention to politics to begin with. Lower knowledge individuals are unlikely to encounter media commentary discussing the Court's judgments, let alone the quality of its reasoning. So, while unreasoned judgments could invoke cynical feelings about government among the less sophisticated, this dynamic seems unlikely to be activated all that often in day-to-day life.

Generally, the results support arguments from Easterbrook (1982), Rogers (1991), and Sunstein (2007), who variously contend that inconsistency in and of itself is not a pathology to be eradicated. Criticisms of the Court arise on many grounds, but inconsistency, in and of itself, does not appear to be a criticism that resonates with ordinary people. Further, the results show that the Court's diffuse support is quite durable, particularly among individuals with high knowledge of the Court. Therefore, while inconsistency may be undesirable for other reasons, this chapter showed that critics of the Court's current institutional setup (Pettit 2001) cannot necessarily rely on the argument that inconsistency reduces the Court's perceived legitimacy in the mass public.

Certainly Pettit's criticism is normative rather than empirical. As such, this lack of an association between unreasoned judgment and diffuse support for the Court should not be viewed as a critique of Pettit's argument. Indeed, if Pettit's views were to become more widespread in society, and group-level consistency were given more primacy in evaluations of courts and other collective-choice bodies, perhaps the results of this study would have been different. As it stands, however, ordinary people do not seem to mind unreasoned judgment all that much. Specific support for decisions in the mass public remains firmly the province of ideological preferences as opposed to logical or legal principles.

These results suggest that future work might consider how exposure to legal reasoning acts as an exposure to the legitimating symbols of the judiciary itself (Bartels, Johnston, and Mark 2015; Gibson and Caldeira 2009*a*; Gibson, Lodge, and Woodson). Perhaps actually reading decisions, regardless of their reasoning, causes individuals to extend the Court more support. In particular, perhaps convoluted or complex opinions motivate individuals to pay greater attention, intensifying the priming effect of legal symbols. Future work should explore this dynamic in more detail.

CHAPTER 8

Do We Need a New "Inferior" Court? Concluding Thoughts

In most matters it is more important that the applicable rule of law be settled than that it be settled right.

—Justice Louis Brandeis, opinion in *Burnet v. Coronado Oil & Gas Co.*, dissenting

While campaigning for the office of president of the United States, Donald J. Trump called publicly for a "'total and complete shutdown' of the entry of Muslims to the United States" (Johnson 2015). Upon winning the office, his first executive order banned travel into the United States from seven majority-Muslim countries. This order blocked citizens of Iran, Iraq, Syria, Libya, Somalia, Sudan, and Yemen from entering the country for ninety days, and permanently blocked the entry of Syrian refugees (Almasy and Simon 2017). Students from these countries studying in the United States were unable to return home from the winter holidays (Rentsch 2017). Protests exploded across the country, with marchers chanting their opposition to, in their words, President Trump's 'Muslim Ban' (Dreyfuss 2017).

Several lower federal courts ruled that this first executive order was motivated by religious animus, likely rendering it unconstitutional on the merits (Almasy and Simon 2017). Injunctions were granted, blocking the ban from being enforced while these issues were litigated. Rather than continue defending the original order, the administration chose to issue a revision. On March 6, 2017, President Trump announced a new travel ban, aimed at defeating the legal difficulties of the original. Iraq was dropped from the list of banned countries (Almasy and Simon 2017), and Syrian refugees were now blocked for 120 days instead of permanently. This order contained language stressing national security concerns as a primary motivator for the action (Order No. 13780, 82 Fed. Reg. 13209), arguing that "nationals [of these countries] continue to present heightened risks to the security of the United States" (§1(e)).

However, lower federal courts continued to rule against the constitutionality of this revised executive order, and injunctions against its enforcement remained in place. Unusually, these opinions cited the president's own Twitter account (@realDonaldTrump) as evidence of religious animus based on statements made during the presidential campaign (*Hawaii v. Trump*, _____ F.Supp. 3d_____, 2017 WL 1167383). The administration filed a petition for a writ of certiorari to the Supreme Court, hoping to overturn these rulings.

On June 26, 2017, the Supreme Court of the United States allowed elements of President Donald J. Trump's ban on travel from six majority-Muslim countries to go into immediate effect.[1] The Court granted certiorari on the question of whether this second ban was constitutional. The justices issued special instructions stipulating that arguments ought to be held in October 2017 (i.e., as soon as typically possible (given that the administration did not request more expedited consideration)). Crucially, the justices had to decide whether to keep the injunctions in place or to allow the ban to go into effect between the date of the cert grant and the announcement of a final decision in the case.

The justices issued their judgment on this issue per curiam. The phenomenon of unreasoned judgment thus arose again at the Court, and again it arose in a salient and controversial case. In a mixed judgment, the per curiam opinion of the Court allowed the ban to go into effect during the intervening period but only for individuals without a "bona fide" connection to the United States—that is, an immediate familial, educational, or occupational connection (Slip Op. at 9).

In this brief, unsigned opinion, the justices cited the need to balance the equities involved over the particulars of the legal doctrine (Slip Op. at 9). The justices resolved this question with a specific focus only on what a reasonable outcome in the instant case would be, eschewing a broader doctrinal analysis. This focus on the reasonableness of the judgment at the expense of the doctrine recalls Justice Breyer's experience on the United States Sentencing Commission, as discussed in chapter 1.

A dissenting opinion by Justice Clarence Thomas, joined by Justices Samuel Alito and Neil Gorsuch, pointed out that the balancing act the per curiam opinion crafted was not a remedy either party asked for. Further, this remedy raised immediate confusion: what exactly counts as a "bona fide" relationship? The per curiam opinion did not rigorously define this class of persons. This decision seemed likely to make the entry of some individuals into the United States subject to idiosyncratic decisions by lower officials, and entry may not therefore be consistently granted or denied to individuals in similar circumstances.

If travelers gain or fail to gain entry inconsistently based on this vague rationale, does this outcome represent a just resolution? Is resolving the uncertainty about the ban's constitutionality worth the price of an unreasoned judgment? Should the Supreme Court have stayed on the sidelines, letting the other branches of government make policy in this fraught area?

Imagine the United States without a Supreme Court. In this world, it wouldn't be clear whose job it was to determine whether, for example, a new Act of Congress violated the Constitution.[2] Disputes over the meaning of the Constitution would fall, perhaps, to various lower federal courts and state courts, each with jurisdiction over different parts of the country. What the national Constitution means, therefore, would be determined in part by an individual's address.

Or perhaps even more dramatically, courts would relinquish (or have taken from them) their province and duty to say what the law is, ceding the role of constitutional review to Congress or other elected representatives. In this world, the rights of people from minority groups would depend on the consideration of representatives elected by a majority that may not share their concerns. Concretely, the rights of American adults to marry whomever they chose, regardless of sexual orientation, for example, would depend on whether representatives elected by predominantly heterosexual constituents would be willing to enact and enforce marriage equality laws. History shows that majorities often elect representatives who fail to respect the rights of the various racial, ethnic, gender, sexual orientation, and religious minorities in a society.

To be sure, in practice it is unclear that the current U.S. Supreme Court can be relied upon to defend minority rights over the will of electoral majorities (Rosenberg 1990). Indeed, the Court at times instead acts on behalf of these majorities (Dahl 1957; Whittington 2005). Recent evidence shows that the Court does tend to reflect the will of electoral majorities with some frequency (Hall and Ura 2015). This argument should not be taken to mean that the Supreme Court adequately defends minority rights, only that electoral majorities seem quite unlikely to consistently do so.

This imagined world without a Court seems undesirable. The resulting society could easily either face an arbitrary fracturing of the meaning of the law in various parts of the country or see the rights of various minorities left subject to the whims of ruling electoral majorities. It seems then that we are stuck with having some sort of a Supreme Court, if we wish to avoid these fates. What, then, do we need our Supreme Court to actually do?

An independent court, free from electoral competition, and speaking for the nation, can theoretically set legal policy that protects minority rights in ways that representative bodies never can. Of course, empowering a court with such authority and independence means that its control over life, liberty, and property must be properly justified. Cries of judicial activism and overreach abound from liberals and conservatives alike whenever courts wade into salient and controversial issues. An unelected court cannot rely upon a mandate from the voters to justify its authority when, for instance, it rules that policies across the nation creating racially segregated public schools are unconstitutional, unlike elected officials (Riker 1982).[3] All judges have are their words. All judges can do is explain to the nation why they exercised authority in the way that they did. It is arguably tyrannical for an un-elected official to exercise authority over life, liberty, and property, without an explanation. More practically, if we expect judges and other people to follow what the Court says, it is helpful and indeed necessary much of the time for the Court to provide some kind of coherent legal doctrine and reasoning alongside its judgments.

Therefore, if we are indeed stuck with some sort of a Supreme Court, it should do, at a minimum, two things. First, it should resolve conflicts about what the Constitution means, telling the country "what the law is." Second, it should provide the nation with public, clear, and logical reasons for these judgments so that its exercises of authority may enjoy normative legitimacy and its doctrine may be easily followed by other judges, politicians, police officers, and everyday people.

As the preceding pages have shown, no one court is capable of simultaneously fulfilling both goals. If the Supreme Court is serious about its business of resolving conflicts, inevitably it will be faced with disputes so complex and controversial that the most the justices can agree on, at the collective level, is *what* the judgment should be, but *not* what the right reasons for that judgment ought to be.

Unreasoned judgment—a decision of a collective choice body that cannot or does not produce a rationale for its judgment that itself carries the support of a majority of the judges in that body—cannot be avoided in collective decision making. It is theoretically impossible to design a system for aggregating individual judgments that avoids the possibility of inconsistency

(List and Pettit 2002). Regarding the United States Supreme Court, some (Pettit 2001) contend inconsistency damages the legitimacy of its exercise of government authority. Others contend that inconsistency alone represents poor grounds for criticism (Easterbrook 1982; Rogers 1991). More strongly, still others contend that partial, potentially inconsistent, collective judgments may be the only means by which society can make progress in areas of divergent preferences (Sunstein 2007).

At the outset of this book, this debate turned on case study evidence, alongside normative and formal theoretical arguments. Two critical items were unknown: first, what is prominence of inconsistency in the modern Court's output? That is, how common is this phenomenon generally? Is it becoming more or less common? Does it occur in especially important cases from a political or legal standpoint? Second, what are the consequences of inconsistent judgments? How do judges utilize inconsistent precedents? Is the federal judicial hierarchy, as currently organized, capable of correcting inconsistency as it arises? Do ordinary people view inconsistency as illegitimate, as Pettit (2001) argues normatively should be the case?

While the literature on social choice and judgment aggregation is quite rich, there are very few systematic empirical studies of collective choice problems to address these two issues. This research shows first that unreasoned judgment empirically is far more than a theoretical curiosity. Inconsistency occurs regularly, though its frequency at the Court has declined thanks to institutional reforms. Unreasoned judgments comprise a significant minority of the Supreme Court's output between 1946–2010. Moreover, inconsistency inefficiently utilizes the limited space on the Court's docket, as inconsistent precedents are not always corrected, or corrected quickly, by future opinions. That said, it is unclear that inconsistency poses any threats to the Court's diffuse support in the mass public or its institutional well-being relative to the other branches of government.

The research reported here centered on five analyses. The first two analyses focused on understanding unreasoned judgments as a phenomenon: their correlates in individual cases, their dynamics over time, and their multiple manifestations. First, an investigation of the case-level correlates of inconsistency showed that the most visible form of unreasoned judgment, the doctrinal paradox, arises with unsettling frequency in politically salient cases and in exercises of judicial review. Then, the second analysis showed that the frequency of inconsistency at the Supreme Court fell considerably after 1988, when the Supreme Court was granted virtually total discretion to set their own agenda. This finding shows that stability-enhancing institutions in legislative committees, like agenda control, can also improve the consistency of a collegial court's output. In sum, the first half of the book shows that unreasoned judgments arise with some frequency, in politically and legally important disputes. Certain institutions, such as agenda control, appear capable of limiting its frequency. The Supreme Court appears to have evolved from an institution that prioritized decisiveness into an institution that prioritizes consistency in the modern era.

The second half of the book centered on the consequences of unreasoned judgments. An analysis of Supreme Court precedent showed that unreasoned judgments are followed significantly less often by federals district and circuit court judges in their opinions. From a legal perspective, then, unreasoned judgments have their costs. They consume precious and limited space on the High Court's docket, with little payoff in terms of resolving conflicts or creating precedents that inspire much deference.

Moving on from other judges, Congress is another key audience for the Court's decisions. Following the approach of Clark (2011), I investigated whether members of Congress introduced more legislation to punish or "curb" the Court following a term with a greater frequency of unreasoned judgments. Interestingly, Congress does not curb the Court any differently as a function of unreasoned judgments. Nor do members introduce more curbing legislation after the Court supports an exercise of judicial review with an unreasoned judgment. Congress, perhaps, cares more about what the Court is doing than how it justifies its behavior.

A final key audience for the Court's output is the American public. The last empirical analysis of this book showed that ordinary citizens do not perceive an unreasoned judgment as any less legitimate than other, consistent decisions. Exposure to an unreasoned judgment does not depress specific support for decisions, nor does it depress diffuse support for the Court as an institution.

Taken together, these findings allow for an assessment of the implied health of the American judicial system. Perhaps most importantly, the findings imply that judicial review cannot be justified on the grounds that the Court's decisions are immune from the pathologies of preference aggregation found in legislative settings. Unreasoned judgments also represent an inefficient use of high Court attention and resources from the perspective of the judicial hierarchy writ large. That said, any existential fears about the legitimacy of the Court as an institution arising as a consequence of the production of unreasoned judgments are not supported by the analysis. Inconsistent judgments, in and of themselves, do not depress diffuse support for the Court in the mass public, nor do they attract the ire of Congress.

The implied health of the American judiciary, as it relates to the phenomenon of unreasoned judgment, may rest normatively on two questions. First, given that plurality decisions exhibit a positive and significant association with exercises of judicial review, is this practice justifiable? Second, the findings could be taken to imply that inconsistency cannot be eliminated from a judicial hierarchy at large—reforms which reduce inconsistency at the Supreme Court level may in fact increase arbitrariness, in the form of differential treatment across geographic circuits, at lower levels of the judiciary. If the Court leaves conflicts between circuits undecided because of the potential for inconsistency, then the law may be applied differently according to geography, inviting forum shopping by wealthy, savvy litigants. Is this indecisiveness and arbitrariness an acceptable tradeoff for a reduction of inconsistency at the highest level?

Judicial Review

The Constitution makes no provision for judicial oversight over Acts of Congress. Waldron (2006), among others, argues that judicial review lacks democratic legitimacy. The unelected status of the Court means that it cannot meet even Riker's (1982) minimal concept of liberalism. Waldron (2006) argues that judicial review is undesirable because a group of judges seem no better positioned to protect individual rights than are legislators. While this research does not address the relative suitability of legislators for the protection of rights, it does show that judicial review over Acts of Congress at times fails to meet even a minimal standard for persuasive decision making.

Chapter 3 demonstrated that of all instances of judicial review over Acts of Congress from 1946–2010, over one in ten of these decisions exhibited the most visible form of unreasoned judgment. Whether this rate of inconsistency is sufficient to give credence to Waldron's (2006) argument is a normative question left to future debate. Others might argue that so long as the exercise of judicial review via an inconsistent judgment followed from a legitimate process, then this exercise would itself be legitimate as well (Patty and Penn 2014). Others still rail against the idea that a judicial decision is illegitimate simply because it fails to satisfy logical consistency (Easterbrook 1982), given Arrow's (1951) theorem and similar results.

Nonetheless, it is clear that the Court frequently fails to provide a consistent rationale for its actions when it exercises its most controversial power. Thus, at least a significant minority of the time, the Court exercises judicial review over Congress in an inconsistent fashion, arguably illegitimate from the standpoint of republican theory. Ultimately, are the reforms advocated for by Pettit (2001), Kornhauser and Sager (2004), and even Waldron (2006) justified? This research provides new systematic empirical insight to inform scholars interested in these weighty normative questions. The answer may turn on how undesirable one views inconsistency as a phenomenon in and of itself. Those who view it as anathema would likely view its appearance in the exercise of judicial review as illegitimate. However, why those less bothered by inconsistency in and of itself would express discomfort over its appearance in the justification of judicial review is uncertain.

Circuit Conflicts

The second potential issue associated with unreasoned judgment that, on the whole, implicates the health of the American legal system is its relationship with circuit conflict cases. Considering the literature over unresolved circuit splits with the added knowledge about unreasoned judgment, this research provided sheds new light on this lively debate. Further, this discussion will make explicit an important normative choice that societies face, a choice that may not have been apparent or empirically necessitated prior to this research.

The caseload of the lower federal courts continues to expand.[4] Yet the Supreme Court adjudicates fewer and fewer disputes each term. Scholars and politicians criticize the Court for its shrunken docket (George and Guthrie 2009; Starr 2006; Specter 2010). These criticisms center around the lack of clarity and predictability in federal law that arises when the Court fails to resolve a circuit split (George and Guthrie 2009). Indeed, unresolved splits introduce arbitrary outcomes into the judicial process, as litigants experience different judgments based solely on geography. This arbitrariness in turn encourages strategic forum shopping.

The justices of the Supreme Court dislike producing inconsistencies, as evidenced by their internal communications (see chapter 1). It seems at least possible that the justices might prefer to leave a circuit split in place than to resolve such a split with an inconsistent decision (see figure 3.2). It appears that the Supreme Court's successful drive to control its own agenda had the consequence, either intentionally or instrumentally, of increasing the consistency of the Court's own output, while reducing the decisiveness of its activities.

The mechanism by which the modern Court reduced the emergence of unreasoned judgments in its output appears to be simple avoidance of potentially fractious disputes. This mechanism suggests that some fractious disputes might remain undecided, even if adjudication would resolve a circuit split. This research therefore suggests a possible answer to a question that puzzles scholars (Hellman 1995; Clark and Kastellec 2013): why does the Court allow these splits to persist? The answer may be that the Court might prefer to leave splits in place indefinitely if such splits cannot be resolved with a consistent opinion or set of opinions.

The Court may therefore delay adjudication and allow disputes to "percolate" (Beim, Clark, and Patty 2017; Clark and Kastellec 2013) for an indefinite amount of time until the Court's membership changes such that the justices no longer anticipate disordered coalitions over the various issues in a split, allowing for a consistent resolution. Of course, there is no guarantee that a new justice will have preferences such that a consistent resolution is achievable; splits may therefore persist for quite some time.

Generally, scholars who criticize the Court for failing to provide clarity when the circuits are divided seem to be assuming that a consistent resolution is easily achieved if the Court would only "work harder" (Starr 2006). Yet when the Court does resolve a split with an inconsistency, the lower courts struggle to follow the inconsistent precedent, as shown by Leonard (1984), Post and Salop (1992), and chapter 5. So, is it fair to criticize the Court for failing to resolve all circuit splits, if the justices may be avoiding disputes that cannot be consistently resolved? Whether an unresolved circuit split or an inconsistent precedent represents a worse outcome for the legal system writ large seems to be an open question.

To be sure, the avoidance of inconsistency is not the only reason for why the justices avoid settling circuit disputes. Simple workload pressures and desire for leisure may explain some avoidance. Further, some circuit splits may be of little national relevance and may not be worth the justices' time. But these explanations would have held in earlier decades when the Court was adjudicating more than twice as many cases per term as they do today. Yet only recently has the Court enjoyed nearly total agenda control. Owens and Simon (2012) credit this institutional change for much of the reduction in docket size. And critics (Starr 2006) argue the modern Court resolves fewer splits than previous Courts. As such, the ability to avoid certain disputes seems a strong candidate for the maintenance of some circuit splits. Indeed, chapter 3 showed that the Court rarely resolves a circuit split with an inconsistent decision.

If the justices are indeed avoiding complex or fractious cases at the agenda stage, then the overall health of the American judiciary may be implicated; again, depending on one's views of inconsistency in and of itself. The avoidance of inconsistency may in fact induce arbitrariness elsewhere in the legal system in the form of unresolved circuit splits. Justice Brandeis, as evidenced in the epigraph to this chapter, seems to think that inconsistent resolutions are preferable to no resolutions at all, as might Sunstein (2007). But given the difficulties associated with inconsistent precedents, in terms of their subsequent treatment by federal judges, Brandeis's maxim may or may not in fact be the best advice for the modern Court.

Implications for Judicial Behavior

Scholars of judicial behavior, prominently Epstein and Knight (1998), persuasively argue that the justices make strategic calculations regarding the preferences and likely behavior of their brethren when making decisions. In their seminal book, Epstein and Knight (1998, 97) show "opinion writers will put aside their most preferred position to generate a definitive ruling of the Court." Yet at times justices find themselves unwilling to defer to their brethren on legal doctrine, even when a definitive majority opinion is at stake.

As the case studies in this book demonstrate, at times a justice allows the promulgation of an unreasoned judgment in order to avoid capitulation on a point of doctrine. Justice Blackmun's refusal to concede to Justice Scalia the viability of historical tradition as a stand-alone justification in *Burson* exemplifies this practice. Conceding this point wouldn't have changed the policy outcome of *Burson* away from Blackmun's preferred position. Yet the inclusion of Scalia's preferred justification could have weakened Blackmun's bargaining position in future cases. More systematically, as I show in chapter 5, the logical consistency of a Court opinion partially determines its precedential impact.

Therefore, while "law, as it is generated by the Supreme Court, is the long-term product of short-term strategic decision making" (Epstein and Knight 1998, xii), these short-term strategic decisions are not myopically confined only to a particular case at hand. Instead, justices must calculate whether securing a definitive ruling of the Court in a particular case, therefore strengthening its precedential value, is worth sacrificing a doctrinal position that may come back to haunt them in future cases.

As I show here, at times this far-sighted consideration constrains the ability of the justices to successfully bargain and coalesce on a majority opinion. Moreover, this constraint likely will arise more frequently in politically volatile, complex, and contentious areas of the law (see chapter 3). This tendency implies that the law will be least coherent in policy areas of great public importance and salience. Indeed, the unreasoned judgments discussed here concern, variously, death penalty jurisprudence (*Lockett* and *Resweber*), gun control (*McDonald*), and presidential politics (*Bush v. Gore*).

Moving forward, scholars could consider further developing the strategic model, both theoretically and empirically, to account more explicitly for the far-sighted doctrinal considerations demonstrated here. Indeed, in later work Epstein and Knight (2013) call for a fuller theoretical depiction of how and why judges change the law. The dynamics shown in this book could potentially inform such an account in future scholarship.

Where Do We Go from Here?

A single court of last resort cannot both resolve all the important legal questions that arise in a large and diverse society while simultaneously providing coherent collective reasons for those judgments. Therefore, while the U.S. Supreme Court appears now to prioritize logically consistent reasoning above dispute resolution in many instances, the preceding analysis shows that this shift in focus may not be universally beneficial. Indeed, the costs of unreasoned judgment fall unequally: the lower courts appear to ignore these judgments and struggling to engage with them, while Congress and the mass public does not appear to mind unreasoned judgments any more or less than than well-crafted, logically consistent opinions.

Therefore, on balance, the evidence shows that the Court may have some justification for its attempts to minimize unreasoned judgments in its output. However, these attempts may have gone too far by introducing substantial indecisiveness into the business of the Court. Some unreasoned judgments are likely inevitable somewhere in a judicial hierarchy (Easterbrook 1982; Sunstein 2007). Further, given that unreasoned judgments, in and of themselves, do not threaten the broader legitimacy of the judicial system, some more satisfactory arrangement seems both possible and potentially even politically feasible.[5]

The paradoxical tension between unreasoned judgment and indecisiveness arises out of the dual nature of our expectations of the Supreme Court. Society demands both the resolution of legal conflicts as well as coherent, easy to apply legal doctrine. Asking a single court to prioritize both tasks positions that court for failure no matter what it does. If it prioritizes decisiveness, then at times its unreasoned judgments will attract fierce criticism, especially from the elite peers judges may be most responsive to. Yet if the court prioritizes coherent collective legal reasoning, then it surely will come under attack for failing to resolve important conflicts in society.

What then is to be done? One simple solution, discussed and ultimately discarded at earlier points in history, is the creation of a new, national Court of Appeals above the circuits and below the Supreme Court. The Freund Commission (appointed by Chief Justice Burger), for example, imagined just such a court several decades ago (The National Court of Appeals: A Constitutional "Inferior Court"? 1973). Such a new court could potentially screen all petitions for certiorari that would have previously gone to the Supreme Court. This court could then adjudicate cases that it deemed both worthy of resolution but not worthy of the Supreme Court's limited and precious time and resources. Its decisions would be reviewable by the Supreme Court but would be final otherwise.

Such a new court could prioritize dispute resolution; indeed, that could be part of its mandate upon creation. The housekeeping functions of the Supreme Court's business (Gizzi and Wasby 2012) could be largely absorbed by this body. If it promulgated unreasoned judgments itself, the Supreme Court could review elements of its decisions via limited grants of certiorari when necessary. Such a bifurcation of responsibility could clarify the Supreme Court's role as a primarily doctrinal one, leaving decisiveness to another set of judges.

Of course, the creation of any new Article III court, with its affiliated lifetime appointees, would represent an opportunity for whichever political party controlled the White House and Senate upon its creation. The minority party would likely oppose such a reform vigorously for this exact reason. Whether such a reform would be feasible politically or not is far from clear; indeed, the Freund Commission's original proposal to create such a court was, of course, never implemented.

If the political process will eternally prevent the bifurcation of the Court's responsibilities, then easing this tension might require an internal solution at the Court itself. At times, different decision problems likely require different procedures (List 2006). The Court might explore flexibly deciding certain problems according to different aggregation rules and opinion structures, depending on the demands of the particular problem before them (List 2006).

What could such a different procedure look like? Consider, for example, the method of dispute resolution practiced by the Supreme Court of the United Kingdom: issuing opinions seriatim, in certain instances. That is, each Justice (formerly Law Lord) on the Court issues her own separate opinion in virtually every case. This practice was utilized frequently in the United States Supreme Court around the time of its founding but was abandoned under Chief Justice John Marshall (Kelsh 1999).

The practice of delivering individual speeches in support of or dissenting from a judgment seriatim dates back centuries. Le Sueur (2008) reports on six seminars held at the Queen Mary School of Law at the University of London regarding the institutional design of a new (as of 2009) U.K. Supreme Court. This Court removed the judicial function from the House of Lords, where it had previously sat for centuries, thus ensuring greater judicial independence from the legislative branch (Paterson 2013). A number of unnamed Law Lords participated in these debates, giving their views on the seriatim practice.

The arguments in favor of the seriatim system proceeded along two avenues. First, that judges should have the independence to write as they see fit. Quashing separate opinion writing stifles the development of the law and the job satisfaction of judges (Le Sueur 2008). Second, the intellectual richness of the common law in enhanced by many judgments. Multiple conflicting rationales for a judgment reflect the complexity and nuance of the law and should be viewed as a continuing attempt to understand a given area of the law. This argument about the necessity for high courts to make progress on complex and fractious issues in society, even if total agreement cannot be reached, is echoed in the work of Sunstein (2007).

As such, perhaps the transparency and individuality of the seriatim system enhance the legitimacy of an unreasoned judgment moreso than papering over the inconsistency with an opinion per curiam (or even total preference subordination), at a minimum. And allowing for opinions seriatim would lay bare the complex disagreements at the heart of many such cases rather than having a single justice's opinion stand as the controlling rationale simply because it happens to be the "narrowest grounds." Further, Steinberg (2017) argues that ascertaining the "narrowest grounds" is far from a straightforward procedure in the first place; the American *Marks* doctrine presents substantial complexities to appellate judges.

However, delivering opinions seriatim in all decisions is likely inadvisable for the U.S. Supreme Court. Rather, the device could be utilized in rare and unusual circumstances in which the Court prioritized reaching a judgment in a high-profile case but could not cohere on a rationale. By shining a light on the messy and complicated nature of such cases, the justices might actually enhance the legitimacy of their high-profile judgments by exposing the public to the complexities and vocabulary of the law (Gibson and Caldeira 2009*a*). Such a public airing of disagreement over doctrine would enter the competing viewpoints into the market of legal discourse, so to speak, and scholars, judges, and lawyers could debate and refine the various positions over time. Hiding these disagreements behind an opinion per curiam, or in a tortured, abbreviated attempt at cohering a majority, may not serve the development of the law in the long run.

Would the justices of the U.S. Supreme Court be willing to air their disagreements and collective incoherence in such a way? Given that the justices are likely sensitive to the views of their elite peer group of judges, law professors, and attorneys, the acceptance and promotion of the seriatim device by this elite group seems likely to be a necessary (though not sufficient) condition for such a change to occur.

Alternatively, of course, the Court could return to its norms of unanimity (Epstein, Segal, and Spaeth 2001), suppressing separate opinion writing altogether. Of course, such a strategy would inevitably result in a great deal of invisible preference subordination over doctrine by the justices (Epstein, Segal, and Spaeth 2001). That is to say, unreasoned judgments undoubtedly occurred, probably with some frequency, at the Court in the nineteenth century with respect to the justices' sincere preferences over legal doctrine. The norms of the period artificially masked these judgments from public view.

As the debate over the seriatim device in the United Kingdom demonstrates, the development of law may be better served by injecting competing perspectives into the market, so to speak, for legal doctrine. Then, attorneys and judges could evaluate these perspectives and continue to shape the law rather than attempt to apply an arbitrarily constrained, artificially unanimous precedent.

Of course, there are no panaceas for resolving complex problems like the irreconcilability of consistent doctrine and decisiveness at the Court. Either proposed reform above will certainly carry its own costs and unintended consequences, and future scholars should continue to vigorously engage the question of reforming the judicial system of the United States to better understand these tradeoffs.

Future Directions

This research suggests several questions for future investigation. First, how do citizens behave when litigating disputes in areas governed by an inconsistent precedent compared with areas involved in an unresolved circuit conflict? Does one arrangement encourage more forum shopping than the other? Are litigation outcomes more predictable under one arrangement or the other? It may be the case that wealthy and powerful litigants use conflicts to their advantage by engaging in forum shopping, undermining democratic ideals of equal representation (Schattschneider 1960). Answering this question will provide evidence as to whether it is normatively desirable to give constitutional courts unfettered agenda control.

Related to this question, how do circuit court judges behave in their own merits decisions when adjudicating a dispute governed by an inconsistent precedent? Is it, as Brandeis suggests, better for lower courts to have a fractious and contradictory precedent as opposed to none at all? Are circuit decisions in a given issue area any more predictable following the issuance of an inconsistent precedent, or does the availability of an inconsistent precedent allow judges to cherry-pick a rationale to legitimate their own attitudinal choices at the appellate court level?

In the executive branch, does the president criticize inconsistent decisions? Does the executive branch enforce inconsistent rulings? Hall (2010) makes a distinction between vertical and lateral policy issues at the Court. Vertical issues are those that lower court judges are most responsible for enforcing—meaning that the Court can oversee the enactment of its ruling. Lateral issues, however, rely on the other branches for enforcement. Does the executive branch enforce inconsistent decisions in these lateral issues, particularly if those decisions are politically unpopular? Does the Court anticipate problems with enforcement in lateral issues and therefore prioritize consistency in these cases? Perhaps the Court exercises its agenda control powers to avoid making rulings in lateral issues when the justices anticipate that they will not be able to come to a consistent ruling.

Finally, this research dealt with two observable manifestations of unreasoned judgment. Yet, as chapter 1 mentions, other manifestations undoubtedly exist at the Court. At times, justices may ignore their true preferences over doctrine and support reasoning they disagree with in order to avoid the appearance of inconsistency in the Court's judgment; this preference subordination over rationales anchors the least transparent end of the spectrum of inconsistency presented in figure 2.1.

National Federation of Independent Business v. Sebelius (132 S. Ct. 2566), the "Obamacare" decision, may be an example of such a case—four justices wrote a lengthy concurrence upholding the Affordable Care Act based on a commerce clause rationale. Chief Justice Roberts wrote his own opinion upholding the Act's individual mandate to purchase health insurance based on Congress's power of taxation. At the very end of their opinion, the four concurring justices inserted two sentences joining Roberts's taxation rationale. As such, this rationale carried a majority, and *Sebelius* did not technically meet the requirements for a doctrinal paradox. Yet something seems amiss about this decision—clearly only Chief Justice Roberts thought the taxation rationale was the best reason for upholding the Act. In this unusual case, some justices joined a less-preferred rationale to promote a consistent outcome. Why might justices engage in this behavior? What are the conditions under which this less visible form of inconsistency emerges as opposed to the doctrinal paradox? Could close textual analysis of concurring opinions determine how frequently this form of inconsistency emerges? Future work should explore these difficult but important questions.

Where Do Societies Want Inconsistency?

Without resorting to autocracy, inconsistency theoretically cannot be escaped in any political system (Arrow 1951). This research suggests that societies should debate and study where in a governmental system inconsistent outcomes will do the least damage. It is not obvious that a legislative body or any other group of political actors would fare better than an independent constitutional court when attempting to resolve complex and fractious policy questions. Theoretical work shows that it is generally impossible to guarantee stable or consistent outcomes from any kind of judgment or preference aggregation system (Arrow 1951; List and Pettit 2002; McKelvey 1976).

Given this fact, is it preferable to adjudicate important questions of individual rights in an elected body that is at least minimally legitimate (Riker 1982)? Or, as argued in "Federalist No. 78," is it preferable to enshrine this power in a body insulated from the prospect of removal? These questions carry sizable normative implications, and this work cannot (and does not seek to) dispositively address them. This work instead shows that inconsistency in the United States Supreme Court occurs regularly, it occurs in politically salient cases, and its value as precedent is questionable. Granting the Court agenda control reduced inconsistency's emergence but at the cost of indecisiveness that increases the amount of unresolved conflicts between lower courts. Yet unreasoned judgments do not appear to pose a structural threat to republican governance in America, given that exposure to an inconsistent judgment does not reduce diffuse support for the Court in the mass public, nor does Congress react negatively to these inconsistencies. Indeed, the declines in unreasoned judgments in the modern era shown in chapter 4 coincide instead with a secular decline in the Court's aggregate favorability/approval rating in the mass public (Gibson and Nelson 2017).

The inescapable prospect of inconsistency in collegial courts, shown empirically in this research, demonstrates that societies on the whole have a choice to make. They can enshrine the function of constitutional review into a legislative body, as in some systems. This solution ensures that constitutional decisions will enjoy at least the minimal legitimacy conferred by democratic election (Riker 1982), though these "judges" may be overly susceptible to public pressure as well as influence by other politicians.

Alternately, societies may create an independent constitutional court and empower it with judicial review. A society with such a court must also determine, at some level, to what extent this court should control its own agenda. This research shows that with agenda control comes fewer instances of inconsistency. Agenda control does not eliminate all inconsistent outcomes. Elimination is virtually impossible in under any minimally reasonable system for aggregating judgments (List and Pettit 2002). Rather agenda control allows the constitutional court an escape valve from disputes that the court identifies in advance as potentially fractious and multidimensional.

The tradeoff of greater agenda control for a constitutional court is that these complex and fractious issues then fester in the lower levels of the judicial hierarchy. Litigants confronted with similar disputes face a volatile and arbitrary fate when they bring their grievance to court. Agenda control may reduce inconsistency at the apex of a judicial hierarchy. Yet agenda control may in fact introduce more overall arbitrariness into a legal system on the whole.

Forcing the constitutional court to adjudicate every appeal, however, is also fraught with tradeoffs. When the High Court resolves a complex, fractious issue with an inconsistent outcome, lower courts may still struggle to follow the confusing and contradictory opinions (Post and Salop 1992). Do litigants experience more predictable and nonarbitrary outcomes when lower courts are left without guidance or when the lower courts are guided by an inconsistent precedent? Ultimately, that question requires an empirical answer beyond the scope of this research. If, in fact, litigants were to experience better (i.e., less arbitrary and more predictable) outcomes even when the lower courts have only an inconsistent precedent to guide them, then agenda control at the Supreme Court would actually harm the overall health of the American judiciary. Future work should explore this question.

Ultimately, this research suggests that societies ought to recognize explicitly that inconsistency cannot be avoided. Importantly, reforms that enhance stability in one arena may in fact induce greater arbitrariness in another. Thus, perhaps the most significant contribution this research makes is encouraging scholars, politicians, and citizens to avoid asking how they might eliminate inconsistency from this institution. Instead, the right question to ask is *where* and *how* inconsistent judgments in a political system might do the least damage in both a theoretical and empirical sense. On balance, the evidence suggests that reducing inconsistency at the Supreme Court level through enhanced agenda control likely facilitated more systematic uncertainties in the form of unresolved conflicts. Given the limited societal consequences of unreasoned judgments, this tradeoff therefore may have left the state of American governance worse off than it was in a more decisive era.

APPENDIX A

Unreasoned Judgment Mathematical Definitions

Let there be a finite set of actors $N = \{1, 2, ..., n\}, n \geq 2$, and a finite set of propositions X. Both atomic propositions, $\{p, q, r\}$, and so forth, and their logical connectives $(\neg, \wedge, \vee, \rightarrow)$ are contained in X.[1] The connectives are used to form compound propositions (such as $(p \vee q)$, read: p or q). In the instance of collegial courts, the set X contains propositions that are premises for a judgment (e.g., the Fourth Amendment bars this search), as well as propositions that are judgments in cases (e.g., find for the petitioner).

Define a nonempty *agenda* $A \subseteq X$, where A is *closed under negation*, meaning that for every proposition that the actors in N form judgments over, atomic or compound, $\{p, q, r, ...\} \in A$, so too is its negation $\{\neg p, \neg q, \neg r\} \in A$. The *agenda* contains every proposition that the actors must make judgments over. Since it must be possible for actors to both affirm or reject a proposition, the negation of every proposition is also included on the agenda.

An individual *i's judgment set* over the propositions on the agenda are denoted $\Phi_i \subset A$. Generally, it is assumed that every individual *i's* judgment set is both *complete* ($\forall \{p, \neg p\} \in A$, either $p \in \Phi_i$, or $\neg p \in \Phi_i$) and *consistent* (if $p \in \Phi_i, \neg p \notin \Phi_i$)—each individual forms judgments over each proposition on the agenda. Individuals must have a judgment affirming or negating each proposition on the agenda *(completeness)* and may not simultaneously affirm and negate any proposition *(consistency)*.

Logical entailment distinguishes work on judgment aggregation from the preference aggregation literature (Arrow 1951). A set $S \in X$ *logically entails* some proposition $p \in X$ (written $S \vdash p$) if $S \cup \{\neg p\}$ is *inconsistent*. For instance, if an individual's personal judgment set $\Phi_i = \{p, q\}$, then $\Phi_i \vdash$

$\{(p \wedge q)\}$. In this example, if an individual decides in favor of both proposition p and proposition q, then the compound proposition $(p \wedge q)$ (read: p and q) is logically entailed, because the proposition $\neg(p \wedge q)$ is *inconsistent* with the set Φ_i. The proposition $\neg(p \wedge q)$ is *inconsistent* because both p and $q \in \Phi_i$; hence if $\neg(p \wedge q) \in \Phi_i$, then $\{(p \wedge q), \neg(p \wedge q)\} \in \Phi_i$, violating *consistency*—since the individual judged in favor of both propositions p and q, the compound proposition p and q is logically entailed. If the individual did not judge in favor of the proposition p and q, then the individual would be saying: "definitely p, and definitely q, but definitely not p and q" simultaneously, which violates *consistency*.

An *aggregation rule* is a function F mapping the individual judgment sets into a collective judgment set Φ, $F(\Phi_1, \Phi_2, ..., \Phi_n) = \Phi$. Φ may be interpreted as the set of propositions accepted by the entire collective. The judgment aggregation rule is the mechanism used by the group to aggregate their judgments on every proposition into a single set of judgments for the entire group.

Majority voting is one such aggregation rule. Under majority voting, each proposition is collectively accepted if and only if it is accepted by a specified majority of individuals, for example $F(\Phi_1, \Phi_2, ..., \Phi_n) = \{p \in X : |i \in N : p \in \Phi_i| > n/2\}$. That is, only propositions that are in the individual judgment sets of more than half of the individuals are accepted by the group. Under pure majority voting, every proposition, whether it is a premise or a conclusion, on the agenda receives the same treatment. The proposition receives a vote, and if it carries a majority, the group accepts it. Other aggregation rules weigh some propositions more heavily than others, due to the possibility of incoherence associated with majority voting.

A *premise-based judgment aggregation rule* is a rule that determines the set of collective judgments by applying majority voting (or some other method) to a privileged subset of propositions (premises), then taking the logical enclosure of the results, for example, $F(\Phi_1, \Phi_2, ..., \Phi_n) = \{p \in X : G(\Phi_1, \Phi_2, ..., \Phi_n) \cap Y \vdash p\}$. $G(\Phi_1, \Phi_2, ..., \Phi_n) \cap Y$ being the set of accepted propositions from the privileged subset of premises, $Y \subseteq X$. Under this rule, the group chooses some premises, votes only on these, and commits to accept whatever other judgments are *logically entailed* by the result.

A *conclusion-based judgment aggregation rule* also privileges a subset of propositions (conclusions) and comes to a judgment based on their votes only over these propositions but does not take the logical closure of the resulting judgments, for example, $F(\Phi_1, \Phi_2, ..., \Phi_n) = G(\Phi_1, \Phi_2, ..., \Phi_n) \cap Z$, where $G(\Phi_1, \Phi_2, ..., \Phi_n) \cap Z$ is the set of accepted propositions from the privileged subset (conclusions), $Z \subseteq X$. Under the conclusion-based approach, there is no notion of logical entailment; rather, the collective makes its judgments based upon the aggregation of individual judgments over a subset of privileged propositions, independently of whether their final outcome is consistent.

Reasoned Judgment obtains when the final collective judgment set Φ is *consistent*—by which it is meant that every proposition included in the final outcome set is logically entailed by the group's judgments on all the other propositions. If the final set of collective judgments Φ under a conclusion-based aggregation rule is the same as the set of judgments obtained with a premise-based voting rule, then the set of judgments obtained under the conclusion-based rule does not violate *consistency*, and thus the outcome exhibits *consistency* (Pettit 2001). However, unless some propositions on the agenda are privileged (which both premise-based and conclusion-based rules require), neither majority voting, nor any other method of aggregating judgments, guarantees consistency (List and Pettit 2002).

APPENDIX B

Technical Details and Supplemental Analyses

This appendix presents the results of the various statistical analyses discussed in this book in greater technical detail for interested readers. Except as otherwise noted, all analyses performed in Stata 12.1 and 14.1 on personal computers running Windows 10.

Chapter 2

Table B.1 shows the results of tests of proportions and tests of distributions (Kolmogorov-Smirnov tests) between two categories of opinions per curiam at the Court. Throughout, I consider only a subset of opinions per curiam to be a form of unreasoned judgment. Opinions per curiam issued following oral argument and accompanied by at least one separate opinion arguably show the signs of genuine controversy, while others do not. To test that conjecture, table B.1 shows that this coding strategy appears to distinguish cases that are disposed of routinely from those that generated controversy. Indeed, for only one variable in table B.1, multiple substantive issues, do I fail to reject the null hypothesis that the proportions do not differ between the two categories of opinions per curiam.

Chapter 3

In this chapter, unreasoned judgment is analyzed both as a binary phenomenon (unreasoned vs. consistent) and as an unordered phenomenon (consistent vs. per curiam vs. plurality). I consider the latter variable unordered for a simple reason: it is unclear that one manifestation of

TABLE B.1. Differences Between Argued and Nonargued Per Curiam Opinions

Variable	Comparison	Mean/Proportion diff.	K-S test $P > \|z\|$	Prop. test $P > \|z\|$	N
Interest group power	Argued - Not	0.003	**< 0.001**	–	513
NY Times front page	Argued - Not	0.10	–	**< 0.001**	550
Combined citations	Argued - Not	0.16	**0.003**	–	550
Combined follows	Argued - Not	0.07	**0.009**	–	550
Nonsingle-peaked	Argued - Not	0.46	–	**< 0.001**	550
Multiple substantive issues	Argued - Not	0.02	–	0.60	550

Note: Bolded entries represent $p < 0.05$. Tests performed using the prtest and ksmirnov commands in Stata 13.1.

unreasoned judgment is more severe or extreme than the other. Treating this variable as ordered would assume that the covariates exert a similar influence on the emergence of both manifestations of inconsistency. Yet, as the theory of chapter 1 shows, there may be important differences in the data-generating processes for these various manifestations. As such, two different statistical models are required. A simple logit model is utilized to determine the correlates of unreasoned judgment. A multinomial probit is preferable for analyzed unreasoned judgment as an unordered phenomenon. The multinomial logit, the common alternative, requires an assumption of independence of irrelevant alternatives (IIA). That is, the fact that the plurality opinion is a possibility should have no bearing on a judgment's probability of being resolved with an opinion per curiam. This assumption seems particularly untenable here, as the manifestations of unreasoned judgment are presumed to arise from a common latent theoretical issue. Indeed, diagnostic testing Stata 12.1 indicates that the multinomial logit is inappropriate for these data.

Results are robust to estimation via penalized maximum likelihood estimatation, a necessary check given the relative sparsity of unreasoned judgment in the data (King and Zeng 2001). Standard errors are clustered on natural courts accounts for dynamic and membership change effects.

Table B.2 shows the results of these two models. The results of column one are robust to estimation via penalized-maximum likelihood for rare events, using the firthlogit command in Stata 14.1.

Estimation results are generally robust to using natural court or term-fixed effects instead of clustered errors. The only sensitive findings relates to mandatory jurisdiction cases. Mandatory caseloads fell at the Court dramatically after 1988. As such, while the association between mandatory cases and inconsistency remains positive in all specifications, a natural court fixed effects specification introduces collinearity with mandatory jurisdiction.

TABLE B.2. Logit and Multinomial Probit Estimates of the Case-Level Correlates of Unreasoned Judgment

	Logit β (se)	Multinomial probit β (se)
Judicial review	0.654 (0.350)	
Mandatory case	0.087 (0.140)	
Legal issues	−0.237* (0.103)	
Civil liberties	0.348* (0.097)	
Salient case	0.295* (0.151)	
Disordered coalition	0.755* (0.097)	
Circuit conflict	−1.283* (0.154)	
Per curiam		
Judicial review		−0.070 (0.517)
Mandatory case		0.118 (0.122)
Legal issues		−0.316* (0.119)
Civil liberties		−0.075 (0.072)
Salient case		−0.072 (0.125)
Disordered coalition		0.460* (0.111)
Circuit conflict		−1.174* (0.165)
Plurality		
Judicial review		0.658* (0.289)
Mandatory case		−0.021 (0.104)
Legal issues		−0.017 (0.056)
Civil liberties		0.665* (0.091)
Salient case		0.425* (0.128)
Disordered coalition		0.529* (0.067)
Circuit conflict		−0.408* (0.108)
N	8268	8268
BIC	3753.243	4422.520

* $p < 0.05$. Robust standard errors, clustered by natural Court, in parentheses. Dependent variable in the Logit column equals one for cases resolved with an unreasoned judgment. Dependent variable in the Multinomial probit column takes on three categorical values: consistent, per curiam, and plurality.

Chapter 4

Chapter 4 analyzes dynamic (time series) data. I model the dependent variable (inconsistency) as a function of contemporaneous values of the independent variables, while accounting for the dynamic properties of the dependent variables. To account for these properties, it is first necessary to pretest each series for their order of integration (Box-Steffensmeier and Helgason 2016; Grant and Lebo 2016; Keele, Linn, and Webb 2016).

Both dependent variables are not fully integrated (I(1)) (Box-Steffensmeier et al. 2014; De Boef and Keele 2008) per standard time series diagnostics. Specifically, both the rate and incidence series can be considered fractionally integrated based on the results of Dickey-Fuller, augmented Dickey-Fuller, Kwiatkowski-Phillips-Schmidt-Shin (KPSS), and Lo-MacKinlay variance ratio tests. I estimate ARFIMA (autoregressive fractionally integrated moving average) models to account for this property. In both models below, the estimate of fractional integration, d, is both statistically significant and different from either 1 or 0. This result buttresses the appropriateness of the ARFIMA approach.

Further, it is crucial to ensure that all variables in a time series regression model are integrated of the same order. The ARFIMA approach directly estimates d, ensuring that the resulting series is integrated of order 0 and is stationary. The independent variables in the model were also pretested for stationarity, using the same tests as mentioned above. The Court's discretionary caseload is likely fractionally integrated. Therefore, in the models below, I preprocessed this series by estimating a constant-only ARFIMA model and using this residual from this estimation as a "pre-whitened" series for the multivariate model to follow (Grant and Lebo 2016). Interestingly, the divergence of ideology series appears likely to be a unit root based on these same tests. Therefore, I simply took the first difference of this variable to render it stationary (Box-Steffensmeier et al. 2014). For these independent variables, I follow the advice of Keele and Kelly (2006) and include both contemporaneous and lagged values of the independent variables in the model in the initial estimation.

White noise portmanteau (Q) tests on the residuals of these models confirms that the ARFIMA modeling strategy adequately addressed the dynamic properties of the data (Box-Steffensmeier et al. 2014). The residuals of both ARFIMA models are indistinguishable from white noise.

Table B.3 replicates the result shown in chapter 4: the 1988 reforms are negatively and statistically significantly associated with the incidence and rate of unreasoned judgment. The control variables and their lags do not attain

TABLE B.3. ARFIMA Estimates of the Effect of the 1988 Agenda Control Legislation on the Incidence and Rate of Unreasoned Judgment

	Incidence β (se)	Rate β (se)
Post-1988	−6.820*	−0.038*
	(2.136)	(0.011)
Differenced preference divergence	−2.212	−0.002
	(2.843)	(0.022)
Discretionary workload	−0.015	
	(0.033)	
Differenced preference divergence$_{t-1}$	−1.243	0.007
	(2.819)	(0.021)
Discretionary workload$_{t-1}$	−0.005	
	(0.033)	
Time series components		
d	0.269*	0.109
	(0.119)	(0.119)
N	63	63
BIC	391.280	−230.522

*$p < 0.05$. Constant not reported. Estimates obtained using the ARFIMA command in Stata 14.1.

statistical significance at convention levels; the lags could be removed from the model, following the advice of Keele and Kelly (2006).

As Caporale and Grier (2005) note, the significance of the 1988 dummy variable is not sufficient to prove that the institutional reform actually caused declines in inconsistency. They advise analysts to determine whether the time point corresponding to a statistically significant intervention falls within the confidence intervals of an endogenously estimated unknown structural break. Using the strucchange package in the R statistical programming language (Zeileis et al. 2001; R Core Team 2014), I estimated the location of unknown structural breaks in the unreasoned judgment rate and incidence series (Zeleis et al. 2001). This procedure estimates the locations and confidence intervals of unknown structural breaks in time series data. Further, the procedure, based on the work of Bai and Perron (1998), suggests an optimal partition of the series in terms of the number of breaks estimated.

These estimates are made both via minimizing Bayesian Information Criterion (BIC) and Residual Sum of Squares (RSS). Confidence intervals for a structural break in both series overlapped 1988, in optimal partitions suggested by BIC and RSS. I therefore reject the null hypothesis of no structural break in 1988 for both unreasoned judgment series.

Chapter 5

In chapter 5, I hypothesized that unreasoned judgments would be negatively and statistically significantly associated with positive treatments and citations in lower federal courts. These citation variables are counts. Moreover, for both positive treatments and citations generally, the mean of these variables is considerably smaller than the variance. This property, as it relates to count variables, is called overdispersion. The commonly used Poisson regression model for count data is inappropriate for overdispersed variables. As such, I utilize negative binomial regression instead, which allows for overdispersion (Cameron and Trivedi 2005, 670). Table B.4 shows the results of the negative binomial regressions on the count of positive treatments and citations accorded to unreasoned and consistent Supreme Court opinions, respectively.

The unit of analysis in all models is a Supreme Court precedent. The dependent variable of the first model in table B.4 is the count of positive lower court treatments each precedent received. The dependent variable in the second model in table B.4 is the count of citations in the lower courts for each precedent.

Fixed effects for the legal issue area and the constant estimates are not reported for brevity. The age of precedents is included as a simple control variable, given that precedents vary by age in terms of their citation counts and depreciation (Black and Spriggs 2013). Results are robust to more complex, nonlinear methods of accounting for age, such as including the squared value of age or controlling for age with a linear or cubic spline. Results are also robust to hierarchical specifications with a random intercept varying by term, as an alternative method of accounting for heteroskedastic effects conditional on precedent age.

Table B.4 shows that unreasoned judgments are negatively and statistically significantly associated with both positive treatments and citations in subsequent opinions of lower federal judges. Regarding the control variables, opinions that resolve circuit conflicts are positively and statistically significantly associated with both positive treatments and overall citations, as are decisions that formally alter precedent, "important cases" (Fowler et al. 2007), and decisions that are later reversed. Mandatory jurisdiction cases

TABLE B.4. Negative Binomial Estimates of the Effect of Unreasoned Judgments on Subsequent Treatments in Lower Federal Court Opinions

	Pos. treatments β (se)	Citations β (se)
Unreasoned judgment	−1.090*	−0.827*
	(0.124)	(0.097)
Resolves conflict	0.298*	0.222*
	(0.123)	(0.094)
Precedent age	−0.044*	−0.035*
	(0.003)	(0.003)
Alters precedent	0.876*	0.767*
	(0.304)	(0.231)
Judicial review	−0.214	−0.117
	(0.147)	(0.099)
Mandatory case	−0.784*	−0.641*
	(0.114)	(0.083)
Dissent	0.145	0.145*
	(0.094)	(0.073)
"Important" case	0.981*	1.027*
	(0.136)	(0.105)
Later reversed	0.765*	0.807*
	(0.339)	(0.224)
N	7418	7417
BIC	66252.957	78365.150

*$p < 0.05$. Constant and issue-area fixed effects not reported. Estimates obtained using the nbreg command in Stata 14.1.

and precedent age are both negatively and statistically significantly associated with both positive treatments and overall citations. Finally, decisions accompanied by dissent are positively and statistically significantly associated with citations, but not positive treatments.

Of course, while the raw sum of total positive treatments and citations may be appealingly straightforward, the district and circuit courts hear different numbers of cases each year and issue different numbers of opinions. To ensure these results are not an artifact of the different businesses of these two levels of the judicial hierarchy, I created a standardized version of the two dependent variables of this chapter. I first standardized a precedent's count of treatments at each level of the judicial hierarchy separately. I then added these two z-scores together for a single aggregated index. Finally, I estimated

TABLE B.5. OLS Estimates of the Effect of Unreasoned Judgments on Subsequent (Standardized) Treatments in Lower Federal Court Opinions

	Pos. treatments β (se)	Citations β (se)
Unreasoned judgment	−0.263* (0.026)	−0.312* (0.033)
Resolves conflict	0.164* (0.079)	0.155* (0.073)
Precedent age	−0.014* (0.002)	−0.015* (0.001)
Alters precedent	0.507* (0.251)	0.670* (0.264)
Judicial review	−0.200* (0.035)	−0.187* (0.044)
Mandatory case	−0.186* (0.026)	−0.240* (0.031)
Dissent	0.089 (0.050)	0.103* (0.051)
"Important" case	0.422* (0.105)	0.740* (0.117)
Later reversed	0.336 (0.261)	0.501* (0.259)
N	7418	7417
BIC	28097.928	28221.161

*$p < 0.05$. Constant and issue-area fixed effects not reported.

OLS models on these standardized indices of positive treatments and citations using otherwise the same specification as the models in table B.4. Table B.5 shows the results of these OLS models.

Table B.5 shows that the negative and statistically significant association between unreasoned judgments and subsequent treatments was not driven by workload or other differences between the two levels of the judicial hierarchy. Results for the control variables are also largely similar: decisions that exercise judicial review become negatively and statistically significantly associated with positive treatments and citations under this specification.

Finally, in chapter 5, I considered the relationship of unreasoned judgment to negative treatments in the opinions of other federal judges. Table B.6 shows the results of these estimates. The first column of Table B.6 is a negative binomial regression on the raw count of negative treatments, while

TABLE B.6. Negative Binomials Estimates of the Effect of Unreasoned Judgments on Subsequent Treatments in Lower Federal Court Opinions

	Count of neg. treatments β (se)	Standardized neg. treatments β (se)
Unreasoned judgment	−0.201 (0.165)	−0.072 (0.069)
Resolves conflict	0.316* (0.134)	0.073 (0.052)
Precedent age	0.003 (0.005)	0.001 (0.001)
Alters precedent	0.188 (0.180)	0.476 (0.288)
Judicial review	−0.236 (0.134)	−0.061 (0.080)
Mandatory case	−0.583* (0.132)	−0.170* (0.048)
Dissent	0.102 (0.109)	0.029 (0.050)
"Important" case	1.041* (0.180)	0.423* (0.164)
Later reversed	3.156* (0.164)	6.468* (1.097)
N	7418	7418
BIC	15491.884	29465.899

*$p < 0.05$. Constant and issue-area fixed effects not reported.

the second column is an OLS estimate of the sum of standardized negative treatments in the district and circuit courts, as above.

Table B.6 shows that unreasoned judgments are not statistically significantly associated with critical treatments in the lower courts. Further, the statistically significant association between conflict cases and negative treatments is sensitive to the metric chosen: the association becomes nonsignificant when measuring negative treatments with the standardized sum instead of the raw count.

Chapter 6

As in chapter 4, chapter 6 analyzes time series data. Therefore, a similar suite of diagnostic tools for stationarity are employed here as well. The key empirical question of this chapter is the extent to which members of Congress respond to the promulgation of unreasoned judgments and judicial review by the Court with proposals to limit or "curb" the Court (Clark 2009; Elliott 1958).

The dependent variable under analysis is the number of Court-curbing bills introduced in an a given year, logged. I pretested all the nonbinary variables under analysis for their univariate properties (stationarity) before estimating a multivariate model (Box-Steffensmeier and Helgason 2016; Keele, Linn, and Webb 2016). Per the standard advice in the literature, I triangulated the results of multiple unit root tests before reaching conclusions on the order of integration of each individual variable.

I estimated Dickey-Fuller, Augmented Dickey-Fuller, KPSS, and Lo-MacKinlay Variance ratio tests for each variable in the analysis (Box-Steffensmeier et al. 2014). The dependent variable series, logged curbing bills, shows signs of fractional integration, a very common outcome with political science data (Lebo, Walker, and Clarke 2000).[1] That is, the series is neither stationary nor is it fully integrated. The order of integration, d, sits somewhere between 0 and 1. As such, table B.7 presents the results of an ARFIMA regression model, so the persistence in the dependent variable can be adequately modeled. Postestimation analysis of the residuals using white noise tests demonstrated that an ARFIMA(1,d,0) specification fit the data best while successfully transforming the residuals into white noise (Box-Steffensmeier et al.).

Further, following the advice of Keele and Kelly (2006), I included lags of the independent variables as well. I then tested the restrictions of this more general model, finding that the lags do not significantly improve model fit. Table B.7 presents the results of both the more general model and this more parsimonious specification. Both models presented in table B.7 show that the estimated d is statistically significant—just under 0.50 in both cases. This result indicates that the ARFIMA specification is appropriate for these data; the confidence interval for the estimated d does not cross either 0 (for stationarity) or 1 (for a unit root) in both models presented.

Table B.7 shows that the rate of unreasoned judgment does not exhibit a statistically significant relationship with Court-curbing by Congress. A similar null result obtains for the exercise of judicial review via unreasoned judgment. Interestingly, none of the control variables exhibit statistically significant relationships with Court-curbing either. It seems, interestingly, that if the Court could provoke Congress with its rulings, judicial review and/or logical inconsistency fail to grab members' attention. Perhaps other types of judgments—ones ideologically displeasing to certain extremist members, for instance—better explain the emergence of curbing legislation. At

TABLE B.7. ARFIMA Estimates of the Effect of the Unreasoned Judgment on Court-curbing

	Full model β (se)	Restricted model β (se)
Rate of unreasoned judgment	1.919	2.258
	(2.611)	(2.374)
Rate of unreasoned judgment$_{t-1}$	0.716	
	(2.806)	
Unreasoned judicial review last term	0.299	0.358
	(0.256)	(0.223)
Total laws overturned	−8.449	−7.018
	(5.195)	(4.958)
Total laws overturned$_{t-1}$	−1.380	
	(5.322)	
Court-public divergence	−0.032	−0.157
	(0.266)	(0.247)
Court-public divergence$_{t-1}$	−0.350	
	(0.268)	
Opposing congress	−0.114	−0.111
	(0.186)	(0.182)
Time series components		
AR(1)	−0.764*	−0.753*
	(0.098)	(0.098)
d	0.470*	0.467*
	(0.041)	(0.045)
N	46	47
BIC	134.617	126.553

*$p < 0.05$. Constant not reported. Estimates obtained using the ARFIMA command in Stata 14.1.

a minimum, Congress does not respond to the overruling of its own bills, or the aggregate quality of the Court's reasoning, with greater criticism in the years under study here.

Chapter 7

In chapter 7, individual differences in knowledge about the Supreme Court and politics were hypothesized to moderate the effect of unreasoned judgment on diffuse and specific support for the Court, as well as trust in government more broadly. Generally, knowledge did not moderate the

TABLE B.8. OLS Estimates of the Moderating Effect of Political Knowledge on Exposure to an Unreasoned Judgment

	Diffuse support	Trust in government	Agreement	Acceptance
	β	β	β	β
	(se)	(se)	(se)	(se)
Per curiam	−0.015	−0.376*	−0.018	−0.275
	(0.293)	(0.163)	(0.282)	(0.281)
Plurality	−0.404	−0.267	0.326	−0.031
	(0.312)	(0.174)	(0.301)	(0.299)
Political knowledge	0.407	−0.240	0.389	−0.349
	(0.298)	(0.166)	(0.287)	(0.285)
Per curiam X Political knowledge	0.163	0.339	0.141	0.609
	(0.376)	(0.209)	(0.362)	(0.360)
Plurality X Political knowledge	0.508	0.280	−0.416	−0.077
	(0.415)	(0.231)	(0.400)	(0.398)
N	265	265	265	265
BIC	792.527	481.645	772.666	769.543

*$p < 0.05$. Constant not reported.

null effects shown. However, political knowledge did appear to moderate the effect of exposure to opinions per curiam on trust in government, and Supreme Court knowledge moderated the effect of exposure to a doctrinal paradox on trust in government.

This section explores the robustness of those findings to an alternative strategy of measuring knowledge. In particular, while chapter 7 treats knowledge as a binary, high/low median split variable, here I consider knowledge as a single continuous moderating variable. For each knowledge scale, I constructed a single composite variable based on the first factor resulting from an iterated principal factor analysis performed on the polychoric correlation matrix of the individual question items.

Tables B.8 and B.9 show the results of simple OLS models where the four dependent variables of chapter 7 are regressed on indicator variables for the two treatments and an interaction between these treatment indicators and the continuous composite knowledge scale.

Table B.8 suggests the same conclusion as presented in chapter 7: political knowledge generally does not moderate the treatment effect of exposure to unreasoned judgment. However, knowledge does moderate the effect of exposure to an opinion per curiam on trust in government. When knowledge is at 0 (a value that is supported in the data), there is a negative and statistically significant association between exposure to an opinion per curiam and

TABLE B.9. OLS Estimates of the Moderating Effect of Supreme Court Knowledge on Exposure to an Unreasoned Judgment

	Diffuse support β (se)	Trust in government β (se)	Agreement β (se)	Acceptance β (se)
Per curiam	−0.226 (0.523)	−0.415 (0.290)	−0.747 (0.504)	−0.547 (0.501)
Plurality	−0.042 (0.564)	−0.679* (0.314)	0.496 (0.544)	0.618 (0.541)
Supreme Court knowledge	1.049* (0.412)	−0.087 (0.229)	0.234 (0.398)	0.134 (0.395)
Per curiam X SC knowledge	0.326 (0.547)	0.302 (0.304)	0.836 (0.528)	0.715 (0.525)
Plurality X SC knowledge	−0.100 (0.592)	0.669* (0.329)	−0.515 (0.571)	−0.730 (0.568)
N	266	266	266	266
BIC	792.180	479.753	773.251	769.796

*$p < 0.05$. Constant not reported.

trust in government (relative to the control condition, the baseline). This negative effect vanishes as knowledge rises.

Moving on, table B.9 presents the results of similar OLS models, but with Supreme Court knowledge included as the moderating variable. Table B.9 replicates the results presented in chapter 7 as well. Exposure to a plurality opinion for individuals with a Supreme Court knowledge score of 0 (supported in the data) is negatively and statistically significantly associated with trust in government. As knowledge rises, trust in government increases following exposure to a plurality opinion. Moreover, table B.9 shows that Supreme Court knowledge is positively and statistically significantly associated with higher levels of diffuse support.

Finally, Hainmueller, Mummolo, and Xu (2017) caution researchers to interrogate the robustness of estimates from multiplicative interaction terms. In particular, they recommend testing the linearity assumption of the interaction term by binning a continuous moderating variable into terciles. Then, a joint Wald test is conducted to determine with these additional tercile interaction terms are jointly equal to 0. Xu et al. (2017) provide a useful Stata package, "interflex," to implement these recommendations. For each statistically significant linear interaction term reported in tables B.8 and B.9, this Wald test failed to reject the null that the additional tercile interaction terms were jointly equal to 0. As such, the linearity assumption holds in this particular case.

APPENDIX C

Experimental Materials

Demographic Materials

1. Demographic Introduction: Below are a series of background questions that will assist us in our research. Thank you for your responses.
2. What is your education level? [Did not complete high school–Postgraduate degree]
3. What is your family's annual income [Less that $10,000–More than $70,000]
4. When you think about your ethnic background, which category do you fall into? [White European; Jewish; Latino; Asian; African–American (Black); Other; I prefer not to answer]
5. What is your sex? [Male; Female]
6. What is your age? [0–100 slider]
7. Generally speaking, do you think of yourself as a Republican, Democrat, an Independent, or what? [Democrat; Republican; Independent] If IND is selected: Do you think of yourself as closer to the Democratic or Republican Party? [Democratic; Republican; Neither]
8. Some people don't pay much attention to political campaigns. How about you? Regarding the last presidential election, would you say you were very much interested, somewhat interest, or not much interested in following the campaigns?

Supreme Court Knowledge

1. Do you happen to know who has the last say when there is a conflict over the meaning of the Constitution—the U.S. Supreme Court, the U.S. Congress, or the president? [Multiple Choice]

2. Some judges in the United States are elected; others are appointed to the bench. Do you happen to know if the justices of the U.S. Supreme Court are elected or appointed to the bench? [Multiple Choice]
3. Some judges in the United States serve for a set number of years; others serve a life term. Do you happen to know whether the justices of the U.S. Supreme Court serve for a set number of years or whether they serve a life term? [Multiple Choice]

Political Knowledge

1. What job or political office is now held by Theresa May? [Fill in the blank]
2. How many members are there in the U.S. House? [Fill in the blank]
3. Whose responsibility is it to nominate judges to federal courts? [The president; House of Representatives; The Senate; The Supreme Court]
4. How long is the term for a U.S. Senator? [Fill in the blank]
5. What job or political office does John G. Roberts currently hold? [Fill in the blank]

Experimental Treatments

- Experimental Treatment Introduction: You will now read about a hypothetical decision by the United States Supreme Court, and then be asked to give your opinion about that decision. Please read closely. There will be questions on your comprehension of the case. Please click the continue button (») to proceed.
- Background: The U.S. Supreme Court practices a policy of selective incorporation. That is, while all the individual rights guaranteed in the Constitution may not be limited by federal law, the Court decides on a case-by-case basis which constitutional rights may not be limited by state or city laws.

  The 2010 case of *McDaniel v. Seattle* centered on whether the city of Seattle's ban on handguns violated the Second Amendment to the Constitution.

  Federal law cannot bar individuals from owning handguns, but before this case was heard at the Supreme Court, the Second Amendment had not yet been incorporated, meaning that while the Second Amendment protected the right to keep and bear arms from being infringed

by federal law, it had not yet been decided that states could also not infringe on the individual right to keep and bear arms.
The lower courts ruled that because the Second Amendment had not yet been incorporated, the city of Seattle's handgun ban was legal.
The Supreme Court then considered two possible reasons for overturning the lower court's decision, which would incorporate the Second Amendment and overturn Seattle's handgun ban.
First, whether or not the right to keep and bear arms is a fundamental right protected by the due process clause of the Fourteenth Amendment, which says that no state may deprive anyone of "life, liberty, or property without due process of law."
Second, whether or not the right to keep and bear arms is a fundamental privilege of American citizenship protected by the privileges or immunities clause of the Fourteenth Amendment, which says that "no state shall make or enforce any law which shall abridge the privileges or immunities of citizens of the United States."

- Congruence Preferences: What do you think the right decision in the case is?

  - The right to keep and bear arms should be incorporated, overturning the handgun ban.
  - The right to keep and bear arms should not be incorporated, leaving the handgun ban in place.

- Treatment: Subjects will be shown one of three conditions. As an example, table C.1 below and accompanying text shows a doctrinal paradox outcome.

The outcome of the case is described above in the table. A judgment of affirm (A) means that the Court would leave the lower court's decision in place, and Seattle will still be allowed to ban handguns. A judgment of reverse (R) means that Seattle's ban would be overturned.

One justice agreed that the privileges or immunities clause means that Seattle's ban should be overturned and voted to reverse. This justice did not agree that the due process clause was a valid reason for overturning Seattle's ban.

Four different justices agreed that the due process clause was a valid reason for overturning Seattle's handgun ban and voted to reverse as well. These four justices did not agree that the privileges or immunities clause was a valid reason for overturning the ban.

TABLE C.1. Plurality Opinion/Doctrinal Paradox Treatment

Justice & Due process? & Privileges or immunities? & Judgment			
Thomas	N	Y	R
Scalia	Y	N	R
Roberts	Y	N	R
Alito	Y	N	R
Kennedy	Y	N	R
Stevens	N	N	A
Ginsburg	N	N	A
Breyer	N	N	A
Sotomayor	N	N	A
Majority	N	N	R

Finally, four justices disagreed with both reasons and voted to affirm.

Thus, there were five votes to reverse the lower court but no reason for the reversal was supported by a majority of the justices. Therefore, the lower court was reversed, and the handgun ban was overturned.

One nonpartisan analyst strongly criticized the Court for failing to agree on a single reason for its judgment. The analyst said,

> "More than a mere agreement on the result is needed; without a majority rationale for the result, the Supreme Court abdicates its responsibility to the institutions and parties depending on it for direction. Each decision such as this one represents a failure to fulfill the Court's obligations. Persistent indulgence in this practice of issuing a judgment without telling the public the reason why has tarnished what has long been considered one of this judicial institution's greatest qualities, the fairness and integrity of its decisionmaking process."

In the per curiam conditions, subjects saw no table and instead read the following passage [result conditional on expressed preferences]:

The result of the case was as follows: five justices agreed that Seattle's ban should be overturned. Thus five of the nine justices voted to reverse the lower court, overturning the handgun ban.

The five justices in the majority could not come to any agreement over the legal reasoning for their judgment.

Four justices disagreed with that judgment and voted to affirm the lower court's judgment.

Instead of issuing several lengthy, contradictory opinions, the five justices in the majority decided to release a very short, unsigned opinion that gave no reasons for why the Court did what it did. This practice is known as issuing an opinion **per curiam**.

One nonpartisan analyst strongly criticized the Court for failing to disclose the reasoning for its decision. The analyst said, "Today, the per curiam is a misused practice that is at odds with the nature of the American common law system, frustrating efforts to hold individual judges accountable and inhibiting the development of the law."

In the consistent control conditions, subjects were instead told that five justices subscribed to the first rationale, giving it a majority of the Court. No nonpartisan analyst was mentioned.

Outcome Variables

1. Agreement: Overall, do you agree or disagree with the Court's decision in this case? [Likert Scale]
2. Acceptance: Do you accept the decision? That is, do you think the decision ought to be accepted and considered the final word on the matter or that there ought to be an effort to challenge the decision and get it changed?

    - Strongly believe that it should be accepted and considered to be final
    - Somewhat believe that it should be accepted and considered to be final
    - Somewhat believe that it should be challenged
    - Strongly believe that it should be challenged

3. Diffuse Support

    - Please rate your agreement with the following statement: It is inevitable that the U.S. Supreme Court gets mixed up in politics; therefore, we ought to have stronger means of controlling the actions of the U.S. Supreme Court. [Likert Scale]
    - Please rate your agreement with the following statement: The U.S. Supreme Court ought to be made less independent so that it listens a lot more to what the people want. [Likert Scale]
    - Please rate your agreement with the following statement: Judges on the U.S. Supreme Court who consistently make decisions at odds with what a majority of the people want should be removed from their position as judge. [Likert Scale]
    - Please rate your agreement with the following statement: Supreme Court Justices are just like any other politician; we cannot trust

them to decide court cases in a way that is in the best interests of our country. [Likert Scale]

- Please rate your agreement with the following statement: If the U.S. Supreme Court started making a lot of decisions that most people disagree with, it might be better to do away with the Supreme Court altogether. [Likert Scale]
- Please rate your agreement with the following statement: The U.S. Supreme Court gets too mixed up in politics. [Likert Scale]
- Please rate your agreement with the following statement: The right of the Supreme Court to decide certain types of controversial issues should be reduced. [Likert Scale]

4. Trust in Government

- Would you say the government is pretty much run by a few big interests looking out for themselves or that it is run for the benefit of all the people?
- How often can you trust the federal government in Washington to do what is right? [Always–Never, five-point scale]
- Do you think that people in government waste a lot of the money we pay in taxes, waste some of it, or don't waste very much of the money we pay in taxes?
- How many of the people running the government are corrupt? [All–None, five-point scale]

5. Issue Salience

We are interested in knowing how important different political issues are to people. We will now present you with a few different issues and ask you how important you think each issue is.

(a) On a scale of 1 to 7, with 7 being extremely important, and 1 being not at all important, how important is the issue of *gun control/gun rights to you?* [1–7 Scale]

(b) On a scale of 1 to 7, with 7 being extremely important, and 1 being not at all important, how important is the issue of *environmental regulation* to you? [1–7 Scale]

(c) On a scale of 1 to 7, with 7 being extremely important, and 1 being not at all important, how important is the issue of *taxes* to you? [1–7 Scale]

(d) On a scale of 1 to 7, with 7 being extremely important, and 1 being not at all important, how important is the issue of *equal treatment for the citizens of the District of Columbia* to you? [1–7 Scale]
(e) On a scale of 1 to 7, with 7 being extremely important, and 1 being not at all important, how important is the *health care* to you? [1–7 Scale]

Manipulation Checks

- In the hypothetical Supreme Court case you read about, what did the nonpartisan analyst criticize the Court for doing? [Multiple Choice: Issuing a very short, unsigned opinion that did not fully explain the Court's reasoning; Reaching an outcome the analyst disagreed with; Failing to agree on a single reason for the Court's judgment; A nonpartisan analyst was not mentioned in the narrative I read]
- What was the issue at stake in the hypothetical Supreme Court case you read about? [Multiple Choice: Abortion; Religious Freedom; Gun Control; Free Speech]

Notes

Chapter 1

* Quantitative and archival replication materials for all analyses presented are available at: https://doi.org/10.5064/F6W7QRSX. If you use these data, please use the following citation: Hitt, Matthew P. 2019. "Replication Data for: Inconsistency and Indecision in the United States Supreme Court." Qualitative Data Repository. https://doi.org/10.5064/F6W7QRSX.

1. District of Columbia v. Heller, 554 U.S. 570 (2008).
2. Of course, others might argue that it is preferable to resolve the complex and fractious disputes in society inconsistently as opposed to leaving such questions unaddressed (Sunstein 2007).
3. Leonard (1984) presents a similar conceptualization of the dual roles of appellate courts. He terms these the "correctness" and "guidance" functions. Compared to this analysis, Leonard does not, however, view these goals as irreconcilable. Further, Leonard's discussion of the "correctness" function focuses less on conflict resolution between lower courts and more on accurate and just dispute resolution in specific cases.
4. All quoted primary source documents in this section can be found in Box 589 of Justice Harry Blackmun's papers, archived at the Library of Congress.
5. Preliminary memorandum dated February 22, 1991.
6. Memo dated January 28, 1992, from Blackmun to Scalia.
7. Memo dated April 29, 1992, from Scalia to Blackmun.
8. Memo dated May 4, 1992, from Blackmun to Scalia.
9. It is reasonable to guess that these memos were written by Ms. Stephanie Dangel, one of Blackmun's clerks during this term. Blackmun's archives on the *Burson* case cannot confirm that Ms. Dangel wrote these memos, however.
10. Memo from "Steff" to Blackmun dated April 29, 1992.

Chapter 2

1. Memorandum to the conference dated January 24, 1978. This memo and other primary sources in the case of Lockett v. Ohio can be found in Box 270 of Justice Harry Blackmun's papers, archived at the Library of Congress.

2. Memorandum to the conference dated June 9, 1978.

3. White would reverse the sentence on the grounds that the Ohio statute allowed a defendant convicted of murder to be sentenced to death without a finding that the defendant intended death to be the result. This rationale is independent from the analysis found in Justice Burger's opinion.

4. Memo dated June 20, 1978, from White to Burger.

5. For the mathematical notation behind these definitions, please refer to appendix A.

6. The logic of judgment aggregation has even been applied to nonhuman actors, notably by computer scientists (Pigozzi 2006).

7. Kornhauser and Sager (2004) and List (2006) variously contend that neither premise nor conclusion based rules should be followed mechanically. Rather, an aggregation rule should be chosen based on the particular needs of the decision problem at hand.

8. As well as the converse that regular concurrences are indeed instances where justices agree with all the majority's reasons and its outcome but wish to pile on in some way.

9. National Mutual Insurance v. Tidewater Transfer (337 U.S. 582 [1949]), Miller v. Albright (523 U.S. 420 [1998]), and Kassel v. Consolidated Freightways (450 U.S. 662 [1981]).

10. All cases that the coders did not find to be a doctrinal paradox are excluded from the analysis. Results are not sensitive to the inclusion or exclusion of these cases.

11. One coder was unable to complete her assigned portion of cases, hence the regrettably small overlap. The author independently coded thirty-one cases using the same protocol, finding 100 percent agreement with both research assistants.

12. Lauderdale and Clark (2012) show that the median justice of the Court at times depends on the substantive issue area of the case. However, prior work (Martin and Quinn 2001) also suggests that approximately 91 percent of the variance in justice voting is explained by a single ideological dimension, captured by the Martin–Quinn scores. The shifts in the median justice documented by Lauderdale and Clark (2012) indicate that this dominant dimension fails to predict voting in a particular issue area. This quantity—the breakdown of the unidimensional model—is also what the nonsingle-peaked variable used here aims to document.

13. Specifically, it is the maximum eigenvector centrality (Bonacich 2007) of an interest group participating in a given case. The network that this centrality is calculated from is the network of cosigners of *amicus* briefs at the Court in a given decade.

14. According to a Fisher's exact test and a test of proportions performed in Stata 14.1.

Chapter 3

1. Would Vice President Gore have won if the Court had ruled the other way and allowed the recounts to proceed? Payson-Denney (2015) summarizes some evidence on this point, mostly compiled by newspapers in the months after the election. While we can never know what would have happened if the recount process had continued, it does appear that if manual recounts of only undervotes (ballots with no candidate clearly chosen) went on in the entire state, as the Gore campaign wanted, Bush still would have won. However, a manual recount of both undervote and overvotes would have given the state and the presidency to Gore, although this strategy was not actively pursued by the Gore campaign (Payson-Denney 2015).

2. Specifically, Congress removed mandatory jurisdiction for appeals when federal courts held federal or state statutes unconstitutional, or when state courts held federal laws

invalid or state laws valid against a challenge under federal law; the 1988 legislation did not change mandatory appeals for reapportionment cases, cases under the Civil Rights and Voting Rights Acts, cases under antitrust laws, or cases under the Presidential Election Campaign Fund Act (Stern, Gressman, and Shapiro 1988).

3. Source: Preliminary hearings on the bill which would become the Supreme Court Case Selections Act of 1988, hearing ID HRG-1983-SJS-0075.

4. In fact, this alignment was the majority coalition in 2017's Cooper v. Harris (No. 15-1262, Slip Op.) ruling overturning the drawing of several North Carolina congressional districts due to racial bias. Contemporary media reports noted the disordered nature of the majority coalition (Liptak 2017, May 23).

5. Black and Bryan (2014) show that the conflict variable in the Spaeth database undercounts the true proportion of circuit conflicts affirmed by equally divided courts. Fortunately, none of the unreasoned judgments in the data (either as pluralities or opinions per curiam) were affirmed by equally divided courts, mitigating this issue.

6. I explore these ramifications of unreasoned judgment on lower courts fully in chapter 5.

7. I focus primarily on exercises of judicial review over Congress. The results below are, however, robust in considering all forms of judicial review, such as over state legislatures.

8. Visit http://scdb.wustl.edu/ for up-to-date data and documentation.

9. See http://epstein.wustl.edu/research/salience.html.

10. See http://mqscores.berkeley.edu/.

11. These marginal effects were obtained following the estimation of a logistic regression model in Stata 14.1, using the margins command. All other variables were held at their modal values for the estimation of marginal effects.

12. If this latter estimate seems high, recall that index values were set at the mode for these estimates. Since civil liberties cases are slightly more common in the data than all other issue areas (52 to 48 percent), this marginal effect estimate is for a civil liberties case that, among other things, does not exercise judicial review.

Chapter 4

1. This new attorney, Bertrand DeBlanc, was a friend of the murder victim. Moreover, he worked on almost nothing other than this case for close to a year with no payment. His primary reward seems to have been the scorn of his white peers in St. Martinville (Miller and Bowman 1982, 10).

2. Memo from Frankfurter to the Conference dated January 11, 1947. This memo, and other primary source materials for this case can be found in Box 157 of Justice Jackson's papers at the Library of Congress.

3. This tap dance around the question of incorporation in the plurality opinion appears to have been the result of maneuvering to keep Justice Black from abandoning the opinion and writing separately (Wiecek 2001, 64).

4. Although, it must be said Justice Frankfurter was not a particularly effusive friend. In introducing Mr. Lemann's letter to his brethren, Justice Frankfurter remarks: "Monte Lemann is, I suppose, unexcelled at the Louisiana Bar. He happens to be an old and close friend and so it is natural for him to send me the enclosure. I thought it might interest the

brethren. -F.F." (Memo to the Conference from Frankfurter dated April 23, 1947. Available in Box 157 of Justice Jackson's papers, Library of Congress).

5. They advise, variously, that the Court should adopt a premise-based judgment aggregation rule in some (Kornhauser and Sager 2004) or all (Pettit 2001) cases.

6. The October term of 1970 enjoys the dubious honor of presenting the highest rate of unreasoned judgment in the data.

7. According to a Spearman rank correlation analysis performed in Stata 14.1.

8. Specifically, Congress removed mandatory jurisdiction for appeals when federal courts held federal or state statutes unconstitutional or when state courts held federal laws invalid or state laws valid against a challenge under federal law; the 1988 legislation did not change mandatory appeals for reapportionment cases, cases under the Civil Rights and Voting Rights Act, cases under the antitrust laws, or cases under the Presidential Election Campaign Fund Act (Stern, Gressman, and Shapiro 1988).

9. Source: Preliminary hearings on the bill which would become the Supreme Court Case Selections Act of 1988, hearing ID HRG-1983-SJS-0075.

10. See http://www.scotusblog.com/wp-content/uploads/2016/06/SB_opinionsbysitting_OT15.pdf.

11. According to a Wilcoxon Rank-Sum test performed in Stata 14.1. The test is a simple nonparametric test, analogous to the more commonly used parametric t-test. The Wilcoxon is preferable for analytic situations such as these where the t-test's assumption of normality does not hold (Wilcoxon 1945).

12. Specifically, this trend line is a smoothed LOWESS line; it is a locally weighted nonparametric smoothed regression line that can be both nonlinear and nonmonotonic. That is, the trend does not have to increase or decrease at a constant linear rate, and the trend line points in either a positive or a negative at different points in time.

13. According to a Wilcoxon Rank-Sum test performed in Stata 14.1.

14. Again, according to a Wilcoxon Rank-Sum test.

15. This finding is largely, but not entirely, statistically robust to analyzing the manifestations of unreasoned judgment separately. The 1988 reforms are negatively and statistically significantly associated with the incidence of both plurality decisions and opinions per curiam, as well as the rate of opinions per curiam. The reforms are not, however, statistically significantly associated with the rate of plurality opinions.

16. Estimate obtained using the margins command in Stata 14.1. Index values set at the mean.

17. According to a Spearman rank correlation analysis performed in Stata 14.1.

18. According to a Wilcoxon Rank-Sum test performed in Stata 12.1.

19. However, much of the potential inconsistency of earlier periods in the Court's history may have been masked by norms of unanimity (Epstein, Segal, and Spaeth 2001; Leonard 1984). As such, unreasoned judgments in this period likely took the form of preference subordination quite often and would be difficult to measure in aggregate.

Chapter 5

1. Diversity jurisdiction may seem like a rather mundane right lacked by citizens residing in the District of Columbia. To put the broader lack of rights of these citizens in proper context, ask yourself: who are the voting members of Congress currently representing

the District of Columbia? Of course, there are none: "Taxation Without Representation" recently graced President Obama's license plates in the District (Craig 2013, January 15).

2. 28 U.S.C. §1332, subsection (e).

3. These notes, and other primary source documents on *Tidewater*, can be found in Box 150 of Justice Jackson's papers at the Library of Congress.

4. I followed a related but distinct line of inquiry on this question in Hitt (2016). There, I utilized a narrower conceptualization of inconsistency and considered the Supreme Court's treatment of precedents as well.

5. In Hitt (2016), I advocate aggregating by summing together a precedent's count of follows at each level after first standardizing these counts at each level. The aggregation is therefore a sum of two z-scores, one for each level. Here I utilize a simpler method, using the raw count for treatments at the district and circuit courts. Results are robust to using either the raw count or the aggregated z-scores; see appendix B.

6. See Hitt (2016) for an analysis of how this metric compares to other common techniques at the Supreme Court level.

7. Fortunately, the results I present below are robust to analyzing the district and circuit courts together or separately. The same empirical patterns persist at both lower levels.

8. Clark and Lauderdale (2012) build on Fowler et al.'s (2007) and Fowler and Jeon's (2008) work by weighting precedents based on how many times a given precedent is invoked in a single opinion. This work represents a sophisticated advance in the literature. As their measure is by definition highly correlated with that of Fowler and Jeon (2008) due to their shared basis on citation counts at the Supreme Court level (Clark and Lauderdale 2012, 346), I focus my discussion moreso on the Fowler et al. (2007) and Fowler and Jeon (2008) method for brevity and clarity.

9. Eigenvector centrality allows for "the centrality of a vertex [to be] proportional to the sum of the centralities of the vertices to which it is connected" (Bonacich 2007, 556). Basically, centrality depends on being connected to other well-connected entities in the network, not just having lots of connections generally.

10. E.g. Followed, Explained, Harmonized, Distinguished, Criticized, Limited, Questioned, Overruled.

11. According to data from Fowler and Jeon (2008).

12. As Corley and Wedeking (2014, 49) focus on linguistic style features, their analysis does not consider directly the clarity of doctrine itself.

13. Specifically, the *Twombly* Court "retired language from *Conley* and announced a new standard"(Hubbard 2013, 37).

14. These marginal effects were estimated using the margins command in Stata 14.1 Index values set at the mean for continuous variables and the mode for discrete and binary variables. Because of the issue area fixed effects in the model, this estimate is for criminal procedure cases (the modal category) only.

Chapter 6

1. Reid v. Covert was heard in consolidation with another very similar case, Kinsella v. Kruger. *Kinsella* also dealt with a military spouse's conviction by court-martial for murdering her husband while overseas.

2. Elliott (1958) also presents a case study of Court curbing in the mid-twentieth century.

3. The data are available at the Harvard Dataverse: https://dataverse.harvard.edu/dataset.xhtml?persistentId=hdl:1902.1/21230.

4. According the results of bivariate Wilcoxon rank-sum tests and Kolmogorov-Smirnov comparison of distribution tests performed in Stata 14.1. These results are also supported by multivariate time series analysis see appendix B.

5. Specifically, terms in the bottom, second, third, and highest quartiles of the rate of unreasoned judgments.

6. These results are robust to considering the raw frequency of unreasoned judgments instead of the rate.

7. According to a Kruskal–Wallis test performed in Stata 14.1, at the $\alpha = 0.05$ level.

Chapter 7

1. Justice Jackson's draft opinion and marginalia notes, along with other primary source material, can be found in Box 157 of Justice Jackson's papers at the Library of Congress.

2. A representative but not exhaustive sample of this literature would have to include Bartels and Johnston (2013); Benesh (2006); Caldeira and Gibson (1992); Gibson, Caldeira, and Baird (1998); Gibson, Caldeira, and Spence (2003*a*, 2005); Gibson and Caldeira (2009*a*,*b*, 2011); Gibson and Nelson 2015; and Nelson and Smith (2014).

3. This finding is conditional on the political salience of the issue. Coalition size and dissensus do little to impact specific support in highly salient cases, such as same-sex marriage.

4. Specifically, the first factor resulting from an iterated principal factor analysis performed on the polychoric correlation matrix (due to the discrete nature of these items) was used as the score for each of these latent variables. In both instances, the eigenvalue associated with this first factor was well above one, with no other factors above one. This result indicates that these sets of items suitably track the latent concept together (Kaiser 1960).

5. According to Kolmogorov-Smirnov comparison of distribution tests performed in Stata 12.1.

6. Moreover, Kruskal-Wallis tests (Kruskal and Wallis 1952) performed in Stata 14.1 confirm that there are no statistically significant differences between treatment and control groups.

7. As with the creation of the diffuse support and trust in government scales discussed, I used the first factor resulting from an iterated principal factor analysis performed on the polychoric correlation matrix as the score for each of these latent variables. It is necessary to use the polychoric correlation matrix due to the discrete nature of these items. For both knowledge scales, the eigenvalue associated with this first factor was well above one, with no other factors above one. As before, this result indicates that these sets of items suitably track the latent concept together (Kaiser 1960).

8. For this section, Kruskal-Wallis tests were employed to determine whether the value of the dependent variable differed significantly across one or more conditions (Kruskal and Wallis 1952). This test is a nonparametric comparison of medians test for more than two groups. Tests were performed using the kwallis command in Stata 14.1.

9. Which would happen if, hypothetically, higher knowledge subjects responded positively to a treatment and lower knowledge subjects responded negatively.

10. This effect is moderately large as Cohen's $d = 0.63$ (Cohen 1992).
11. Again, according to Kruskal-Wallis tests performed in Stata 14.1.
12. According to a χ^2 and Fisher's exact test for categorical data, performed in Stata 14.1.

Chapter 8

1. 582 U.S. ______ (Slip Op.), Trump v. International Refugee Assistance Project.
2. To be sure, the Court does not exist as a supreme arbiter above the rest of the government. The branches struggle against each other for influence, and the Court is no different (Chafetz 2017).
3. Brown v. Board of Education of Topeka, 347 U.S. 483 (1954).
4. See e.g., http://www.fjc.gov/history/caseload.nsf/.
5. For the eternal optimist, anyhow.

Appendix A

1. Read these connectives: not, and, or, implies.

Appendix B

1. These same tests showed that the rate of unreasoned judgment is approximately stationary; the estimated *d* for this series in table B.3 supports this conclusion as well. The rate of laws invalidated by the Court appears to be fractionally integrated as well. Therefore, I preprocessed this series to render it stationary. The divergence between the Court's aggregate liberalism and the public mood appears to be a unit root, according to these same tests. I therefore render this variable stationary by utilizing the first difference of this variable in the analysis to follow.

References

Abramowicz, Michael, and Maxwell L. Stearns. 2001. "Beyond Counting Votes: The Political Economy of Bush v. Gore." *Vanderbilt Law Review* 54(5):1849–1952.

Abramson, Paul R., John H. Aldrich, Paul Paolino, and David W. Rohde. 1992. "'Sophisticated' Voting in the 1988 Presidential Primaries." *American Political Science Review* 86(1):55–69.

Almasy, Steve, and Darran Simon. 2017, March 30. "A Timeline of President Trump's Travel Bans." CNN. Accessed April 18, 2018. https://www.cnn.com/2017/02/10/us/trump-travel-ban-timeline/index.html.

Archer, Susan Joan, and Adam Liptak. 2017. "Neil Gorsuch Confirmed by Senate as Supreme Court Justice." *The New York Times*, April 8. 2015, p. A1.

Arrow, Kenneth J. 1951. *Social Choice and Individual Values*. New Haven, CT: Yale University Press.

Atkinson, Scott E., Alan C. Marco, and John L. Turner. 2009. "The Economics of a Centralized Judiciary: Uniformity, Forum Shopping, and the Federal Circuit." *The Journal of Law and Economics* 52(3):411–43.

Bai, Jushan, and Pierre Perron. 1998. "Estimating and Testing Linear Models with Multiple Structural Changes." *Econometrica* 66(1):47–78.

Baird, Vanessa A., and Amy Gangl. 2006. "Shattering the Myth of Legality: The Impact of the Media's Framing of Supreme Court Procedures on Perceptions of Fairness." *Political Psychology* 27(4):597–614.

Bartels, Brandon L., and Christopher D. Johnston. 2013. "On the Ideological Foundations of Supreme Court Legitimacy in the American Public." *American Journal of Political Science* 57(1):184–99.

Bartels, Brandon L., Christopher D. Johnston, and Alyx Mark. 2015. "Lawyers' Perceptions of the U.S. Supreme Court: Is the Court a "Political" Institution?" *Law & Society Review* 49(3):761–94.

Baum, Lawrence. 1994. "What Judges Want: Judges' Goals and Judicial Behavior." *Political Research Quarterly* 47(3):749–68.

Baum, Lawrence. 2006. *Judges and Their Audiences: A Perspective on Judicial Behavior*. Princeton, NJ: Princeton University Press.

Beim, Deborah, Tom S. Clark, and John W. Patty. 2017. "Why Do Courts Delay?" *Journal of Law and Courts* 5(2):199–241.

Belton, Ian K., Mary Thomson, and Mandeep K. Dhami. 2014. "Lawyer and Nonlawyer Susceptibility to Framing Effects in Out-of-Court Civil Litigation Settlement." *Journal of Empirical Legal Studies* 11(3):578–600.

Benesh, Sara C. 2006. "Understanding Public Confidence in American Courts." *Journal of Politics* 68(3):697–707.

Bickel, Alexander M. 1962. *The Least Dangerous Branch: The Supreme Court at the Bar of Politics*. Indianapolis; New York: The Bobbs-Merrill Company.

Black, Duncan. 1948. "On the Rationale of Group Decision-Making." *Journal of Political Economy* 56:23–34.

Black, Ryan C. and Amanda C. Bryan. 2014. "Explaining the (non) Occurrence of Equal Divisions on the U.S. Supreme Court." *American Politics Research* 42(6):1077–95.

Black, Ryan C., and James F. Spriggs. 2013. "The Citation and Depreciation of U.S. Supreme Court Precedent." *Journal of Empirical Legal Studies* 10(2):325–58.

Black, Ryan C., Maron W. Sorenson, and Timothy R. Johnson. 2013. "Toward an Actor-Based Measure of Supreme Court Case Salience: Information-Seeking and Engagement during Oral Arguments." *Political Research Quarterly* 66(4):804–18.

Black, Ryan C., and Ryan J. Owens. 2009. "Agenda Setting in the Supreme Court: The Collision of Policy and Jurisprudence." *The Journal of Politics* 71(3):1062–75.

Black, Ryan C., and Ryan J. Owens. 2016. "Courting the President: How Circuit Court Judges Alter Their Behavior for Promotion to the Supreme Court." *American Journal of Political Science* 60(1):30–43.

Blake, William D., Hans J. Hacker, and Shon J. Hopwood. 2015. "Season Affective Disorder: Clerk Training and the Success of Supreme Court *Certiorari* Petitions." *Law & Society Review* 49(4):973–97.

Bonacich, Phillip. 2007. "Some Unique Properties of Eigenvector Centrality." *Social Networks* 29:555–64.

Bonnefon, Jean-Francois. 2011. "The Doctrinal Paradox, a New Challenge for Behavioral Psychologists." *Advances in Psychological Science* 19(5):617–23.

Bovens, Luc, and Wlodek Rabinowicz. 2006. "Democractic Answers to Complex Questions—an Epistemic Perspective." *Synthese* 150:131–53.

Bowie, Jennifer Barnes, and Donald R. Songer. 2009. "Assessing the Applicability of Strategic Theory to Explain Decision Making on the Courts of Appeals." *Political Research Quarterly* 62(2):393–407.

Box-Steffensmeier, Janet M., and Agnar Freyr Helgason. 2016. "Introduction to Symposium on Time Series Error Correction Methods in Political Science." *Political Analysis* 24(1):1–2.

Box-Steffensmeier, Janet M., Dino P. Christenson, and Matthew P. Hitt. 2013. "Quality over Quantity: Amici Influence and Judicial Decision Making." *American Political Science Review* 107(3):446–60.

Box-Steffensmeier, Janet M., John R. Freeman, Matthew P. Hitt, and Jon C. Pevehouse. 2014. *Time Series Analysis for the Social Sciences*. New York: Cambridge University Press.

Brady, Henry E., Michael C. Herron, Walter R. Mebane, Jasjeet Singh Sekhon, Kenneth W. Shotts, and Jonathan Wand. 2001. "Law and Data: The Butterfly Ballot Episode." *PS: Political Science and Politics* 34(1):59–69.

Braman, Eileen. 2006. "Reasoning on the Threshold: Testing the Separability of Preferences in Legal Decision Making." *The Journal of Politics* 68(2):308–21.

Brennan, Geoffrey. 2001. "Collective Coherence?" *International Review of Law and Economics* 21:197–211.

Breyer, Stephen. 1988. "The Federal Sentencing Guidelines and the Key Compromises upon Which They Rest." *Hofstra Law Review* 17(1):1–50.

Brief For Respondents City of Chicago and Village of Oak Park, Otis McDonald et al. v. City of Chicago. 2010. American Bar Association Supreme Court Preview. 561 U.S. 742, no. 08-1521.

Budziak, Jeffrey. 2013. "Blind Justice or Blind Ambition? The Influence of Promotion on Decision Making in the U.S. Courts of Appeals." *Justice System Journal* 34(3):295–320.

Bueno De Mesquita, Ethan, and Matthew Stephenson. 2002. "Informative Precedent and Intrajudicial Communication." *American Political Science Review* 96(4): 755–66.

Caldeira, Gregory A. 1987. "Public Opinion and the U.S. Supreme Court: FDR's Court Packing Plan." *American Political Science Review* 81(4):1139–53.

Caldeira, Gregory A., and James L. Gibson. 1992. "The Etiology of Public Support for the Supreme Court." *American Journal of Political Science* 36(3):635–64.

Caldeira, Gregory A., John R. Wright, and Christopher J.W. Zorn. 1999. "Sophisticated Voting and Gate-Keeping in the Supreme Court." *Journal of Law, Economics, and Organization* 15(3):549–72.

Cameron, A. Colin, and Pravin K. Trivedi. 2005. *Microeconometrics: Methods and Applications*. New York: Cambridge University Press.

Caporale, Tony, and Kevin Grier. 2005. "How Smart Is my Dummy? Time Series Tests for the Influence of Politics." *Political Analysis* 13(1):77–94.

Carpini, Michael X. Delli, and Scott Keeter. 1996. *What Americans Know About Politics and Why It Matters*. New Haven, CT: Yale University Press.

Carrubba, Cliff, Barry Friedman, Andrew D. Martin, and Georg Vanberg. 2012. "Who Controls the Content of Supreme Court Opinions?" *American Journal of Political Science* 56(2):400–412.

Chafetz, Josh. 2017. *Congress's Constitution: Legislative Authority and the Separation of Powers*. New Haven, CT: Yale University Press.

Chapman, Bruce. 1998. "More Easily Done Than Said: Rules, Reasons and Rational Social Choice." *Oxford Journal of Legal Studies* 18(2):293–329.

Chilton, Adam, and Dustin Tingley. 2012. "The Doctrinal Paradox & International Law." *Journal of International Law* 34(1):67–81.

Choi, Stephen J., and Mitu Gulati. 2008. "Bias in Judicial Citations: A Window into the Behavior of Judges?" *The Journal of Legal Studies* 37(1):87–129.

Choi, Stephen J., Mitu Gulati, and Eric A. Posner. 2012. "What Do Federal District Judges Want? An Analysis of Publications, Citations, and Reversals." *Journal of Law, Economics, and Organization* 28(3):518–49.

Christenson, Dino P., and David M. Glick. 2015. "Chief Justice Roberts's Health Care Decision Disrobed: The Microfoundations of the Supreme Court's Legitimacy." *American Journal of Political Science* 59(2):403–18.

Christiansen, Matthew R., and William N. Eskridge Jr. 2014. "Congressional Overrides of Supreme Court Statutory Interpretation Decisions, 1967–2011." *Texas Law Review* 92(6):1317–541.

Clark, Thomas S. 2011. *The Limits of Judicial Independence.* New York: Cambridge University Press.

Clark, Tom S. 2009. "The Separation of Powers, Court Curbing, and Judicial Legitimacy." *American Journal of Political Science* 53(4):971–89.

Clark, Tom S., and Benjamin E. Lauderdale. 2012. "The Geneaology of Law." *Political Analysis* 20(3):329–50.

Clark, Tom S., and Clifford J. Carrubba. 2012. "A Theory of Opinion Writing in a Political Hierarchy." *The Journal of Politics* 74(2):584–603.

Clark, Tom S., Jeffrey R. Lax, and Douglas Rice. 2015. "Measuring the Political Salience of Supreme Court Cases." *Journal of Law and Courts* 3(1):37–65.

Clark, Tom S., and Jonathon P. Kastellec. 2013. "The Supreme Court and Percolation in the Lower Courts: An Optimal Stopping Model." *The Journal of Politics* 75(1):150–68.

Claussen, Carl Andreas, and Oinstein Roisland. 2010. "The Discursive Dilemma in Monetary Policy." *Sveriges Riksbank Working Paper Series* (240).

Cohen, David S., and Maxwell Stearns. 2010. "McDonald Typifies Need For Consensus." *The National Law Journal* 32(44). https://www.law.com/nationallawjournal/almID/1202463394661/-typifies-need-for-consensus/.

Cohen, Jacob. 1992. "A Power Primer." *Psychological Bulletin* 112(1):155.

Collins, Todd A., and Christopher A. Cooper. 2012. "Case Salience and Media Coverage of Supreme Court Decisions: Toward a New Measure." *Political Research Quarterly* 65(2):396–407.

Corley, Pamela C. 2009. "Uncertain Precedent: Circuit Court Responses to Supreme Court Plurality Opinions." *American Politics Research* 37(1):30–49.

Corley, Pamela C., Amy Steigerwalt, and Artemus Ward. 2013. *The Puzzle of Unanimity: Consensus on the United States Supreme Court.* Redwood City, CA: Stanford University Press.

Corley, Pamela C., Udi Sommer, Amy Steigerwalt, and Artemus Ward. 2010. "Extreme Dissensus: Explaining Plurality Decisions on the United States Supreme Court." *The Justice System Journal* 31(2):180–200.

Corley, Pamela, and Justin Wedeking. 2014. "The (Dis)Advantage of Certainty: The Importance of Certainty in Language." *Law & Society Review* 48(1):35–62.

Craig, Tim. 2013, January 15. "Obama to Use D.C. 'Taxation Without Representation' License Plates." *The Washington Post* . Accessed June 28, 2017. https://www.washingtonpost.com/local/dc-politics/obama-to-use-dc-taxation-without-representation-license-plates/2013/01/15/f91b09ac-5f5b-11e2-9940-6fc488f3fecd_story.html?utm_term=.db673ac8d423.

Curtis, Charles P. 1949. "A Better Theory of Legal Interpretation." *Vanderbilt Law Review* 3:407–37.

Dahl, Robert A. 1957. "Decision-Making in a Democracy: The Supreme Court as a National Policy-Maker." *Journal of Public Law* 6:279–95.

De Boef, Suzanna, and Luke Keele. 2008. "Taking Time Seriously." *American Journal of Political Science* 52(1):184–200.

Diermeier, Daniel, and Keith Krehbiel. 2003. "Institutionalism as a Methodology." *Journal of Theoretical Politics* 15(2):123–44.

Dietrich, Franz. 2006. "Judgment Aggregation: (im)Possibility Theorems." *Journal of Economic Theory* 126:286–98.

Dreyfuss, Ben. 2017, January 29. "Across the Country, Thousands Protest Trump's "Muslim Ban." *Mother Jones* . Accessed June 27, 2017. http://www.motherjones.com/politics/2017/01/sunday-protests-trump-muslim-ban/

Durr, Robert H., Andrew D. Martin, and Christina Wolbrecht. 2000. "Ideological Divergence and Public Support for the Supreme Court." *American Journal of Political Science* 44(1):768–76.

Easterbrook, Frank H. 1982. "Ways of Critcizing the Court." *Harvard Law Review* 95(4):802–32.

Easton, David O. 1965. *A Systems Analysis of Political Life*. New York: John Wiley & Sons.

Edelman, Paul H., David E. Klein, and Stefanie A. Lindquist. 2008. "Measuring Deviations from Expected Voting Patterns on Collegial Courts." *Journal of Empirical Legal Studies* 5(4):819–52.

Edelman, Paul H., David E. Klein, and Stefanie A. Lindquist. 2012. "Consensus, Disorder, and Ideology on the Supreme Court." *Journal of Empirical Legal Studies* 9(1):129–48.

Elliott, Shelden D. 1958. "Court-Curbing Proposals in Congress." *Notre Dame Law Review* 33:597–616.

Epstein, Lee, and Jack Knight. 1998. *The Choices Justices Make*. Washington, DC: CQ Press.

Epstein, Lee, and Jack Knight. 2013. "Reconsidering Judicial Preferences." *Annual Review of Political Science* 16:11–31.

Epstein, Lee, and Jeffrey A. Segal. 2000. "Measuring Issue Salience." *American Journal of Political Science* 44(1):66–83.

Epstein, Lee, Jeffrey A. Segal, and Harold J. Spaeth. 2001. "The Norm of Consensus on the U.S. Supreme Court." *American Journal of Political Science* 45(2):362–77.

Epstein, Lee, Jeffrey A. Segal, Harold J. Spaeth, and Thomas G. Walker. 2012. *The Supreme Court Compendium*. 5th ed. Washington, DC: CQ Press.

Farganis, Dion. 2012. "Do Reasons Matter? The Impact of Opinion Content on Supreme Court Legitimacy." *Political Research Quarterly* 65(1):206–16.

Flanders, Chad W. 2009, July 15. "Sotomayor and the Art of the Judicial Deal." *Saint Louis Post-Dispatch*, p. A13.

Fowler, James H., and Sangick Jeon. 2008. "The Authority of Supreme Court Precedent." *Social Networks* 30:16–30.

Fowler, James H., Timothy R. Johnson, James F. Spriggs, Sangick Jeon, and Paul J. Wahlbeck. 2007. "Network Analysis and the Law: Measuring the Legal Importance of Precedents at the U.S. Supreme Court." *Political Analysis* 15:324–46.

Frankfurter, Felix, and James M. Landis. 1928. *The Business of the Supreme Court: A Study in the Federal Judicial System*. New York: The MacMillan Company.

Friedman, Barry. 2002. "The Birth of an Academic Obsession: The History of the Countermajoritarian Difficulty, Part Five." *Yale Law Journal* 112(2):153–259.

Friedman, Lawrence M. 2005. *A History of American Law*. 3rd ed. New York: Simon and Shuster.

Gallagher, Ryan J., Andrew J. Reagan, Christopher M. Danforth, and Peter Sheridan Dodds. 2016. "Divergent Discourse Between Protests and Counter-Protests: #BlackLivesMatter and #AllLivesMatter." Accessed November 27, 2018. http://arxiv.org/abs/1606.06820

Gelman, Andrew, and Eric Loken. 2014. "The Statistical Crisis in Science Data-dependent Analysis—a "Garden of Forking Paths"—Explains Why Many Statistically Significant Comparisons Don't Hold Up." *American Scientist* 102(6):460.

George, Tracey E., and Chris Guthrie. 2009. "Remaking the United States Supreme Court in the Courts' of Appeals Image." *Duke Law Journal* 58(7):1439–75.

Gibbard, Allan. 1973. "Manipulation of Voting Schemes: A General Result." *Econometrica* 41(4):587–601.

Gibson, James L., and Gregory A. Caldeira. 2009*a*. *Citizens, Courts, and Confirmations: Positivity Theory and the Judgments of the American People*. Princeton, NJ: Princeton University Press.

Gibson, James L., and Gregory A. Caldeira. 2009*b*. "Confirmation Politics and the Legitimacy of the US Supreme Court: Institutional Loyalty, Positivity Bias, and the Alito Nomination." *American Journal of Political Science* 53(1):139–55.

Gibson, James L., and Gregory A. Caldeira. 2011. "Has Legal Realism Damaged the Legitimacy of the U.S. Supreme Court?" *Law and Society Review* 45(1):195–219.

Gibson, James L., Gregory A. Caldeira, and Lester Kenyatta Spence. 2003*a*. "Measuring Attitudes toward the United States Supreme Court." *American Journal of Political Science* 47(2):354–367.

Gibson, James L., Gregory A. Caldeira, and Lester Kenyatta Spence. 2003*b*. "The Supreme Court and the U.S. Presidential Election of 2000: Wounds, Self-Inflicted or Otherwise?" *British Journal of Political Science* 33(4):535–56.

Gibson, James L., Gregory A. Caldeira, and Lester Kenyatta Spence. 2005. "Why Do People Accept Public Policies They Oppose? Testing Legitimacy Theory with a Survey-Based Experiment." *Political Research Quarterly* 58(2):187–201.

Gibson, James L., Gregory A. Caldeira, and Vanessa A. Baird. 1998. "On the Legitimacy of National High Courts." *American Political Science Review* 92(2):343–58.

Gibson, James L., and Michael J. Nelson. 2015. "Is the U.S. Supreme Court's Legitimacy Grounded in Performance Satisfaction and Ideology?" *American Journal of Political Science* 59(1):162–74.

Gibson, James L., and Michael J. Nelson. 2017. "Reconsidering Positivity Theory: What Roles do Politicization, Ideological Disagreement, and Legal Realism Play in Shaping U.S. Supreme Court Legitimacy?" *Journal of Empirical Legal Studies* 14(3):592–617.

Gibson, James L., Milton Lodge, and Benjamin Woodson. 2014. "Losing, but Accepting: Legitimacy, Positivity Theory, and the Symbols of Judicial Authority." *Law & Society Review* 48(4):837–66.

Gizzi, Michael C., and Stephen L. Wasby. 2012. "Per Curiams Revisited: Assessing the Unsigned Opinion." *Judicature* 96(3):110–18.

Grant, Taylor, and Matthew J. Lebo. 2016. "Error Correction Methods with Political Time Series." *Political Analysis* 24(1):3–30.

Hainmueller, Jens, Jonathan Mummolo, and Yiqing Xu. 2017. "How Much Should We Trust Estimates from Multiplicative Interaction Models? Simple Tools to Improve Empirical Practice." Accessed November 27, 2018. https://www. researchgate.net/profile/Jens_Hainmueller/publication/315530437_How_Much_Should_We_Trust_Estimates_from_Multiplicative_Interaction_Models_Simple_ Tools_to_Improve_Empirical_Practice/links/59c28f1aaca272295a0deccf/How-Much-Should-We-Trust-Estimates-from-Multiplicative-Interaction-Models-Simple-Tools-to-Improve-Empirical-Practice.pdf

Hall, Matthew E.K. 2010. *The Nature of Supreme Court Power*. New York: Cambridge University Press.

Hall, Matthew E.K., and Joseph Daniel Ura. 2015. "Judicial Majoritarianism." *The Journal of Politics* 77(3):818–32.

Hamilton, Alexander, James Madison, and John Jay. 2008. *The Federalist Papers*. New York: Oxford University Press.

Hansford, Thomas G., and James F. Spriggs. 2006. *The Politics of Precedent on the U.S. Supreme Court*. Princeton, NJ: Princeton University Press.

Hasen, Richard L. 2004. "A Critical Guide to *Bush v. Gore* Scholarship." *Annual Review of Political Science* 7:297–313.

Hellman, Arthur D. 1995. "By Precedent Unbound: The Nature and Extent of Unresolved Intercircuit Conficts." *University of Pittsburgh Law Review* 56:693–800.

Hertz, Randy, and Robert Weisberg. 1981. "In Mitigation of the Penalty of Death: *Lockett v. Ohio* and the Capital Defendant's Right to Consideration of Mitigating Circumstances." *California Law Review* 69(2):317–76.

Hitt, Matthew P. 2016. "Measuring Precedent in a Judicial Hierarchy." *Law & Society Review* 50(1):57–81.

Hornsby, D. Brock. 2007. "The Business of the U.S. District Courts." *The Green Bag* 10(4):453–68.

Hubbard, William H.J. 2013. "Testing for Change in Procedural Standards, with Application to *Bell Atlantic v. Twombly*." *Journal of Legal Studies* 42(1):35–68.

Huston, Luther A. 1956, June 24. "Military Upheld on Civilian Trial." *New York Times*, p. 24.

Johnson, Jenna. 2015, December 7. "Trump Calls for 'Total and Complete Shutdown of Muslims Entering the United States'." *The Washington Post* . Accessed June 26, 2017. https://www.washingtonpost.com/news/post-politics/wp/2015/12/07/donald-trump-calls-for-total-and-complete-shutdown-of-muslims-entering-the-united-states/?utm_term=.a9221589dc06

Kaiser, Henry F. 1960. "The Application of Electronic Computers to Factor Analysis." *Educational and Psychological Measurement* 20(1):141–51.

Keele, Luke. 2007. "Social Capital and the Dynamics of Trust in Government." *American Journal of Political Science* 51(2):241–54.

Keele, Luke, and Nathan J. Kelly. 2006. "Dynamic Models for Dynamic Theories: The Ins and Outs of Lagged Dependent Variables." *Political Analysis* 14(2):186–205.

Keele, Luke, Suzanna Linn, and Clayton McLaughlin Webb. 2016. "Treating Time with All Due Seriousness." *Political Analysis* 24(1):31–41.

Kelsh, John P. 1999. "The Opinion Delivery Practices of the United States Supreme Court 1790–1945." *Washington University Law Quarterly* 77:137–81.

King, Gary, and Langche Zeng. 2001. "Logistic Regression in Rare Events Data." *Political Analysis* 9(2):137–63.

King, Gilbert. 2008. *The Execution of Willie Francis: Race, Murder, and the Search for Justice in the American South*. New York: Basic Civitas Books.

Kleinberg, Jon M. 1999. "Authoritative Sources in a Hyperlinked Environment." *Journal of the ACM* 46(5):604–32.

Kleiner, Andreas, and Benny Moldovanu. 2017. "Content-Based Agendas and Qualified Majorities in Sequential Voting." *American Economic Review* 107(6):1477–506.

Kornhauser, Lewis A., and Lawrence G. Sager. 1986. "Unpacking the Court." *The Yale Law Journal* 96(1):82–117.

Kornhauser, Lewis A., and Lawrence G. Sager. 2004. "The Many as One: Integrity and Group Choice in Paradoxical Cases." *Philosophy and Public Affairs* 32(3): 249–76.

Kruskal, William H., and W. Allen Wallis. 1952. "Use of Ranks in One-criterion Variance Analysis." *Journal of the American Statistical Association* 47(260):583–621.

Landa, Dimitri, and Jeffrey R. Lax. 2009. "Legal Doctrine on Collegial Courts." *The Journal of Politics* 71(3):946–63.

Landes, William M., and Richard A. Posner. 1976. "Legal Precedent: A Theoretical and Empirical Analysis." *Journal of Law and Economics* 19(2):249–307.

Lauderdale, Benjamin E., and Tom S. Clark. 2012. "The Supreme Court's Many Median Justices." *American Political Science Review* 106(4):847–66.

Lax, Jeffrey R. 2007. "Constructing Legal Rules on Appellate Courts." *American Political Science Review* 101(3):591–604.

Lax, Jeffrey R., and Charles M. Cameron. 2007. "Bargaining and Opinion Assignment on the U.S. Supreme Court." *Journal of Law, Economics, and Organization* 23(2):276–302.

Lax, Jeffrey R., and Dimitri Landa. 2009. "Legal Doctrine on Collegial Courts." *The Journal of Politics* 71(3):946–63.

Lax, Jeffrey R., and Kelly T. Rader. 2010. "Legal Constraints on Supreme Court Decision Making: Do Jurisprudential Regimes Exist?" *The Journal of Politics* 72(2):273–84.

Le Sueur, Andrew. 2008. "A Report on Six Seminars about the UK Supreme Court." *Queen Mary School of Law Legal Studies Research Paper* (1).

Lebo, Matthew J., Robert W. Walker, and Harold D. Clarke. 2000. "You Must Remember This: Dealing with Long Memory in Political Analysis." *Electoral Studies* 19(1):31–48.

Leonard, David P. 1984. "The Correctness Function of Appellate Decision-Making: Judicial Obligation in an Era of Fragmentation." *Loyola of Los Angeles Review* 17:299–352.

Levi, Edward H. 1948. "An Introduction to Legal Reasoning." *University of Chicago Law Review* 15(3):501–74.

Levmore, Saul. 1989. "Parlimentary Law, Majority Decisionmaking and the Voting Paradox." *Virginia Law Review* 75(5):971–1044.

Lindquist, Stefanie A., and David E. Klein. 2006. "The Influence of Jurisprudential Considerations on Supreme Court Decisionmaking: A Study of Conflict Cases." *Law and Society Review* 40(1):135–62.

Liptak, Adam. 2010, January 28. "Supreme Court Gets a Rare Rebuke, in Front of a Nation." *New York Times*, p. A12.

Liptak, Adam. 2017, May 23. "Justices Reject 2 Gerrymandered North Carolina Districts, Citing Racial Bias." *New York Times*, p. A18.

List, Christian. 2003. "A Possibility Theorem on Aggregation over Multiple Interconnected Propositions." *Mathematical Social Sciences* 45(1):1–13.

List, Christian. 2005. "The Probability of Inconsistencies in Complex Collective Decisions." *Social Choice and Welfare* 24(1):3–32.

List, Christian. 2006. "The Discursive Dilemma and Public Reason." *Ethics* 116(2):362–402.

List, Christian. 2012. "The Theory of Judgment Aggregation: An Introductory Review." *Synthese* 187(1):179–207.

List, Christian, and Philip Pettit. 2002. "Aggregating Sets of Judgements: An Impossibility Result." *Economics and Philosophy* 18(1):89–110.

List, Christian, and Philip Pettit. 2004. "Aggregating Sets of Judgments: Two Impossibility Results Compared." *Synthese* 140(1):207–35.

Lupia, Arthur. 2015. *Uninformed: Why People Seem to Know So Little About Politics and What We Can Do about It.* New York: Oxford University Press.

Lyall, Sarah. 2017, February 19. "For Garland, No Lamenting a Lost Seat." *The New York Times*, p. A1.

Maltz, Earl. 1987. "The Nature of Precedent." *North Carolina Law Review* 66:367–93.

Maltzman, Forrest, Alyx Mark, Charles R. Shipan, and Michael A. Zilis. 2014. "Stepping on Congress: Courts, Congress, and Interinstitutional Politics." *Journal of Law and Courts* 2(2):219–40.

Maltzman, Forrest, James F. Spriggs, and Paul J. Wahlbeck. 2000. *Crafting Law on the Supreme Court: The Collegial Game.* New York: Cambridge University Press.

Martin, Andrew D., and Kevin M. Quinn. 2001. "Estimating Latent Structures of Voting for Micro-Committees, with Application to the U.S. Supreme Court." Paper presented at the Annual Meeting of the Midwest Political Science Association, April 19–22, Chicago, IL.

Martin, Andrew D., and Kevin M. Quinn. 2002. "Dynamic Ideal Point Estimation via Markov Chain Monte Carlo for the U.S. Supreme Court 1953–1999." *Political Analysis* 10(2):134–53.

McAleer, David. 2013. "*United States v. Duvall:* Splintered Decisions and the Narrowest Grounds Interpretation." *American Criminal Law Review.* Accessed June 30, 2017. http://www.americancriminallawreview.com/aclr-online/united-states-v-duvall-splintered-decisions-and-narrowest-grounds-interpretation/

McGuire, William J. 1960. "Cognitive Consistency and Attitude Change." *Journal of Abnormal and Social Psychology* 60(3):345–53.

McKelvey, Richard D. 1976. "Intransitivities in Multidimensional Voting Models and Some Implications for Agenda Control." *Journal of Economic Theory* 12(3):472–82.

Mérola, Vittorio, and Matthew P. Hitt. 2016. "Numeracy and the Persuasive Effect of Policy Information and Party Cues." *Public Opinion Quarterly* 80(2):554–62.

Miller, Arthur S., and Jeffrey H. Bowman. 1982. "Slow Dance on the Killing Ground: The Willie Francis Case Revisited." *DePaul Law Review* 32(1):1–75.

Miller, Joanne M., Kyle L. Saunders, and Christina E. Farhart. 2016. "Conspiracy Endorsement as Motivated Reasoning: The Moderating Roles of Political Knowledge and Trust." *American Journal of Political Science* 60(4):824–44.

Moorhead, Thomas B. 1960. "Reid v. Covert and Its Progeny: The Practical Problem of Punishment." *Syracuse Law Review* 12:18–25.

Murphy, Walter F. 1964. *Elements of Judicial Strategy*. Chicago, IL: University of Chicago Press.

Nash, Jonathon R. 2003. "A Context-Sensitive Voting Protocol Paradigm for Multimember Courts." *Stanford Law Review* 56(1):75–159.

Nash, Jonathon R. 2017, February 9. "Trump is not the First President to Criticize Judiciary." Accessed November 27, 2018. https://thehill.com/blogs/pundits-blog/the-judiciary/318783-trump-is-not-the-first-president-to-criticize-judiciary

Nelson, Michael J., and Steven S. Smith. 2014. "Change and Stability in Diffuse Support for the Supreme Court." Working paper. Accessed November 27, 2018. http://mjnelson.org/papers/HCLegi t.pdf.

Owens, Ryan J., and David A. Simon. 2012. "Explaining the Supreme Court's Shrinking Docket." *William and Mary Law Review* 53(4):1219–85.

Paterson, Alan. 2013. *Final Judgment. The Last Law Lords and the Supreme Court*. Oxford: Hart.

Patty, John R., and Elizabeth Maggie Penn. 2014. *Social Choice and Legitimacy: The Possibilities of Impossibility*. New York: Cambridge University Press.

Patty, John W., Elizabeth M. Penn, and Keith E. Schnakenberg. 2013. "Measuring the Latent Quality of Precedent: Scoring Vertices in a Network." In *Advances in Political Economy*, edited by Norman Schofield, Gonzalo Caballero, and Daniel Kselman, 249–62. Berlin: Springer-Verlag.

Paulsen, Monrad G. 1954. "The Fourteenth Amendment and the Third Degree." *Stanford Law Review* 6:411–37.

Pauly, Marc, and Martin Van Hees. 2006. "Logical Constraints on Judgement Aggregation." *Journal of Philosophical Logic* 35:569–85.

Payson-Denney, Wade. 2015. "So, Who Really Won? What the *Bush v. Gore* Studies Showed." *CNN*. Accessed June 17, 2017. http://www.cnn.com/2015/10/31/politics/bush-gore-2000-election-results-studies/index.html.

Perry, H.W. 1991. *Deciding to Decide: Agenda Setting in the United States Supreme Court*. Cambridge, MA: Harvard University Press.

Pettit, Philip. 2001. "Deliberative Democracy and the Discursive Dilemma." *Philosophical Issues* 11(1):268–99.

Pigozzi, Gabriella. 2006. "Belief Merging and the Discursive Dilemma: An Argument-Based Account to Paradoxes of Judgment Aggregation." *Synthese* 152(2):285–98.

Pinello, Daniel R. 1999. "Linking Party to Judicial Ideology in American Courts: A Meta-analysis." *Justice System Journal* 20(3):219–54.

Post, David, and Steven C. Salop. 1992. "Rowing Against the Tidewater: A Theory of Voting by Multijudge Panels." *The Georgetown Law Journal* 80(3):743–74.

Poznyak, Dmitriy, Bart Meuleman, Koen Abts, and George F. Bishop. 2014. "Trust in American Government: Longitudinal Measurement Equivalence in the ANES, 1964–2008." *Social Indicators Research* 118(2):741–58.

R Core Team. 2014. *R: A Language and Environment for Statistical Computing*. Vienna, Austria: R Foundation for Statistical Computing. http://www.R-project.org/

Randazzo, Kirk A. 2008. "Strategic Anticipation and the Hierarchy of Justice in U.S. District Courts." *American Politics Research* 36(5):669–93.

Raustiala, Kal. 2007, June 9. "Bill of Rights Without Borders." *Los Angeles Times*. Accessed June 27, 2017. http://articles.latimes.com/2007/jun/09/opinion/oe-raustiala9

Ray, Laura Krugman. 2000. "The Road to Bush v. Gore: The History of the Supreme Court's Use of the Per Curiam Opinion." *Nebraska Law Review* 79:517–76.

Rentsch, Julia. 2017, January 31. "Ph.D. Student Stranded in Airport with Baby Following Executive Order Deported Back to Libya, Still Barred from U.S." *The Rocky Mountain Collegian*. Accessed June 27, 2017. https://collegian.com/2017/01/ph-d-student-stranded-in-jordan-airport-with-baby-following-executive-order/

Riker, William. 1982. *Liberalism Against Populism: A Confrontation Between the Theory of Social Democracy and the Theory of Social Choice*. San Francisco, CA: WH Freeman.

Rogers, John M. 1991. "I Vote This Way Because I'm Wrong: The Supreme Court Justice as Epimenides." *Kentucky Law Journal* 79(3):439–75.

Rosenberg, Gerald. 1990. *The Hollow Hope: Can Courts Bring About Social Change?* Chicago: The University of Chicago Press.

Rostow, Eugene V. 1952. "The Democratic Character of Judicial Review." *Harvard Law Review* 66(2):193–224.

Salamone, Michael F. 2014. "Judicial Consensus and Public Opinion: Conditional Response to Supreme Court Majority Size." *Political Research Quarterly* 67(2):320–34.

Satterthwaite, Mark Allen. 1975. "Strategy-proofness and Arrow's Conditions: Existence and Correspondence Theorems for Voting Procedures and Social Welfare Functions." *Journal of Economic Theory* 10(2):187–217.

Scalia, Antonin. 1989. "The Rule of Law as a Law of Rules." *The University of Chicago Law Review* 56(4):1175–88.

Schattschneider, E.E. 1960. *The Semi-Sovereign People: A Realist's View of Democracy in America*. New York: Holt, Rinehart, and Winston.

Schauer, Frederick. 1987. "Precedent." *Stanford Law Review* 37:571–605.

Schurr, Richard A. 1994. "Burson v. Freeman: Where the Right to Vote Intersects with the Freedom to Speak." *Whittier L. Rev.* 15:869–920.

Segal, Jeffrey A., and Harold J. Spaeth. 1993. *The Supreme Court and the Attitudinal Model*. New York: Cambridge University Press.

Segal, Jeffrey A., and Harold J. Spaeth. 1996. "The Influence of Stare Decisis on the Votes of United States Supreme Court Justices." *American Journal of Political Science* 40(4):971–1003.

Segal, Jeffrey A., and Harold J. Spaeth. 2002. *The Supreme Court and the Attitudinal Model Revisited*. Cambridge University Press.

Shapiro, Carolyn. 2006. "The Limits of the Olympian Court: Common Law Judging Versus Error Correction in the Supreme Court." *Washington & Lee Law Review* 63:271–337.

Shapiro, Carolyn. 2009. "Coding Complexity: Bringing Law to the Empirical Analysis of the Supreme Court." *Hastings Law Journal* 60(3):478–540.

Shepsle, Kenneth A., and Barry R. Weingast. 1981. "Structure Induced Equilibrium and Legislative Choice." *Public Choice* 37(3):503–19.

Silver, Nate. 2012. "Poll Averages Have No History of Consistent Partisan Bias." *FiveThirtyEight*. Accessed June 17, 2017. https://fivethirtyeight.com/features/poll-averages-have-no-history-of-consistent-partisan-bias/

Specter, Arlen. 2010. "Letter to the Honorable Elena Kagan, Solicitor General of the United States." Accessed February 21, 2014. http://votesmart.org/public-statement/520457/letter-to-the-honorable-elena-kagan-solicitor-general-of-the-united-states.

Spill, Rorie L., and Zoe M. Oxley. 2003. "Philosopher Kings or Political Actors—How the Media Portray the Supreme Court." *Judicature* 87(1):22–29.

Spriggs, James F., and Thomas G. Hansford. 2000. "Measuring Legal Change: The Reliability and Validity of Shepard's Citations." *Political Research Quarterly* 53(2):327–41.

Spriggs, James F., and Thomas G. Hansford. 2001*a*. "Explaining the Overruling of U.S. Supreme Court Precedent." *The Journal of Politics* 63(4):1091–111.

Spriggs, James F. and Thomas G. Hansford. 2001*b*. "The U.S. Supreme Court's Incorporation and Interpretation of Precedent." *Law and Society Review* 36(1):139–160.

Starr, Kenneth W. 2006. "The Supreme Court and Its Shrinking Docket." *Minnesota Law Review* 90(5):1363–85.

Staton, Jeffrey K., and Georg Vanberg. 2008. "The Value of Vagueess: Delegation, Defiance, and Judicial Opinions." *American Journal of Political Science* 52(3): 504–19.

Stearns, Maxwell. 2000. *Constitutional Process: A Social Choice Analysis of Supreme Court Decision Making*. Ann Arbor: University of Michigan Press.

Stearns, Maxwell L. 1999. "Should Justices Ever Switch Votes? *Miller v. Albright* in Social Choice Perspective." *Supreme Court Economic Review* 7:87–156.

Steinberg, Asher. 2017. "A Sixth Circuit-Themed Primer on the Marks Doctrine, and an Endorsement of a Proposal to Overhauls Marks." *The Narrowest Grounds*. Accessed June 30, 2017. http://narrowestgrounds.blogspot.com/2017/06/a-sixth-circuit-themed-primer-on-marks.html

Stern, Robert L., Eugene Gressman, and Stephen M. Shapiro. 1988. "Epitaph for Mandatory Jurisdiction." *ABA Journal* 74(12):66–71.

Storing, Herbert J. 2008. *The Complete Anti-federalist*. Vol. 2. Chicago, IL: University of Chicago Press.

Stras, David R., and James F. Spriggs. 2010. "Explaining Plurality Decisions." *The Georgetown Law Journal* 99(2):515–70.

Sunstein, Cass R. 2007. "Incompletely Theorized Agreements in Constitutional Law." *Social Research: An International Quarterly* 74(1):1–24.

Taber, Charles S., and Milton Lodge. 2006. "Motivated Skepticism in the Evaluation of Political Beliefs." *American Journal of Political Science* 50(3):755–69.

"The National Court of Appeals: A Constitutional 'Inferior Court'?" 1973. *Michigan Law Review* 72(2):290–312.

Tullock, Gordon. 1981. "Why so Much Stability?" *Public Choice* 37(2):189–204.

Volden, Craig, and Alan E. Wiseman. 2014. *Legislative Effectiveness in the United States Congress*. New York: Cambridge University Press.

Waldron, Jeremy. 2006. "The Core of the Case Against Judicial Review." *The Yale Law Journal* 115(6):1346–406.

We Want Them Accountable. 1955. *Time* 66(23):32.

Whittington, Keith E. 2005. "'Interpose Your Friendly Hand': Political Supports for the Exercise of Judicial Review by the United States Supreme Court." *American Political Science Review* 99(4):583–96.

Wiecek, William M. 2001. "Felix Frankfurter, Incorporation, and the Willie Francis Case." *Journal of Supreme Court History* 26(1):53–67.

Wilcoxon, Frank. 1945. "Individual Comparisons by Ranking Methods." *Biometrics Bulletin* 1(6):80–83.

Wold, John T., and Gregory A. Caldeira. 1980. "Perceptions of 'Routine' Decision-Making in Five California Courts of Appeals." *Polity* 13(2):334–47.

Wood, Lewis. 1947, May 8. "Youth Due to Go to Chair Again Today as High Court Denies Plea." *New York Times*, p. A1.

Woodson, Benjamin. 2015. "Politicization and the Two Modes of Evaluating Judicial Decisions." *Journal of Law and Courts* 3(2):193–221.

Xu, Yiqing, Jens Hainmueller, Jonathan Mummolo, and Licheng Liu. 2017. "INTERFLEX: Stata Module to Estimate Multiplicative Interaction Models with Diagnostics and Visualization." Statistical Software Components, Boston College Department of Economics. https://ideas.repec.org/c/boc/bocode/s458314.html.

Yule, G. Udny. 1926. "Why Do We Sometimes Get Nonsense-Correlations between Time-Series?–A Study in Sampling and the Nature of Time-Series." *Journal of the Royal Statistical Society* 89(1):1–63.

Zeileis, Achim, Friedrich Leisch, Kurt Hornik, and Christian Kleiber. 2002. "Strucchange: An R Package for Testing for Structural Change in Linear Regression Models." *Journal of Statistical Software* 7(2):1–38. http://www.jstatsoft.org/v07/i02/

Zeleis, Achim, Christian Kleiber, Walter Kramer, and Kurt Hornik. 2003. "Testing and Dating of Structural Changes in Practice." *Computational Statistics and Data Analysis* 44:109–23.

Zilis, Michael A. 2015. *The Limits of Legitimacy: Dissenting Opinions, Media Coverage, and Public Responses to Spureme Court Decisions*. Ann Arbor: University of Michigan Press.

Zink, James R., James F. Spriggs, and John T. Scott. 2009. "Courting the Public: The Influence of Decision Attributes on Individuals' Views of Court Opinions." *Journal of Politics* 71(3):909–25.

Index

Printed and bound by CPI Group (UK) Ltd, Croydon, CR0 4YY
16/09/2026
14963487-0001